POLITICAL GROUPS IN CHILE

The Dialogue between Order and Change

LATIN AMERICAN MONOGRAPHS, NO. 21
INSTITUTE OF LATIN AMERICAN STUDIES
THE UNIVERSITY OF TEXAS AT AUSTIN

Political Groups in Chile

THE DIALOGUE BETWEEN ORDER AND CHANGE

by Ben G. Burnett

Published for the Institute of Latin American Studies by the University of Texas Press • Austin and London

International Standard Book Number 0-292-70084-9
Library of Congress Catalog Card Number 70-135759

Manufactured in the United States of America
Typesetting by G&S Typesetters, Austin
Printed by Capital Printing Company, Austin
Bound by Universal Bookbindery, Inc., San Antonio

TO MY PARENTS,

Cora S. and Ben H. Burnett

AND TO MY PARENTS-IN-LAW,

Ingrid S. and J. Scott Jensen

CONTENTS

CHARTS

TABLES

PREFACE

Generations of observers of the Latin American scene have been attracted to Chile, charmed by its hospitable people and magnificent scenery, and intrigued with its long, almost unbroken history of constitutionalism. Early in the republican era, the aristocracy established order in the political system; a century later the emergent middle sectors infused politics with wider democratic practices, and, relative to most of Latin America, a level of pluralism came to characterize group politics. The military developed along professional lines, making requests of government but rarely dominating it; the Church in time performed more and more as a religious and less as a political institution; student elements sought to air their grievances primarily by peaceful means; and management and labor structures came to be the principal competitors for political resources.

However, despite the distinctive advantages that embellished Chile's political system, certain unfulfilled promises still marred the actual picture in the early 1960's. In particular, the lower economic strata of society had been passed over by most of the social reforms and economic advances that periodically bettered the general outlook of the nation. Virtually all the agricultural workers and a large proportion of urban labor remained outside trade unions. Possessing no bargaining agents, they largely went ignored by the rest of society. Furthermore, even organized workers found their claims upon the policy-formation process usually falling upon deaf ears. Over and over again, labor encountered decision makers in the executive and legislative branches "talking but not acting." As political alienation grew among these societal strata, compounded by a worsening economic situation, their frustrations were brought into the open and their votes were catered to by reformist and radical political parties anxious to break the political hegemony of moderates and conservatives.

Thus, the 1960's stood out as a high-water mark in the confrontation between, on the one side, those desirous of maintaining the status quo, or at most admitting to prescriptive change, and, on the other side, progressive elements demanding deep structural alterations in the entire social fabric. This study seeks to analyze the sources of alienation, the styles and objectives of the participants in the confrontation, and the relative ability of groups to gain satisfaction of their claims upon the political system. The bulk of the present study delineates this dialogue between order and change as it inexorably pushed toward a showdown in the presidential elections of 1964 and the congressional elections of 1965. The concluding chapter views events since those elections and attempts to appraise tendencies and directions of the group process.

Field research was carried out in Chile during 1963 and 1964 under a grant from the Social Science Research Council, to whom I should like to extend my most appreciative expression of thanks. The research design included a questionnaire largely made up of open-end questions, which permitted comparative evaluations of the several score of respondents contacted and, at the same time, allowed for flexibility in pursuing subject areas that were especially relevant to the specific types of leaders interviewed. The interviewees included high officers of most managerial and labor centrals as well as a cross section of political party leadership. In addition, conversations and interviews transpired with a number of government officials, journalists, professors, and students, and with a sprinkling of clerical, military, and other leaders.

Most of the interviews were held in metropolitan Santiago, though interviews also were obtained with ranking officials in Valparaíso-Viña del Mar, in Concepción, and in the more important cities south as far as Punta Arenas. An interview schedule planned for northern cities at the end of my stay in Chile was cancelled when an opportunity to interview Eduardo Frei, Salvador Allende, and several other leading politicians developed. Nevertheless, some northerners were interviewed while they were in Santiago.

Chile's capital, Santiago, is particularly well endowed for research purposes. It claims some of the finest libraries in Latin America, with major collections in the University of Chile and the Catholic University as well as in the National Library, the Central Bank, offices of the Economic Commission for Latin America, and the Library of Congress, to mention only a few. One branch of the Congressional Library contains a press-clipping service modeled after the Library of Congress in Washington, D.C., that is outstanding and unique for Latin America. Moreover, most of the central headquarters of economic, social, and political organizations reside in a relatively small area of downtown Santiago, thus facilitating mobility among offices. This is especially important in a Latin context because of the long midday meal break, which necessitates catching interviewees in the mornings and evenings, and in a city whose U.S.-owned telephone company is ineffective in so many ways that it often acts as a hindrance to arranging interviews.

Another obvious advantage to carrying out a research design in Chile derives from the comparatively stable political environment. For the most part, there is an absence of violence, though anomic activity is not completely absent; this general stability permits scrutiny of structures and processes of more than an ephemeral nature. Further, the Chileans have achieved a level of political literacy and activism that is very high for Latin America. As a consequence, it is possible to locate informed citizens among all societal strata. Finally, it should be noted that, though problems certainly exist for the researcher in Chile, the Chileans by and large must rank among the kindest and most helpful people to be found anywhere.

Untold numbers of people have contributed to bringing this book to fruition. Many of their names are noted in the footnotes; others remain anonymous at their request. There are a few names, though, that should be singled out for personal kindnesses and that, for the most part, do not appear in the footnotes. They are the Amador Charad, Paul Crasemann, Gonzalo Biggs, Myron Glazer, Peter Gregory, Henry Landsberger, Moisés Poblete Troncoso, Enrique Sánchez Ossandon, Jean-Paul Sudreau, Hernán Troncoso, and Adolph Vorwerk families as well as Juan Guzmán Cruchaga, Benjamin Martin, Julio Pinto, and Rodrigo Santa Cruz. The director of the Chilean Library of Congress, Rubén A. Bulla, was most helpful as were the staff of the Congressional Library's newspaper-clipping service: Raquel Arancibia Blanco, Betsabé Cortés, Teresa Isla Hevia, and Raquel Veloz Román. At Whittier College, I am indebted to President Paul S. Smith, former Dean Harold F. Spencer, Dean W. Roy Newsom, J. William Robinson, and Benjamin Whitten for their help; Kathy Harmon and Lynne Frankel were generous of their time to do the typing. Also, I should like to thank the Institute of Latin American Studies, especially Thomas F. McGann, and the University of Texas Press for their helpfulness and professionalism. Above all, I owe my most profound gratitude to my wife, Dorothy, for her contant encouragement and support.

Whittier College

POLITICAL GROUPS IN CHILE

The Dialogue between Order and Change

CHAPTER ONE

Political Foundations

Geographic Context

Anyone gaining an acquaintanceship with Chile for the first time cannot help but be struck by its singular shape on the map: a long, thin ribbon of land almost crushed between the towering Andes and the massive Pacific. Its great length of some 2,600 miles and a narrowness that averages approximately 110 miles have led writers to dub Chile the "shoe-string republic" or, as one of its countrymen prefers, "simply a cartographical coquetry to prevent the chilly water of the Pacific from wetting the Argentine frontiers."[1] In more personal terms, the Chilean worker describes his country as being "as long as Monday," a reference to his discomfiture following a day of excessive imbibing.

In addition to this metropolitan territory, Chile's domain stretches out over Pacific holdings that range from the coastal islands of Juan

[1] Benjamín Subercaseaux, *Chile: A Geographic Extravaganza*, p. 17.

Fernández to distant Easter Island. Antarctic claims contribute more to national pride than material gain, though Chileans like to contemplate on their future significance in facilitating south polar airline routes between Africa and Australasia.[2]

Just within the confines of continental Chile, however, can be found extraordinary topographical variances and climatic changes. Indeed, if Chile were inverted and placed in North America, it would reach from La Paz in Baja California to Juneau, Alaska—replete with an equivalent diversity of land forms and climate. As a consequence, several different regions are quite clearly distinguishable.[3]

Between the Peruvian boundary and the province of Coquimbo lies the Northern (or Atacama) Desert Region, much of it devoid of precipitation during all of recorded history. Only sparsely settled anciently by Indians who located along scarce water sources, in modern times Chile receives the lion's share of its export revenues from the copper, fish-meal, and nitrate industries found there. The scattered seaports of Arica, Iquique, Antofagasta, and Coquimbo-La Serena service the area.

Next, Northern Middle (or Mediterranean) Chile runs south to Concepción, a region labeled "the cradle of Chilean nationality." In this area, originally populated by Spaniards attracted by the mild climate and fertile soil, *latifundia* soon swallowed up the best land as they spread throughout the Central Valley. Later, the feudal calm was pierced by the intrusion of commerce and industry, which gradually agglomerated most Chileans in the major metropolises of Santiago, Valparaíso, and Concepción.

The third principal region, Southern Middle Chile, halts at the island of Chiloé. A land of heavy rainfall and dense forests, it sheltered the largest grouping of Indians who survived the colonial era. The effective development of the district, though, dates from the middle nineteenth century with the arrival of European immigrants and

[2] See Oscar Kaplan C., *Geografía de Chile*, p. 9.

[3] Because of Chile's great diversity, several divisions of the country are possible. The four-fold division used here is convenient for the general purpose of the book and it follows the regions noted in Preston E. James, *Latin America*, pp. 213–263.

then with a spillover from the Central Valley of pioneers drawn mostly from the tenant-farmer class. Since that time it has carried on an agricultural and pastoral tradition that relies upon the urban clusters of Temuco, Valdivia, Osorno, and Puerto Montt for processing and marketing its products.

Finally, the South is a land of rugged terrain and inhospitable climate. Natural obstacles have inhibited colonization so greatly that the population of the entire southern extremity reaches only slightly more than 100,000. Punta Arenas, the single important city, is gaining new significance with the recently discovered oil fields nearby. Otherwise, there appears to be little room for optimism regarding the early settlement of the remainder of this region.

Chile's boundaries with two of its three neighbors, Argentina and Bolivia, follow along the Andean range as a generally secure line of demarcation. Only in the extreme south where the mountain barrier diminishes and in the north, bordering Peru, has it been necessary to mark out arbitrary lines in the absence of natural ones. Historically, the definition of these frontiers evolved from highly problematic circumstances in which Chile engaged in one major war, nearly was drawn into others, and finally required the good offices of several foreign intercessors as well as almost continuous negotiations with the respective countries.

In the case of Argentina, more than a half century of litigation and numerous near wars culminated in 1902 with a compromise that ended most of the dispute.[4] Disagreements with Peru and Bolivia grew out of the inconclusive settlements that followed the War of the Pacific, which Chile had waged against its two neighbors between 1879 and 1882.[5] Whereas a treaty in 1929 with Peru demarcated the northern

[4] Much of the argument raged over whether the water divide, which Chile favored, or a line running along the highest peaks, a particularly complex solution and one that would have carried Argentina to the Pacific, should serve as the boundary separation. King Edward VII offered a compromise between these proposals that allocated claims almost equally between the two nations (Luis Galdames, *A History of Chile,* trans. and ed. Isaac J. Cox, pp. 405–407).

[5] See Isaac J. Cox, "Chile," in *Argentina, Brazil, and Chile since Independence,* ed. A. Curtis Wilgus, pp. 336–348.

border once and for all, a seemingly conclusive arrangement with Bolivia never really did placate the Bolivians' hard feelings over the loss of their seacoast to Chile.[6]

Even as early as colonial times the stirrings of Chilean national self-identity became manifest. Public documents referred to the area as the "kingdom of Chile," thus boasting a spatially definable and viable political entity.[7] At first, self-identity took the form of patriotism or simple love of country, which the early Europeans felt as they discovered and finally settled in Chile's Central Valley:

As the territory was explored and became better known, the people were persuaded that the subsoil contained enormous riches and that the cultivated soil had unlimited possibilities. The gentle climate, the absence of poisonous reptiles and insects, the abundance of forest vegetation, the fertility of the cultivated fields, the stimulating yield of the mines, the landscape of the forests and mountains, the well-defined demarcation of the country—between the deserts of the north, the great cordillera, and the sea —all stimulated regional pride among the Creoles and furthered a patriotic restlessness, as was shown by their love for their native land and their desire for progress.[8]

In the nineteenth century, the War of the Pacific, occasional boundary flare-ups, and a still somewhat isolated geographic position combined to instill a deep-rooted nationalism in the Chilean character. Furthermore, war and threats of conflict turned the nation's attention away from almost entirely considering domestic issues to a greater cognizance of the international scene. Now nationalism acquired new dimensions as Chile entered international conferences, engaged in an

[6] A choice, but probably apocryphal, story tells of then-President Carlos Ibáñez' state visit to Bolivia. Although everyone present had only one subject on his mind—Bolivia's desire for a seaport—Ibáñez carefully steered all discussion away from this topic. Finally, after dinner over cognac, a high Bolivian official brought the issue into the open with the question: "Mr. President, when are you Chileans going to return our seaport to us?" Ibáñez mused for a moment and then replied: "Why do you want a seaport? You don't even have a seacoast." Astonished by the reasonableness of the query, the Bolivians dropped the topic (related by Gonzalo Biggs).

[7] Galdames, *History of Chile*, p. 143.

[8] *Ibid.*

arms race and in power relationships, and achieved a heightened awareness of the outside world. Hence, the spirit of Chilean nationalism came to be "cultural and economic as well as political and military, and outward-looking rather than introspective."[9]

Today Chile ranks among only a very few Latin American republics (the others being Uruguay, Argentina, and Costa Rica) that have developed farthest along the path to nation statehood. Kalman Silvert suggests that the principal test of such a status is the presence of empathy "as it is structured in patterns of loyalty toward fellow citizens, legitimated in terms of an apposite set of symbols, and enforced and mediated by the state."[10] Despite the obvious presence of such mutual identification, Chilean nationalism has not been marred by the aggressiveness or xenophobia that characterizes some other peoples, who seem to have their nerve ends protruding ready to flail out at any real or fancied slur on their nation.

Of course, as in other lands, nationalism can be an important mobilizer of the Chilean people; but the call to patriotic feelings ordinarily is couched in muted tones. Thus in 1964, when Argentina issued postage stamps and an Argentine publishing house brought out an encyclopedia that contained maps showing Chilean Antarctic claims as part of Argentine national territory, opposition was largely expressed in formal, legal terms rather than in emotion-charged verbiage. *El Mercurio* of Santiago, Chile's largest and most influential newspaper, decried the acts as appearing "to contravene the spirit, if not the letter" of international conventions regarding Antarctica.[11]

A more serious alleged violation of Chilean national territory also involved Argentine actions. Late in 1963, an Argentine police detachment penetrated the frontier area of Palena in southern Chile. When the police remained and carried out normal functions as though they were on Argentine soil, Chile protested and rebuked Argentine aggressiveness. Nevertheless, no Chilean troops moved in to contest Argentina and a serious crisis was thus averted.

[9] Arthur P. Whitaker, *Nationalism in Latin America*, pp. 22–23.

[10] Kalman H. Silvert, "Nationalism in Latin America," *Annals of the American Academy of Political and Social Science* no. 334 (March 1961): 4.

[11] *El Mercurio* (Santiago), February 29, 1964.

About the same time, elements in a small northern town, located in a zone taken from Bolivia in the War of the Pacific, raised the Bolivian flag in protest against the lack of attention the central government had given to their needs. Of course, the perpetrators of this act were severely chastised for their unpatriotic act. But this occurrence as well as the Palena incident produced a number of articles in leading newspapers specifying grievances in out-of-the-way places and, as a consequence, stimulated a reappraisal of policies toward these regions. In brief, Chileans "exude a love of country that is childlike in the finest sense of the word: genuine and unquestioning, but free from the wild exaggerations and psychopathic quirks that have vitiated much of modern nationalism."[12]

The Human Factor

Chilean nationality is remarkably similar in its ethnic composition throughout the length and breadth of the land. Something over one-third of the population is European and most of the rest mestizo (and even these tend to be more European than Indian in their racial makeup). In the early sixteenth century indigenous peoples perhaps numbered as high as 1.5 million, but following the conquest they were nearly obliterated by warfare, flight into Argentina (for survival or economic reasons), and intermingling with the Spaniards.[13] Today only 1.6 per cent of Chileans (130,000) reside on reservations and even these Indians generally speak Spanish and live much like other Chilean peasants.[14]

Another factor contributing to the generally homogeneous racial quality characterizing Chile stems from the nature of immigration in the republican era. The Germans, British, Italians, French, Yugoslavs, and Middle Easterners who came to Chile's shores never constituted such a massive wave at one time that they could not be absorbed into national life. Moreover, in the last 150 years, they probably totaled

[12] Fredrick B. Pike, *Chile and the United States, 1880–1962*, p. xx.

[13] Julian H. Steward and Louis C. Faron, *Native Peoples of South America*, pp. 267–283.

[14] Kaplan, *Geografía de Chile*, p. 89.

no more than 100,000.[15] As a consequence, most of the newcomers blended in with the older Spanish society and quickly assumed leadership roles in both urban and rural areas. (A German concentration in the lake country persists as something of a residual exception to this general rule.) An example of this intermingling of Spanish and other European families was evident in paternal and maternal lineages of all four presidential nominees who began the 1964 campaign: Eduardo Frei Montalva, Salvador Allende Gossens, Julio Durán Newman, and Jorge Prat Eschaurren.

Despite the small Indian population and modest immigration, Chile is beleaguered by demographic problems endemic to so much of the hemisphere. Its growth rate of 2.5 per cent is well above the world average of 1.8 per cent and is dramatically observable in terms of the tremendous increase in absolute numbers over a half century:

1920	3,785,000
1930	4,365,000
1940	5,063,000
1950	6,073,000
1960	7,340,000
1970	9,800,000
1980	est. 12,200,000

Following World War I, Latin America launched a major attack on communicable diseases with aid from international health agencies and the Rockefeller Foundation. Programs of sanitation, vaccination, and the spraying of insecticides over large areas reduced the prevalence of dysentery, smallpox, and other maladies that had taken a heavy toll of human life.[16] At the same time that the death rate dropped, fertility remained high. In Chile the number of births per one thousand mostly held between thirty-five and forty during the period from 1935 to 1960, while the number of deaths per one thousand dropped from twenty-four to half that number in the same time span. New medicines

[15] Pedro Cunill, *Geografía de Chile*, pp. 74–75.

[16] T. Lynn Smith, "The Population of Latin America," in *Population: The Vital Revolution*, ed. Ronald Freedman, pp. 178–190.

and somewhat more accessible medical services continued to lower the death rate.[17]

With the lessening death rate, more children grew to maturity and in turn produced more children; but the health of the Chilean population is still far from satisfactory. Malnutrition afflicts great numbers of people and many Chileans are unable to eat every day. The average daily caloric intake (2,150) falls below the normal minimum of 2,400 established by world health recommendations and considerably behind the average of more than 3,000 calories a day consumed by Europeans and North Americans. The typical diet is excessively given over to carbohydrates, with a deficiency of fruits, vegetables, and dairy products. Swollen stomachs, short stature, and rapid aging testify to this condition among countless of the poorest people in society. And while the population expands, Chile's ability to feed itself declines—thus compounding the malnutrition problem and further opening the door to debilitating diseases. Tragically, not only is preventive medicine inadequate in many areas, but there also exists a dearth of medical facilities to care for the ill and infirm. Five hospital beds for every one thousand inhabitants and nineteen hundred persons per doctor is a good ratio for a Latin American country, but less than half the number of beds and more than twice the number of inhabitants to each doctor than is found in the United States and Canada.[18] All this suggests a human tragedy as well as a labor problem—weak and ill people do not make the best workers. This situation is further exacerbated by the chronic drunkenness to be found among a high percentage of laborers, who find wine or *chicha* cheaper than food and an antidote to their wretched lives.

The Chilean term for the unfortunate slum dweller is *roto*, implying the broken nature of his existence in the proliferating city slums. Urbanization, and especially the incredible expansion of Santiago, is a principal contributing factor to Chile's already grave social problems. The rural poor often are enticed to the cities in the usually misguided belief of certain economic advancement. Actually, most of them fare no better in the urban environment than they did in the farm areas.

[17] Cunill, *Georgrafía de Chile*, pp. 71–74.

[18] John Gerassi, *The Great Fear in Latin America*, pp. 35–38.

Such natural disasters as earthquakes and tidal waves uproot others who trudge to the larger cities seeking a new stake. Moreover, Santiago houses an overabundance of the nation's economic, political, and social institutions; as these institutions expand and new enterprises set up their plants and headquarters, even more people migrate to the sprawling capital.

The statistics of urbanization are striking. A majority of Chileans lived in cities by 1940; only twenty-five years later the percentage had jumped to 70 per cent of the population and half of these resided in Santiago alone. Santiago in particular among the burgeoning urban centers faces mammoth problems resultant from the inexorable migrations. It has the distinction of being one of the world's four worst metropolitan sites from the standpoint of air pollution: automobile exhaust, industrial pollutants, and smoke and debris from burning rubbish contaminate the air. Public transportation is overcrowded and often antiquated, and traffic jams the streets during the working day; telephones, gas, water, and electricity are in short supply; and housing for the poor is a national disaster as 650,000 of Greater Santiago's 2,400,000 people bunch together in the *poblaciones callampa*s ("mushroom settlements"), slums that wrap a ribbon of blight, disease, and crime around the city.[19]

Despite the apparent hopelessness of the urban dispossessed, the slum dweller at least can view some possibilities for his (or, more realistically, his progeny's) betterment. Schools are more plentiful and an individual's chance at a few years of education is more likely than in the semifeudal rural region. However, located on the fringes of economic advancement and political power, his expectations unfulfilled, he surveys his own miserable living and working conditions and may become a severely alienated member of society. Thus, whereas the agricultural worker began to display glimmerings of political activism in the early 1960's, the *rotos* stood closer to the center of political action. Reformers and radicals played on this discontent to support their

[19] The phenomenon of urbanization and its problems in Chile are well set out in Cunill, *Geografía de Chile*, and in Bruce H. Herrick, *Urban Migration and Economic Development in Chile.*

programs of social renovation, and oligarchic dominance of the nation's political and economic resources was vigorously contested.

Economic Factors

In a continent where incongruities abound, Chile stands out as one of the most paradoxical in that it possesses great quantities of natural resources and, yet, has been unable to resolve deep economic troubles. Rich land and abundant mineral deposits simply have not proved sufficient to meet the nation's needs. In no small measure this has been due to antiquated methods, a heavy drain of profits out of the country, and the concentration of economic control in a very small element of society.

Agriculture

It is an accepted fact in Chile that agriculture constitutes a sick partner in the national economy. Statistics abound to demonstrate its inability to fulfill national consumption requirements: In the decade of the 1950's, its contribution to the national income dropped from 18.6 to 13.5 per cent of the total, and the value of farm exports was halved relative to the cash value of total national exports. Alimentary requirements during the same period grew at an average rate of 2.3 per cent while agricultural production increased by only 1.6 per cent. According to minimum food requirements established by the National Health Service, in 1960 Chile failed to produce enough milk (−65%), meat (−11.2%), eggs (−17%), legumes (−13.4%), potatoes (−46.8%), and fruit (−20.9%) to supply the minimum national needs for these commodities.[20]

Obviously, such a low agricultural yield relative to the population growth contributes measurably to Chile's tremendous systemic difficulties in the economic sphere. The need to import staples drains other sources of revenue and is a significant cause of an unfavorable balance; an imbalance of demand to supply pushes up food prices, contributing to the inflationary spiral, and keeps a large percentage of the popula-

[20] These data can be found in Carlos Fredes, *Curso de economía: Elementos de economía chilena*, p. 89, and in Corporación de Fomento de la Producción (hereafter referred to as CORFO), *Geografía económica de Chile*, pp. 63–69.

tion in a substandard level of caloric intake; and, since numerous farm workers remain on the margin of the money economy, they are unable to assume any important role as consumers of manufactured goods and thus delimit domestic industry's markets.[21]

About the only comment favorable to the farm situation that is widely heard in Chile is that land is owned and produce is marketed by Chileans rather than foreigners. Otherwise, a myriad of forces interact to aggravate agriculture's difficulties. The three most commonly offered reasons are governmental farm policies, abuse and misuse of the land, and the land-tenure system.

The Sociedad Nacional de Agricultura, which speaks for big agriculture (most small farms being marginal and only producing for their own consumption), has come to be philosophical about government intervention in farm matters—a situation the farmers do not prefer, but cannot do much about. What the SNA does oppose is the application of government policy that seems to engage in too rigid and often arbitrary price fixing, that purchases foreign farm products and then sells them at a loss—to the detriment of domestic production, and that maintains an unfair and unequal ratio between the price of domestic farm products (i.e., by keeping prices low) and the high cost of imported machinery and implements essential to raise productivity.[22] Undoubtedly, there is much truth in the claim that "all of this conspires against agricultural development."[23]

One exception to the usual status of Chilean farms is a model *fundo* ("farm") near Valdivia. The workers are provided with sanitary and comfortable living quarters and land productivity is high (in part resulting from the importation of quality seeds and an adequate supply of farm machinery). This was made possible because the landowner invested all the profits from his farm in improvements and lived off his pension as a retired general.[24]

21 Fredes, *Curso de economía*, pp. 87–88.

22 Interview with César Sepúlveda Latapiat, secretary general of the Sociedad Nacional de Agricultura, in Santiago, March 31, 1964.

23 Editorial in *El Mercurio* (Santiago), October 27, 1963.

24 Interview with General (retired) Alfonso Cañas Ruíz Tagle, in Valdivia, March 9, 1964.

Usually, farmers believe that the government penalizes them by setting a low price for their products and yet insists upon imposing astronomical customs taxes on imported farm machinery. Supporters of the government program point out that agriculture does not produce enough to meet Chilean needs, necessitating buying food abroad and so creating an unfavorable trade balance, which in turn must be met at least partially by high customs duties. Obviously one argument vitiates the other.

Another suggested cause of Chile's agrarian difficulties is the abuse and misuse of land. Man-made erosion damages a great deal of land where protecting trees are slashed with no regard for reforestation and, in some areas, crops (e.g., cereals in the south) are planted that diminish the soil's fertility. There are many instances where a better utilization of land, such as turning over more soil in the Central Valley to fruit orchards, would bring in higher returns; but old ways are resistant to change.

One of the most serious defects in land usage occurs in the rich Central Valley where in places the earth is not cultivated, but held for speculative or status purposes—the landowner simply not being interested in planting. Furthermore, urbanization gobbles up land mercilessly. In the absence of planning, Santiago has spread over good land and even buried former producing farms as large vacant spaces within the city limits.

Finally, the land-tenure system has drawn widespread criticism as one of the most grievous flaws in the entire Chilean economy.[25] Large

[25] Countless Chilean and foreign studies have been produced dealing with agricultural problems and agrarian reform. A sample includes: Hernán Navarrete and Gastón Carvallo, "Agricultura," in CORFO, *Geografía económica de Chile*, pp. 2–99; Francisco Rojas Huneeus, "Chile en su aspecto agrícola," in *Desarrollo de Chile en la primera mitad del siglo XX*, I, 151–188; Horacio Serrano Palma, *¿Por qué somos pobres?*; Oscar Domínguez C., *El condicionamiento de la reforma agraria*; Rafael Baraona, Ximena Aranda, and Roberto Santana, *Valle de Putaendo: Estudio de estructura agraria*; Luis Correa Vergara, *Agricultura chilena*; Francisco Encina, *La reforma agraria*; Extensión Cultural de la Biblioteca Nacional, *Chile: Su futura alimentación*; Aníbal Pinto Santa Cruz, *Chile: Un caso de desarrollo frustrado*; Robert R. Kaufman, *The Chilean Political Right and Agrarian Reform*; and the excellent work by William C. Thiesenhusen, *Chile's Experiments in Agrarian Reform.*

estates (those with more than 200 hectares) encompass 87.38 per cent of the farmland, whereas medium-sized farms (50–200 hectares) claim only 7.60 per cent, and small land plots (under 50 hectares) 5.02 per cent. The degree of concentration of landownership is evidenced in the fact that 0.4 per cent of the total number of farms—all over 5,000 hectares—constitutes 54 per cent of the farmland of Chile. Or to put it another way, a tiny minority of 2 per cent controls 72 per cent of occupied farm land.[26]

Not only can serious questions be raised respecting the present efficiency of many of these *latifundia*, but about the semifeudal relationships of the peon to his master and the grossly inequitable distribution of farm income as well. Recent findings indicate that the wealthiest 1 per cent of the entire farm population takes 25 per cent of farm income, while all the farm workers (that is to say, 87 per cent of the farm population) obtain only another 25 per cent of agriculture's cash return.[27] To make matters worse, the farm worker's economic plight has been deteriorating. In the decade of the 1950's, the landowners' real income rose by almost 50 per cent at a time when farm labor's income fell more than 5 per cent; in the next five years, the agricultural workers' purchasing power plummeted by a third.[28]

Supposedly, the farm labor force is protected from exploitation by a guaranteed minimum salary. But this is largely meaningless when some landlords ignore the minimum wage and when the government itself has been slow to raise the minimum wage to compensate for the national currency's never-ending drop in value. Apologists for the system argue that the farm worker's income is greatly amplified by special perquisites granted him by the landowner in the form of a dwelling, a plot to farm, and food. Overwhelmingly, though, the dwelling is a shoddy pile of debris mounted above an earthen floor and festooned with flies from a nearby pigsty or manure pile; the farm plot is practically worthless land that offers a pathetically small bounty

[26] Center of Latin American Studies (hereafter referred to as CLAS), *Statistical Abstract of Latin America*, p. 32.

[27] William Thiesenhusen, "Latin American Land Reform: Enemies of Promise," *Nation*, January 24, 1966, pp. 90–94.

[28] *Ibid.*, p. 90; CORFO, *Geografía económica de Chile*, pp. 86–88.

for so much scratching; and the food is acquired from vouchers exchangeable in the latifundist's store at 80 per cent of value. Beginning in 1961, inroads were being made into altering this insidious arrangement by legal edict—the cash portion of a worker's income to be at least 25 per cent by 1962, 35 per cent in 1963, 50 per cent in 1964, and so forth.[29] Nevertheless, in the middle 1960's the farm workers' average annual cash income of $150 kept them at a bare subsistence level and at the bottom of the economic ladder for employed labor.[30]

For more than thirty years land reform laws have been on the books and in 1962–63, the most liberal of these to that date was enacted. But even then, agrarian reform lagged pitifully. In the three decades combined, Chile distributed half as much land as Mexico parceled out in the single year of 1962.[31]

Mining

Chile's abundant minerals, distributed throughout its Andean and Coastal ranges, have served vitally in the history and growth of the nation. During the colonial period Chile stood only second to the Viceroyalty of Peru in the production of gold; silver was mined in significant quantities until well into the nineteenth century.[32] Late in the last century, Chileans fanned northward through their own lands and onto Bolivian soil in their search for additional minerals—finally, seizing rich copper and nitrate beds from Bolivia as an outgrowth of the War of the Pacific. Ultimately, the great copper stores superseded in importance a virtual monopoly of the world's natural nitrates when in World War I a process was found for creating synthetic nitrate that made it widely and cheaply available.

In modern times, copper brings in more than 60 per cent of the return gained from all mining activities.[33] Other principal metals and minerals are iron ore, most of which is consumed by Chile's steel in-

[29] *El Mercurio* (Santiago), April 11, 1964.
[30] Thiesenhusen, "Latin American Land Reform," p. 90.
[31] John F. Wheeler, "Agrarian Reform Program Moves into Forward Motion," *South Pacific Mail* (Santiago), December 6, 1963.
[32] Francisco Frías Valenzuela, *Geografía de Chile*, pp. 88–89.
[33] Kalman H. Silvert, *Chile: Yesterday and Today*, p. 127.

dustry; the largest deposits of coal in Latin America, though of low grade; enormous quantities of nitrates, a product that continuously declines in its marketability; and petroleum, recently discovered in the extreme south and having great import for the general economy. Some gold is still mined, but the known silver mines are almost totally depleted. In addition, there exist measurable deposits of manganese, lead, sulfur, and mercury as well as lesser amounts of more than a score of other minerals and metals—all and all an impressive selection of industrial and precious metals and fuel minerals.[34]

There can be no question about the significance of the mining industry's role in the nation's economy. Some 100,000 persons labor in the mines, among whom a large number make up the main part of the working force in the north. Moreover, mining accounts for 50 per cent of direct taxes accruing to the state and contributes around 75 per cent of the revenues garnered from exports.[35] Nevertheless, the relationship of mining to the over-all economy is not without its troubled aspects. First of all, Chile's dependence upon mining (and particularly copper) is excessive, producing a monocultural situation with all the dangers inherent therein. When the international demand for Chilean copper rises, production and revenues increase; on the other side of the coin, a drop in demand pushes prices down and drastically affects the entire economy. Since Chile suffers from the uncertainty of copper prices, it is next to impossible for the government to be assured of a balance of trade in the coming year or of its capacity to pay on foreign loans.

Second, despite the obvious predominant position of mining in the economy of the northern regions—in direct employment as well as in its contribution to ancillary service industries—scarcely 5 per cent of the national labor force is employed by mining enterprises. A larger number could be hired if more ore processing were to take place in Chile proper (though this has increased greatly in recent years) and if added quantities of finished products, such as wire and tubing, could be manufactured for export.[36]

[34] See CORFO, *Geografía económica de Chile*, pp. 273–380.
[35] Fredes, *Curso de economía*, p. 126.
[36] Silvert, *Chile*, pp. 127–129.

Third, before the Christian Democrats assumed power in 1964, foreign capital all but monopolized copper production. Just two U.S. firms, Anaconda and Kennecott (through subsidiaries), turned out 90 per cent of Chile's copper. This situation was supported by some who argued that Chile could not possibly have accumulated the capital necessary to develop its mines. They also pointed to the fact that the U.S. companies furnished better housing, hospitals, and schools and paid higher salaries than existed among any other group of Chilean workers.

On the other hand, critics rebelled against the tremendous drain of Chile's national wealth into foreign coffers. The U.S. companies already had accumulated a return of considerably more than three times their total investment. John Gerassi estimates that if the foreign-held mines had been nationalized in 1950 and the companies paid back full value for their book investment, twelve years later Chile would have been $1.5 billion richer: a sufficient quantity to expunge all foreign debts.[37] This argument was taken up by both the leading political contenders in the 1964 elections, and, whether the specific proposal was the Christian Democrats' plan to "Chileanize" copper (i.e., for Chile to obtain a share of ownership) or the Socialist-Communist coalition's plank for outright nationalization, the idea was widely applauded as a significant forward step in Chile's quest for economic security.

Manufacturing

Manufacturing has had a long, though irregular, history in Chile. In the colonial era, Chile's industrial pattern was primitive and limited mainly to artisan and home manufacturing. In line with Spanish mercantilist doctrine of the time, Chile remained a closed economic system—such trade as was permitted being with Spain, Peru, and Argentina. For the most part, the nation lived in a subsistence economy. Then, in the first fifty years of the republican period, leaders endeavored to pull the nation together by concentrating on political and economic consolidation. Largely dominated by the Conservatives, the government entered the economy in a protectionist sense and opened the country to foreign trade.

[37] Gerassi, *Great Fear in Latin America*, pp. 364–366.

From 1860 to the end of the century, Liberal regimes reversed the protectionist policies by admitting competition of products from abroad. At times this fostered a certain amount of industrial development, but as often as not there was no expansion and even some retrenchment. For example, the 507 mills operating in 1868 grew to 553 in 1878 and dropped to 360 in 1888; tanneries numbered 177, 302, and 281 and copper furnaces 250, 127, and 69 respectively in the same three industrial censuses.[38]

The period from 1900 to 1930 marks another definable change in government's treatment of industry. Then, a moderately protectionist approach replaced the free-exchange policy of the previous epoch and the government's policies often seemed to harbor inner contradictions. For example, around the turn of the century a number of laws were passed to subsidize certain specific industries (including beet sugar, finished steel, alcohol, sulfuric acid, linen, and fishing boat construction enterprises); shortly afterward, the government turned around and lowered import duties on several foreign products, permitting them to compete more advantageously with those made in Chile, and destroying a number of domestic factories.[39]

Despite shifting government policies toward the manufacturing sector and a generally uneven growth pattern, Chilean industry became firmly established early in this century when a rather impressive array of consumer goods was domestically produced. The production of consumer products was considerably augmented as a result of the two world wars, which cut off supplies from the major industrial powers and thus necessitated their replacement domestically, and as a consequence of the sudden drop in nitrate exports in the 1920's and of copper in the depths of the depression—both of which eradicated the luxury of importing foreign consumer items.

The depression, in particular, created a disastrous situation in Chile; some economists even go so far as to suggest that Chile suffered a greater shock in 1929 than any other nation. (Using 1929 as an index of 100, Chile's ability to import fell to 40 in 1931.)[40] In any case, the

[38] CORFO, *Geografía económica de Chile*, p. 153.

[39] *Ibid.*, pp. 147–167; Fredes, *Curso de economía*, pp. 139–140.

[40] CORFO, *Geografía económica de Chile*, p. 168.

world depression forced the government to move strongly to preserve what it could of the nation's economic capacity by imposing severe controls on monies leaving the country and by encouraging some foreign and many domestic enterprises to reinvest profits into the economy that previously could have been freely taken out of Chile. In addition, the government offered various incentives to the industrial sector, so that the 1930's saw a steady climb in manufacturing. This was topped off in 1939 with the formation of Latin America's first government development corporation, Corporación de Fomento de la Producción, or CORFO, which pushed Chile into new areas of industrial expansion.

CORFO has been widely lauded as an exceptionally effective example of state planning. Its diversified undertakings encompass electrification, metallurgy, fertilizers, chemicals, lumber, food products, tires, cement, and a host of other basic industries.[41] Sometimes CORFO assumes the full financial burden for promoting the creation of an enterprise; at other times, it joins with private capital to make a specific developmental endeavor possible. Its flexibility in approaching areas of development is further exemplified by differing styles of ownership. Some enterprises are held by the state alone (e.g., electricity), others are controlled by a mixture of governmental and private ownership (e.g., the steel industry in Concepción), and, in still other instances, the government has sold off its original investment to private stockholders (e.g., the tire company).[42] CORFO's tremendous initial impact on the economy declined somewhat during the 1950's as a consequence of reduced governmental support, though this trend was reversed in the 1960's.

Recent Trends and Problems

One of the most striking characteristics of the Chilean economy has been its slow rate of growth since World War II. Between 1945 and 1955, Latin America's gross national product advanced at an average of 6.3 per cent annually; in contrast, Chile's growth rate held at about

[41] *Ibid.*, p. 173.
[42] Silvert, *Chile*, pp. 140–141.

2.7 per cent.[43] This gloomy picture altered only slightly in the early 1960's when the rate nudged upward to approximately 3 per cent.[44]

At the same time, Chile suffered a serious trade imbalance that ran close to $150 million a year and required credits from the United States to fill the gap. The nation's industry imports the bulk of its new machinery and a substantial percentage of its raw materials; on the other hand, revenues from exports accrue from a very limited segment of the national economy—70 per cent from big mining, 20 per cent from lesser mines, and a paltry 10 per cent from farm products and a few industrial items.[45]

As has been noted, agriculture's chronic failure or inability to modernize and to enlarge its productive capacity stands at the center of the problem. Furthermore, industry, which expanded markedly during the 1950's, slumped significantly in the early 1960's. Kalman Silvert summed up the dilemma of industry as a circular problem: "The uncertainties of the world market, added to a gross maldistribution of income within Chile, limit demand and thus make unattractive the investment of further capital in industry. The resulting failure to enlarge industry then further weakens Chile's bargaining position in the world market and in turn makes it extremely difficult to raise the incomes of persons at the bottom of the occupational scale."[46] Thus, not only is an infinitesimally small percentage of the population in a position to accumulate savings that could be turned into capital investment, but those who do acquire savings tend to back away from investing them because of existing economic conditions.

Compounding this pernicious predicament is the debilitating effect of endemic inflation, which has battered Chile for most of the last eighty years and in recent decades has soared to astronomical heights: 94 per cent in the 1930's, 412 per cent in the 1940's, and 2,089 per cent in the 1950's.[47] A few of the more salient factors contributing to

[43] F. Benham and H. A. Holley, *A Short Introduction to the Economy of Latin America*, p. 112.

[44] CLAS, *Statistical Abstract of Latin America*, p. 106.

[45] Silvert, *Chile*, pp. 141–146.

[46] *Ibid.*, p. 134.

[47] Albert O. Hirschman, *Journeys toward Progress*, pp. 159–223; a statisti-

price increases include agricultural production continually falling behind the population increase; the necessity for importing foodstuffs not being countered by the ability of other economic sectors to export; the modest level of investment being inadequate to meet expanding employment needs; deficiencies in the tax system; and a government policy of yearly wage hikes to compensate for jumps in the cost of living.[48] The inflationary spiral encourages those with savings to convert their holdings into hard foreign currencies and to hoard them in safes or in safety deposit boxes and as investments abroad. (Chile's black market in money is notorious in the hemisphere.) It also has induced investment in such speculative endeavors as residential dwellings, which accounted for 45 per cent of all fixed investment in 1955, "a very high proportion, even for Latin America."[49]

Conclusion

The environmental backdrop to the Chilean political system, even in this brief introduction, offers a picture of considerable complexity. Chile is highly cohesive, with relative ethnic homogeneity and strong ties of nationalism. It abounds in great natural resources and possesses varied soils, climate, and terrain—permitting a great variety of economic endeavors. On the other hand, problems growing out of the inordinately high population increase and urbanization; desperate living conditions in the urban and rural slums; malnutrition, debilitating diseases, and alcoholism; under- and unemployment; and economic stagnation coupled with inflation are only a few indicators of long-time societal ailments still demanding resolution.

By 1964, the greater portion of the population had moved to the peak of disaffection and, more and more, they clamored for political answers to society's problems. The dynamism of group activity in the political system closely reflected this condition.

---

cal summary can be found on p. 159. Also, see Alvin Cohen, *Economic Change in Chile, 1929–1959.*

[48] Benham and Holley, *Short Introduction to the Economy*, p. 110.

[49] *Ibid.*, pp. 112–113.

CHAPTER TWO

Communications and Politics

ALTHOUGH THE PROCESS of political communication is quite simple diagrammatically—someone sends a message by means of a medium to a receiver—quantitive and qualitative factors largely condition the efficiency and effectiveness of that process. Chile is one of the more fortunate Latin American nations on all counts. The sources of information generally are open and manifold, message styles vary, competition exists at most levels, and the ability of the receivers to perceive information is high. In some respects, such as the spectral spread of views presented in printed publications, Chile compares very favorably with the most pluralistic of societies. As far as propaganda penetration of all societal strata and the perceptive levels of receivers are concerned, Chile lags behind the more affluent countries of Europe and North America while still standing high relative to the rest of Latin America.

For some decades, more than lip service has been paid in Chile to expanding educational facilities and upgrading the quality of classroom instruction. Deep concerns exist among educators as to the level of this education, but impressive gains have been registered in recent years and the climate of opinion conduces to improvements in the system.[1] As a result, in the century between 1865 and 1965, the ratio of illiterates to literates almost exactly reversed—from 83 per cent illiteracy to approximately 81 per cent of the population being classed as literate.[2] Moreover, even allowing for a certain inaccuracy in official statistics, the proportion of national income earmarked for public education (4.23%) is exceptional. This is at least as much as any Latin American nation and only slightly behind the United States (4.31%).[3]

Among the total population between seven and fifteen years of age, the extent of students enrolled in public or private elementary and secondary schools is close to two-thirds—again, very high for Latin America.[4] Of course, as in all of the continent, disparities persist between urban and rural areas. The farmers' labor needs keep as many as half of the school-age children from the schoolroom in such agricultural provinces as Bío-Bío, Cautín, and Malleco.[5] The law sanctions this procedure by requiring urban children to matriculate seven years (six in primary grades and one in secondary or vocational school), whereas in the rural areas the minimum is reduced to the first four years of elementary school.[6] In fact, many rural children fail to fulfill even these low requirements due to inaccessibility of schools or demands upon their time by the landowner. Nonetheless, while problems obtain educationally in both quantitative and qualitative ways, a sound basis exists for the bulk of the citizenry to perceive political information of the most varied types and styles.

Chile enjoys an additional advantage in the communications function in that virtually all of the population depends upon the Spanish language for the dissemination of information. Most of the Indians

1 See Eduardo Hamuy *et al.*, *El problema educacional del pueblo de Chile.*

2 *Ibid.*, p. 10.

3 Center of Latin American Studies (hereafter referred to as CLAS), *Statistical Abstract of Latin America*, p. 28.

4 Hamuy, *El problema educacional*, p. 8.

5 Gilbert J. Butland, *Chile: An Outline of Its Geography, Economics, and Politics*, pp. 26–27.

6 Hamuy, *El problema educacional*, pp. 13–14.

residing in Chile when the Spaniards arrived eventually were absorbed by the Spanish culture. Today, the indigenous population living in *reducciones* probably is not more than 130,000,[7] and most of them communicate in the Spanish idiom as a first or second language.[8] Furthermore, immigration of non-Spanish-speaking people has not been numerically great, and almost without exception these, too, understand Spanish. Hence, the ethnic and linguistic dualism that inhibits a free flow of information between elements in many hemispheric societies does not pertain to Chile.

Media of Communication

The Printed Word

If political communication is to operate at a high level of effectiveness, the disseminating instruments must continually probe at the sources of information and provide the citizenry with competing interpretations of events. The Chilean press considerably overshadows other media in performing such functions. Indeed, it can be classed among the most lively, provocative, and significant in Latin America. The kiosks and bookstalls are replete with newspapers, magazines, and other publications representing every partisan view and from most corners of the earth. *Peking Review*, *Time*, and *The Economist* hang side by side to attract the passers-by. This helps to side-step at least one obstruction to competing information and that results from the press's tendency to stress news and to publish commentary that reflect a given newspaper's bias.

Importantly, too, the major Santiago newspapers contribute substantially to providing a sort of national outlook for the country as a whole. This is not an easy matter, because of the nation's topography. Mountains, fjords, and its great length limit the effective span of such media as radio and television to quite small regions. Thus, while regionalism and particularism do prevail, newspapers, and especially the Santiago press, assist in pulling the country together. Since the principal newspapers of the capital are dispersed by train, airplane, and boat

[7] Oscar Kaplan C., *Geografía de Chile*, p. 89.
[8] Butland, *Chile*, p. 14.

throughout all provincial urban centers, they bring attention to bear on important national issues, trends, and personalities as a vital adjunct to the weaker national coverage found in the regional press.

Santiago's most prestigious newspaper and one that enjoys an international reputation is *El Mercurio*, founded at nearby Valparaíso in 1827. Often it is cited as the *New York Times* of Chile. If this is somewhat exaggerated, certainly its appearance and tone are conservative and its coverage of national and international events is the most impressive of the Chilean press. The preponderance of the play given to overseas news—and it is in great abundance—has its origins in releases from the United States (both Associated Press and United Press International) and European (mostly Agence France-Presse) newsgathering associations. In addition, *El Mercurio* publishes the official record of debate and procedures in the Senate as well as outdistancing all other Santiago newspapers combined in advertising copy. Its circulation reaches 100,000 daily and nearly double that amount on Sunday. Long associated with the Liberal party, editorially it tends to support the regime in power. In 1964, it favored the Democratic Front (a coalition of Liberal, Conservative, and Radical parties) by advocating on behalf of its candidate for the presidency until it became obvious that the race had effectively narrowed down to the Socialist-Communist and Christian Democratic nominees. Then it swung its allegiance to the latter.

El Mercurio, a morning newspaper, owns two other dailies in Santiago—*Las Ultimas Noticias*, a midday tabloid, and *La Segunda*, an evening tabloid. Other moderate to right-wing newspapers in the capital are *El Diario Ilustrado*, the Conservative party's voice and extremely pro-Church; *Tercera de la Hora*, a Radical party publication with a big circulation; and *La Nación*, a government organ that publishes the official record of the lower house of the national Congress.

Of Santiago's three left-wing newspapers, *Clarín* claims the largest circulation with some 65,000 copies daily. Much of its popularity stems from the major attention it gives to murder, assault, and sexual improprieties—all colored with a highly sensationalist tone. Politically, it considers itself independent left and in the 1964 presidential campaign it enthusiastically joined the other leftist newspapers in aiding the cause of Salvador Allende, the Socialist-Communist nominee.

Socialists publish *Las Noticias de Ultima Hora*, an evening tabloid that sketchily covers the international scene and, in fact, only thinly reports national news. Much of it comprises feature articles of a highly polemic nature.

In several ways, the Communists' *El Siglo* merits the greatest interest and attention of the radical press. Its level of writing is the most sophisticated and it delineates the doctrine and programs of Chilean radicalism in a generally intelligent fashion. Its Sunday edition—the only one among the left-wing press—is rich in ideological discussions and information regarding trade unions and socialist politics. Furthermore, the influential voice of *El Siglo*, speaking for the dominant pro-Moscow wing of the Communist party, largely subverted efforts of the Peking-oriented Communists to push a more militant line of action in the 1964 campaign.

Numerous periodicals augment the large circulation of Santiago's dailies.[9] Many of these are pictorial news magazines that take an independent political stand. *Vea* and *Ercilla*, the most widely read, feature stories of current interest about all political personalities and groups as well as countless articles of nonpolitical, popular appeal. *Topaze* aims its biting satire at the best-informed elements of Chilean society. On the other hand, a number of weeklies openly espouse partisan causes. The Communists draw upon the facilities of *El Siglo* to bring out their hard-hitting publication, *Vistazo*, and the Christian Democrats, lacking a daily newspaper aside from the official government organ, rely heavily upon *Flecha Roja* and *Boletín PDC* to publicize their views, and they gain sympathetic attention from the Archbishopric's *La Voz*. More esoteric are the Trotskyites' biweekly *Vanguardia Proletaria*, the

[9] Statistics on the circulation of Latin American newspapers and magazines vary widely, as individual publications customarily exaggerate figures on total copies sold. One yearbook indicates that forty-eight newspapers in Chile have a daily circulation of 520,000, while another lists twenty-one dailies with an aggregate of 609,000. See S. H. Steinberg, ed., *Statesman's Yearbook*, p. 833, and Walter Mallory, ed., *Political Handbook and Atlas of the World*, pp. 48–49.

Castroites' weekly *El Rebelde*, and a number of foreign-language newspapers and periodicals directed to specific nationality groups—of these the Arab community's *El Mundo Arabe* and *Al Watan* are the most significant.[10]

Collectively, then, Santiago's dailies and weeklies represent every shade of partisan persuasion, though individually they heavily favor given groups. Not surprisingly, leftist newspapers emphasize socialist labor and political news and print stories prejudicial to management and the opposition political parties; whereas the moderate and conservative press demonstrate a reverse bias. When emotion-charged questions arise, this lack of a balanced coverage in any one newspaper becomes fully apparent.

For example, the conservatives and radicals displayed exceedingly opposed interpretations of a strike called in February, 1964, by the nation's biggest labor confederation, Central Unica de Trabajadores de Chile (CUT). *El Diario Ilustrado* blasted the strike as a politicial move and one that aborted ("The Political Strike Convoked by CUT Was a Failure"). Contrariwise, *El Siglo* exclaimed "Great Strike."[11] The truth fell somewhere in between. CUT called for work stoppages by some one dozen unions. For the most part, these federations obliged and, hence, the strike could be labeled a success. Still, labor hoped for sympathy demonstrations from additional unions. To the extent that they did not materialize, the effort failed.[12]

Finally, a word is in order regarding the regional press. Geographic factors accentuate the importance of provincial capital cities. Each of these not only acts as an administrative center, but additionally serves as an economic and transportation funnel to and from the tributary countryside. Inasmuch as there are few newspapers outside the capitals, the provincial press constitutes the main clearinghouse for regional information. Most of the newspapers contain few pages—

10 For a brief survey of the press in Chile, see Ronald Chilcote, "The Press in Latin America, Spain, and Portugal," *Hispanic American Report* (Special Issue, [1963?]): xxix–xxxii.

11 Both headlines appeared in the February fourteenth editions.

12 Interview with Oscar Núñez, president of CUT, in Santiago, February 20, 1964.

commonly ten during the week compared with sixty pages in the daily *El Mercurio* of Santiago—and necessarily devote little space to events of a nationwide scope.[13] Occasionally, a Santiago editorial or feature story finds its way into the provincial press, but only the presence of several of the Santiago newspapers in most of the Chilean urban centers truly nurtures a national outlook.

Radio, Television, and Motion Pictures

Next to the press, radio performs most materially as a mass medium in Chile. Being infused with private capital and sustaining operating costs far below those of, say, television, ensure radio a generally superior level of programming and technical competence. A variety of content reaches most interests.

In 1960, there were more than one hundred radio stations spread throughout the republic, some two dozen short-wave broadcasters, and eight transmitting on frequency modulation.[14] According to the only official source for statistics on radio consumption, the Dirección General de Servicios Eléctricos, 95 per cent of the nation's territory is covered by at least one transmitter.[15] The number of receivers that fall under this transmission blanket seems to be between 1 million and 1.1 million.[16] Uncertainty exists as to how these are dispersed nationally, though in Santiago the coverage is immense. One study taken in 1957 concluded that the proportion of dwellings possessing a radio might reach 77 per cent among workers and as high as 98 per cent in homes of the well to do. In effect, it showed that almost all homes that were electrified (i.e., 87%) claimed a set.[17] Undoubtedly this erred to the

[13] The more important provincial dailies include *El Mercurio* (Antofagasta), *La Discusión* (Chillán), *La Patria* and *El Sur* (both of Concepción), *La Prensa* (Osorno), *El Llanquihue* (Puerto Montt), *La Prensa Austral* and *Magallanes* (both in Punta Arenas), *La Mañana* (Talca), *El Diario Austral* (Temuco), *El Correo de Valdivia* (Valdivia), and *La Estrella*, *El Mercurio*, and *La Unión* (all of Valparaíso).

[14] Corporación de Fomento de la Producción (hereafter referred to as CORFO), *Geografía económica de Chile*, p. 432.

[15] Ralph Marienberg F., *Algunas sugerencias respecto a combinaciones de medios de propaganda en Chile*, p. 93.

[16] *Ibid.*, pp. 87–91; CLAS, *Statistical Abstract*, p. 73.

[17] In a survey carried out by the Institute of Sociology of the University of

low side, especially in the slum areas where individuals regularly tie into electrical lines illegally and, thus, would be reluctant to admit ownership of a radio.

In this regard, a veritable revolution in the mass communications of developing countries has occurred since the appearance of transistor radios. Rather inexpensive, especially with the pervasive smuggling of radios at prices below those tagged in commercial enterprises, they are easily transportable and do not depend upon electricity—so often absent in lower-class homes.

The most serious barrier to an even greater diffusion of radio broadcasting derives from the harsh topographical configurations of the Chilean land, which in many cases restrict its circulation to narrowly defined geographic regions. Mountains act as obstacles to even the strongest signals in some areas. A famous case of this is Casablanca, which lies a little more than twenty miles from Valparaíso and somewhat over forty miles from Santiago, yet receives nothing from either city.

Another physical problem originates in northern Chile where the arid terrain hinders good reception. The same transmitters located there produce weak signals that in the humid south can be heard clearly. By the same token, since moisture aids the passage of radio waves, those population centers situated along the Pacific Ocean reach listeners many miles away up and down the coast, whereas receivers only a short distance inland may be almost completely blocked out. In summary, then, while some of the stronger national broadcasting stations, such as Santiago's Radio Sociedad Nacional de Agricultura and Radio Cooperativa Vitalicia, theoretically could reach more than four hundred miles, physical conditions cause a very uneven coverage.[18]

Despite such limitations, radio does contribute somewhat to nullifying regionalism by imposing nationally oriented information on its

---

Chile, the actual breakdown by occupation was liberal professions and managers (98%), public employees (94%), private employees (94%), merchants and artisans (87%), workers (77%), and retired and without a profession (89%) (quoted in Marienberg, *Algunas sugerencias*, p. 94).

[18] Most broadcasting stations' maximum transmission ranges far less—from ten to under one hundred miles (*ibid.*, pp. 103–114).

listeners. There are no major national networks, but periodically the government preempts prime time from broadcasters throughout Chile to transmit speeches and other information, usually of a political nature.[19] Obviously, this focuses the attention of much of the nation on the same matter simultaneously. Further, although there is a strong tendency for provincial radio to cater to tastes and items of regional interest, some surveys submit that most people who tune in on programs beamed from other cities opt for the largest metropolitan area's broadcast that is available. This gives some built-in strengths to Santiago's more powerful stations and their stress upon national events. This is particularly true with broadcasters transmitting on the lower radio bands, which are inclined to be so forceful as to drown out local broadcasts in some cases.

Besides newspapers and radio, movies and television for one reason or another do not merit a "mass" description. Although movie theaters can be found widely throughout the country and admission prices are not prohibitive for most of the people, there is no important Chilean motion-picture industry to promote national themes. Instead, titles from the United States and Europe dominate the marquees and the sound tracks reflect the language of the film's origin, having recourse to subtitles when the language is not Spanish.

In the mid-1960's, television remained in such an embryonic and problematic stage of its development that it offered little hope for performing importantly in the communications function for some time. It is impossible to do more than offer a rough estimate of the number of receivers presently in existence because of the Chileans' penchant for purchasing such items on the black market. This is because the government's policy of imposing high customs taxes on television receivers, and countless other items that are not manufactured in Chile and thus must be imported, pushes up the retail prices of foreign-made merchandise to extraordinary heights. Most television sets purchased in commercial stores in 1964 began at about $650, with those smuggled in priced somewhat lower. Official statistics calculated the total

[19] Nevertheless, one broadcasting group, Asociación de Radiodifusoras de Chile, engaged in educational extension work beginning in 1942 (see Wilbur Schramm, *Mass Media and National Development*, pp. 167–168).

number of receivers at 35,000 in 1964, though illegal purchases would raise that figure considerably. Still, even allowing for an adjustment the number is not large.[20]

To date, the government limits the installation of television stations to educational institutions. While this appears to contain great merit on the surface, the low funding of these endeavors produces extremely inferior technical and programmatic results. In 1964, perhaps 40 per cent of the total programmed time of Santiago's two channels was filled with propaganda films offered free of charge by the foreign embassies. As the television stations were deficient in sound stages, cameras, and other facilities, these films served to fill in while scenery was changed for live programs. The remainder of television offerings in Santiago seemed to be divided between rather sophisticated adult fare on Channel 9, emphasizing artistic productions, and highly popularized "new wave" music and shows on Channel 13, catering to youth. News and commentary comprised a small portion of both channels' efforts and relied very heavily on amateur talent from the universities and a shifting panorama of professional newspapermen. Due to extremely low remunerations, the skilled technicians and directors abandoned television for other occupations—compounding the problem of poor programming and stressing the need for a major overhaul of the government's policies toward the television industry if it is to expand into a useful medium of mass communications.

Evaluation of the Communication Process

Chile does possess, then, a high proportion of its citizenry educationally competent to evaluate political propaganda that comes from competing sources in the press and to a lesser extent from radio, with television and movies still very unimportant. Newspaper circulation lags behind that in Uruguay and Argentina, but at 134 per 1,000 population it is high for Latin America generally.[21] The number of

[20] A brief summary of events up to 1960 can be found in CORFO, *Geografía económica de Chile*, pp. 432–433. For an excellent editorial discussion regarding many aspects of television, see *El Mercurio* (Santiago), March 1, 1964.

[21] CLAS, *Statistical Abstract*, p. 34.

radio receivers (130 per 1,000 persons) drops Chile to sixth place among the Latin American countries, though it still is considerable.[22] And, as noted, the styles of communication demonstrate great variances —from the sharp satire of *Topaze* to the conservative tone of *El Mercurio,* from the rightist *Diario Ilustrado* and its defense of traditionalism to *El Siglo*'s call for revolution.

Nonetheless, threats to the openness of Chilean communications lurk below the surface and from time to time erupt to challenge its vitality. Since the press is the most open, it also is most subject to circumscriptions. First, some observers object to an inherent danger in the nature of newspaper ownership. Most are held by giant economic trusts, tying together perhaps 70 per cent of Chilean industry.[23] The family of Augustín Edwards together with Banco Edwards, controls *La Estrella* and *El Mercurio* of Valparaíso and *El Mercurio*, *Las Ultimas Noticias*, and *La Segunda* in Santiago. Most of the major newspapers in the south are held by the Sociedad Periodística del Sur and include *La Patria* (Concepción), *El Diario Austral* (Temuco), *El Correo de Valdivia* (Valdivia), and *La Prensa* (Osorno). Two powerful groups own most northern dailies. Sociedad de Publicaciones "El Tarapacá" publishes *El Tarapacá* (Iquique), and *El Día* (La Serena); Compañía Salitrera Anglo-Lautaro issues *La Prensa* (Tocopilla) and *El Mercurio* (Antofagasta).[24]

These great industrial, commercial, and mining enterprises seek a profit for their newspapers, but generally are in a position to underwrite losses in the press by subventions from more financially lucrative branches of their holdings. On the other hand, the radical press relies heavily upon political parties for its support. Necessarily, these seek their main clientele in the remunerative Santiago metropolitan district. Consequently, the provincial press is conservative, and leftist views can only permeate the countryside by means of the Santiago-based radical newspapers.

22 *Ibid.*, p. 73.

23 One of the most influential and controversial studies of this problem is Ricardo Lagos Escobar, *La concentración del poder económico, su teoría, realidad chilena.*

24 Marienberg, *Algunas sugerencias*, pp. 26–27.

Actually, only a few large societal structures believe themselves to be seriously closed off from regular access to the printed media. These primarily consist of the moderate labor organizations—shunned by the conservative press simply because they are trade unions and by the radicals as a threat to their own dominance of the working-class movement. A fairly standard practice to overcome this disadvantage is to buy newspaper space, usually specified as advertising copy. Another method for skirting the problem is to pay reporters to plant stories, but even this approach rarely succeeds in gaining access to the socialist press.[25] Of course, it is extremely regrettable that such a situation should exist at all, though the actual number of such groups does not appear to be significant.[26]

On the positive side, traditional forms of oral communications between interest groups and government are generally quite open. Because most economic, social, and political structures establish their national offices in Santiago proper and the decision-making process has not become so complex as to make direct contact with officialdom difficult if not impossible, it has been customary for group leaders to take their grievances straight to the appropriate governmental officers. Whether they found a response receptive to their wishes is another matter—many labor groups protesting that they did not. Still, government remains rather accessible and this engenders personalized channels of communications and overrides certain shortcomings that may prevail in the mass media.

Importantly, too, these traditional forms of direct persuasion are be-

[25] This was verified by interviews with many labor leaders of all political colors. Among the moderates who substantiated the existence of these practices are Carlos Ibáñez King, president, and Luis Lavín Céspedes, secretary general, of the Confederación Nacional de Trabajadores; Federico Mujica, vice-president of the Confederación de Empleados Particulares de Chile; and José Goldsack, president of the Confederación Latinoamericana de Sindicalistas Cristianos—all interviewed in Santiago during January–February, 1964.

[26] The head of the powerful independent maritime federation, Confederación Marítima de Chile, indicated that his group usually found no difficulty in having stories printed by the newspapers. His reason was that they always offered items of a professional and not of a political sort (interview with Wenceslao Moreno, secretary general of COMACH, in Valparaíso, January 30, 1964).

ing implemented by an extension of such activity into popular sectors of the society. This became strikingly manifest in the by-election at Curicó in March, 1964, when the Christian Democrats and Frapistas (followers of FRAP, the Socialist-Communist coalition) took their cases directly to the slum dwellers and peasants. The result was remarkable. Rural workers voted against the demands of landowners who exhorted them to support the conservative office seeker and, instead, challenged their economic masters by a demonstration of political independence. The FRAP candidate won and the Christian Democrat came in second. Added evidence of the trend to independent political action among the popular sectors became even more demonstrative in the presidential elections of September, 1964, and in congressional balloting in March, 1965. In short, new links between political groups and the lower economic classes currently are bringing deep and basic changes in the traditional communications process.

The gravest threats to freedom of communications in Chile emanate periodically from restrictive actions of the national government. During the 1960's, such pressures became almost chronic. Mario Planet Rojas, correspondent for *Time*, narrowly averted court action in 1961 for writings the government considered slanderous to Chile; the University of Chile's School of Journalism was subjected to official harassment when it sought to name Planet its director. Subsequently, a prison term was meted out to the editor of the leftist publication *Paredón* for suggesting Supreme Court complicity in hiding improper deeds by the administration from public view. In 1962, the Communists' *Vistazo* suffered governmental attacks and one of its reporters received a prison sentence of one and a half years.[27]

But the most menacing occurrence transpired in January, 1964, when the government pushed through a statutory enactment that stimulated furious debate over the future of freedom of press and of other media of communication and information. Officially known as the Law on Norms of Written and Oral Publicity, by its attackers it was soon dubbed the "Gag Law" (Ley Mordaza).

[27] These and other recent instances of government interference in the press are summarized in Chilcote, "The Press in Latin America, Spain, and Portugal," p. xxx.

The antecedents of opposition to this enactment go back a few years to the presidential regime of Gabriel González Videla, which promulgated legal sanctions against speech and assembly as well as the press.[28] González Videla attained the presidency in 1946 with the support of left-wing political elements, including the Communists. Although at first the Communists enjoyed some preeminence in the new regime, even holding three cabinet posts, they and the President became mutually disenchanted within a few months and the Communists were ejected from the government. Then, as the economic situation worsened and labor strife became chronic, González Videla turned harshly against those who seemed to have precipitated the crises—in particular the Communists. His principal legal support rested on new laws that were vague enough to ensure immediate, effective action against dissidents. Entitled Laws for the Defense of Democracy and Defense of the State, they empowered officials with the authority "to arrest and transfer to isolated locations any persons accused of menacing democracy."[29]

If the President's move attracted initial approval from most conservatives and moderates, especially because of irresponsibility in the labor movement at the time, it was not long before arbitrary arrests widened the opposition. Outcries against the laws ranged from "ill-conceived" to "dictatorial." Furthermore, the police net encompassed not just the radicals, but spread over many moderates as well. A leading Christian Democratic labor leader, arrested twice under these laws, spoke for many when he concluded that their intent was "really an effort to divide and weaken the labor movement" and their ultimate effect was "to persecute the democratic trade-union leaders."[30] Many labor leaders, radical politicians, and organs of the press did suffer considerable circumscription. And whatever the justice or alleged need

[28] In fact, beginning as early as 1925, various laws were proposed and a few enacted that aimed at extremism, improper methodology, and political movements controlled by foreign masters. Nonetheless, González Videla's decrees and their applicability evoked the strongest antagonism. For a view supporting these actions, see Florencio Durán Bernales, *El Partido Radical*, pp. 487–506.

[29] Austin F. Macdonald, *Latin American Governments and Politics*, p. 326.

[30] Interview with José Goldsack, in Santiago, February 12, 1964.

for the Laws for the Defense of Democracy, their revocation in 1957 won more than a little applause.

Perhaps it is not too surprising, then, that the proposal of new restrictive legislation in 1964 presaged bitter controversy. In order to place this debate in its fullest meaning, it seems appropriate first to analyze the law itself and then to summarize the contending views.

The first title, devoted to a definition of the law and its application, reiterates constitutional guarantees that the individual is not to be persecuted for his opinions and that he enjoys full rights of investigating, receiving, and diffusing information.[31] It goes on to require that, except for certain technical or scientific journals and foreign-language publications specifically exempted by the President of the republic, owners and directors of newspapers and other periodicals and radio and television stations must possess Chilean citizenship.

But it is Title III, regarding legal transgressions committed by the press, that touches on several more sensitive points. Fines or imprisonment may be imposed upon those publishing or reproducing "false news"—the punishment being more severe for fraud or malice than for imprudence or negligence. Although not clearly defined, false news does include printing spurious or adulterated documents or those attributed to a person inaccurately; altering in substantial form declarations, details about events, discourses, or the contents of documents; and disseminating information about official agreements and documents considered of a restricted nature. Following this dictum, attention is given to acts that are obscene or contrary to good taste and custom as well as slanderous or otherwise injurious statements. Finally, the law prohibits the press from making any pronouncements abusive of foreign representatives or officials; divulging information relating to

[31] For purposes of this law Article 12 states that the following will be considered as the media of diffusion: "Newspapers, magazines, placards, posters, notices, wall inscriptions, leaflets or emblems that are sold, distributed or exposed in public places or gatherings; and radio, television, movies, loudspeakers, phonographs and in general any device apt for affixing, picturing, reproducing or transmitting the word, sounds or images, whatever the form of expression that is utilized" (Luis Rosso, ed., *Ley No. 15,576 sobre normas de publicidad escrita y oral*).

crimes committed by minors; publishing news or photographs (unless specifically sanctioned by the courts) of a sensational character that stress delinquency, crime, or suicides; or disclosing the proceedings of secret sessions of Congress. In each instance, the precise punishment is stipulated and publishers, editors, reporters, and photographers all fall under the law's purview.

The press debate for and against the legal measure intriguingly exemplifies the types of responses to be expected from the Santiago newspapers when faced with an issue of such magnitude and one that touches them so directly. Opponents of the "Gag Law" used the occasion of its passage to dramatize the main issue—censorship. *Clarín* left its front page blank, suggesting the inevitability of censorship. The Communists' weekly, *Vistazo*, showed a photograph of such accouterments of newspapermen as cameras, a typewriter, and a press card; the mouth of the reporter pictured on the press card was covered by a cloth gag. The Christian Democrats' periodical, *Flecha Roja*, offered a montage of national and foreign newspaper headings on its cover—then cancelled these symbols of press freedom with an X in red and the words "Requiem for the Press."[32]

Enrique Ortúzar Escobar, the minister of justice under whose guidance the law evolved, claimed that his sole interest in this matter was to update an old statute largely unimproved since its promulgation in 1925. Toward this end he only sought to readjust fines, to extend sanctions to cover radio and television, and to restrain the flood of crime reporting. In essence, the new law would protect the honor and dignity of all the citizenry:

> The mothers of Chile can be certain that there is not going to be the daily penetration into their homes of the poison of sensationalist and morbid exploitation which, with motives of profit, certain publications bring out the lowest and most base acts that affect society, without concern for the grave damage that it causes to our youth.
>
> This law constitutes the triumph of liberty over license; of truth over the lie; of honesty over blackmail; of the dignity and honor of persons over

[32] All these issues were from late January and early February, 1964.

insult and defamation; and of decency over pornography and outrage to all spiritual values.[33]

El Diario Ilustrado agreed, naming the statute, "The Law for the Defense of Decency."[34] *La Nación* also expressed general satisfaction and a sigh of relief that the "now tedious discussion" over its passage was at an end.[35] Santiago's senior newspaper, *El Mercurio*, followed suit with a series of editorials lengthily explaining reasons for the law. In particular, it contended that the inefficiency of the old statute was proved by the prevalence of widespread irresponsibility among the extremist press and the absence of appropriate legal procedures against these acts.[36]

Several periodicals concluded otherwise and expressed complete disbelief that *El Mercurio* could ignore the fact that during the Alessandri regime (1958–1964) there had been more than seventy cases brought against newspapermen. Of these, approximately thirty suffered punitive action ranging from fines to jail sentences.[37] Furthermore, the opposition press insisted that the government had been politically motivated in pushing passage of the "Gag Law." It being an election year, the law was intended to serve the conservatives well by hampering the radicals' campaigns.[38]

The Communists summed up the government's true motivations for pushing through the law as (1) liquidating freedom of the press, in particular, and freedom of expression, generally; (2) aiding and protecting the conservatives' presidential candidate; (3) persecuting and threatening newspapermen and publishers of the opposition with severe jail sentences and huge fines; and (4) spreading a curtain of silence and immunity over the scandals commonly involving large landowners, monopolists, government officials and their political supporters, and

[33] *El Mercurio* (Santiago), January 16, 1964.
[34] Quoted in *Vistazo* (Santiago), February 4, 1964.
[35] *La Nación*, February 9, 1964.
[36] *El Mercurio* (Santiago), January 28, 1964.
[37] *Vistazo* (Santiago), February 4, 1964.
[38] Manuel Cabieses Donoso, "La ley mordaza," *Aurora* 1, no. 1 (January–March 1964): 96–99.

agents of United States imperialism.[39] *El Siglo*, lambasting the law, emitted a clarion call to newspapers to refuse to abide by its restrictions. It editorialized that "we newspapermen who are in the service of the popular cause are not going to abandon our duties, we are not going to fall into an abetting silence nor or we going to adopt the attitude of cowards."[40]

While the socialist press defined the bases of their antagonism to the "Gag Law" in flamboyant and sometimes even absurd terms (such as *Vistazo*'s Communist party-line approach), the Christian Democrats expressed their concern in a much more sober tone. They affirmed the need for some reform in the old basic law. Nonetheless, the new statute struck them as a desperate political maneuver by the Conservative, Liberal, and Radical parties to contain their antagonists—in the process chopping away at press freedom.

The articles dealing with "false news" and "defamation" called for particularly sharp criticism. Since mere carelessness or simple negligence could place in print items classifiable as false news, the fear of punishment might impede reporting other events that are true but difficult to prove. Besides, newspapermen would be at the mercy of lies and of those who purvey falsehood. Defamation was defined in terms so wide as to severely limit or even halt discussion of certain topics vital to the public interest. Taken as a whole, the law failed to make guarantees to protect "the sacred right and the ineludible duty of the press to watch out for the common good, making errors, evils, and anti-social attitudes known."[41]

Many foreign newspapers joined in expressing their dismay over the law. *El Mercurio* responded to criticism from abroad with a generally accurate appraisal of the traditional freedoms enjoyed by the Chilean press: "For those who live in Chile and are witnesses of the amplitude with which all ideas and opinions are expressed, by the most diverse media, there is no room for doubt that we are a nation respectful of the right of discussion and that in this sense we cannot be considered less worthy than any of the democracies of the world, in which,

[39] *Vistazo* (Santiago), February 4, 1964.
[40] *El Siglo* (Santiago), February 22, 1964.
[41] *La Flecha Roja* (Santiago), January, 1964.

moreover, laws and rules exist which prevent and limit excesses of publicity, at times more severe than the resolutions that have just been dictated."[42]

But the major point of foreign and Chilean criticism of the law was that the customary freedoms might now be threatened by the dangers inherent in restrictive legislation and especially enactments that only generally and rather vaguely defined the punishable acts. At any rate, probably due to the strong criticism, the government was reticent to move very fast to effectuate the law. The first action taken was directed against an encyclopedia published in Argentina that contained a map picturing Antarctic territory claimed by Chile as belonging to Argentina.

With all of this, some considered the government and its partisans terribly myopic. For, by raising the question of press circumscription in a time of maximum political activity, they ran the risk of retaliation by the radicals should the Socialist-Communist coalition achieve control of the presidency. As it turned out, the Christian Democrats carried the election by an absolute majority and they committed themselves to overhauling the law in order to remove its more odious and ambiguous sections. Thus, hopes ran high that an unfettered and uncoerced press would still be one of the attributes of Chilean democracy.

[42] *El Mercurio* (Santiago), January 16, 1964.

CHAPTER THREE

Interest Groups: Military, Clergy, and Students

THROUGHOUT MOST OF LATIN AMERICA, three of the groups that chronically intrude in the political process are the armed forces, the clergy, and the students. Chile is quite exceptional in this regard in that none of these three sectors can be characterized as being guilty of such pernicious involvements. This is not to say that they warrant an apolitical classification, but rather that they rarely have been accessories to social disorientation nor have they regularly sought to dominate the decision-making councils of government. Certainly, this has both resulted from and contributed to the democratic forms so firmly implanted in Chile.

MILITARY

In the entire history of Chile since independence military men have assumed a major political role on only a few occasions.[1] In 1851, civil disorders broke out when Liberals, stimulated by radical doctrines from France in the late 1840's, clashed with the authoritarian Conservative regime. When their presidential candidate, General José María de la Cruz, lost to the Conservatives' Manuel Montt, the Liberals took to the barricades in protest against what they considered an oppressive political environment. Government troops crushed the rebellion by the end of the year.

Another forty years were to pass before a serious domestic rupture involved the military again—and then it pitted the navy against the army. In 1891, civil war broke out between the navy-supported Congress and mostly army-backed President José Balmaceda in a test of power between the two governmental branches. Ultimately the navy, which had secured control of the rich northern resources and created a land-based component, carried the day—a unique accomplishment in the annals of Latin American civil-military relations.

The last example of direct military entrance into the political sphere turned around disruptive events in the middle 1920's. Unquestionably, this was the single most serious breach of civilian authority in that the army went along with Colonel (later General) Carlos Ibáñez del Campo's manipulation of the political process beginning in 1924 and in

[1] General studies of the military in Latin America include Víctor Alba, *El militarismo*; Robert Alexander, "The Army in Politics," in *Government and Politics in Latin America*, ed. Harold E. Davis, pp. 147–165; Irving Louis Horowitz, "The Military Elites," in *Elites in Latin America*, ed. Seymour Martin Lipset and Aldo Solari, pp. 146–189; John J. Johnson, *The Military and Society in Latin America*, and ed., *The Role of the Military in Underdeveloped Countries*; Edwin Lieuwin, *Arms and Politics in Latin America*, and "The Changing Role of the Military in Latin America," *Journal of Inter-American Studies* 3, no. 4 (October 1961): 559–569; Lyle N. McAlister, "Civil-Military Relations in Latin America," *Journal of Inter-American Studies* 3, no. 3 (July 1961): 341–350, and "The Military," in *Continuity and Change in Latin America*, ed. John J. Johnson; Theodore Wyckoff, "The Role of the Military in Latin American Politics," *Western Political Quarterly* 3, no. 3 (September 1960): 745–763.

his creation of an outright military dictatorship between 1927 and 1931. This era ended so disastrously that the military retired to the sidelines, and civilian antipathy to a politically active armed forces greatly inhibited the possibility of a sequel to the aberration.

Excepting the episodes of 1851, 1891, and that of the 1920's, the military remained generally aloof from politics and very few presidents even came out of the armed forces. As a consequence, the military's public image in recent times has been good—most Chileans seeming to consider their army, navy, air force, and police (*carabineros*) as generally well-trained, nonpolitical professionals. Political cartoons, which can be vicious in Chile, almost never view them as apt subjects. And it is virtually impossible to solicit an officer's opinion on current national issues.

Reasons for a Nonpolitical Military

A variety of factors have combined to encourage the military's present nonpolitical stance. Some are historical, others can be defined by the nature of the armed forces themselves, and reasons also can be detected in the Chilean sociopolitical system.

Historical Factors. The early years of Chile's republican history were marked by great turbulence and chronic military dictatorship. Then beginning in 1830, for a little more than a half-dozen years, Diego Portales ruled the nation as a powerful civil dictator bent on one cause—establishing order. In fulfilling his goal, Portales not only brought about a long era of stability that would outlive him by decades, but also utterly crushed the military as a freewheeling power institution. This was accomplished by dismissals, demotions, and death to recalcitrants and ended in firmly placing the armed forces under civilian hegemony and imbuing them with a respect for civilian authority. Thus in all of Spanish America during the nineteenth century, only Chile (along with Costa Rica) escaped an epoch of a virtual monopoly of power by the triad of military, clergy, and landowners.

Portales' compulsion for order and his reshaping of the officer class toward that purpose additionally contributed to a close correlation between civilian and military elites in the early years of the republic. That is to say, that those who filled the officer ranks tended to come from the same social background as those civilians who governed; consequently, there existed a similarity in values held by both elements.[2] In time, however, immigrants seeking status in a foreign society and middle- and lower-class sectors entered the officer corps, where opportunities for social mobility were more prevalent than in most other occupations. The net result of these changes in the class background of the military meant that the army did not stay tied to the upper class; in fact, on a number of occasions it categorically rebuffed oligarchical pleas for support. The military's single major drive to the center of political power, in the 1920's, seems to have been more a disgust for civilian feuding and governmental ineptness—not unrelated to Portales' inculcation of a desire for order almost a century earlier—than because of siding with any particular social group. As has been noted, that episode greatly reduced the army's fascination for a repeat performance.

Inhibiting Features in the Military. A second over-all explanation for a military behavior pattern that has been largely apolitical resides in many attributes of the military itself. First of all, both the army and the navy assumed high standards of training and discipline at the end of the last century. From 1885 until World War I, German influence over the army was immense and brought such a thorough overhaul of organization and training procedures, from officers through enlisted men, that around the turn of the century the Chilean army was based upon the first universal conscription law in Latin America and its military standing was so high that it was dispatching training teams to other hemispheric nations as well as receiving officers from abroad to study in its highly esteemed military academies. The navy experienced a parallel boost in professional standing beginning in the 1890's and, early in this century, came under the mantle of British instruction. More recently, U.S. influences have been felt, especially in the air force.

All of this conduced to an enduring professionalism among officers, whose "sense of discipline . . . is stronger than political sympathies."[3]

[2] Luis Galdames, *A History of Chile*, trans. and ed. Isaac J. Cox, p. 238; Lyle N. McAlister, "The Military," p. 145. For an opposing view, see Federico Gil, *The Political System of Chile*, pp. 94–95.

[3] Gil, *Political System of Chile*, p. 296.

Also, while the impatience of junior officers toward their superiors is not unknown, internal mobility is based upon military considerations rather than political determinants; frictions between ranks, though not unknown, are uncommon.

Organizational checks and decentralization also are contributory to the armed forces' nonpolitical stance. Chile's extraordinarily long coastline early engendered attention to naval expansion. Consequently, only in Chile of the Latin American nations did a naval service develop as a really effective counterforce to the army's more customary dominance of coercive power. Indeed, the aforementioned naval defeat of the army in 1891 remains as the solitary instance of such a happening in Latin America. This could have led to a history of interservice rivalries, but instead it sent each military branch into its own bailiwick.

Today, the three armed services total some 47,000 troops.[4] In addition, *carabineros* comprise another 22,000 well-trained officers and men. The large population concentration in the central part of the country necessarily demands the presence of the greatest number of police, though they are to be found in every corner of the republic. On the other hand, the army, navy, and air force tend to be dispersed more widely. The army is grouped into six divisions, of which the cities of Iquique, Antofagasta, Santiago, Concepción, Valdivia, and Punta Arenas serve as headquarters; the navy is centered at six bases—Mejillones, Valparaíso, Talcahuano, Puerto Montt, Punta Arenas, and Puerto Williams; and the air force is more or less similarly scattered. Each area headquarters is commanded by a general officer and has a full component of troops.[5] This decentralization certainly does not prevent a division, say near Santiago, from moving into the capital and seizing control; but the existence of the navy and air force as well as strong army units spread throughout the nation clearly would make

[4] Although there is some disagreement regarding the number of troops in each branch of service, the following figures seem quite accurate: 21,875 in the army, 17,512 in the navy, and 7,432 in the air force (*Vistazo* [Santiago], May 18, 1964).

[5] Military organization is discussed in Oscar Kaplan C., *Geografía de Chile*, pp. 101–110; supplementary material provided by interview with Colonel Dan S. McMillan, United States Army Attaché to Chile, in Santiago, February 24, 1964.

such a move more dangerous than in countries where the army is overwhelmingly powerful and congregated near the nation's capital.

Another aspect of military life that aids the armed services' image and that, at the same time, seems to strengthen their professional, nonpolitical nature is the many basically nonmilitary functions performed by all four branches of service. Simply to catalog all these activities would be a major undertaking; but it may clarify the point being made to explain something of the variety of services carried out.

One area of such operations is countless public works projects. The army in particular engages in building roads, airfields, irrigation systems, and bridges; it also erects telephone and electrical lines, widens river channels, and promotes reforestation.[6] In these activities it is aided by the air force, which utilizes B-26 bombers for taking aerial views of the land and then reduces these photographs to scale models—permitting better planning for dams, flood control, irrigation projects, and similar public works. All this has spurred development, especially in the more remote areas of the country. At times the military has made a direct contribution to the nation's economic health. This occurred during World War II when Chile was cut off from its normal access to certain important supplies from abroad and the army stepped into the breach and manufactured bicycles and agricultural equipment.

When natural disasters strike—and they happen altogether too frequently in Chile in the form of earthquakes, volcanic eruptions, floods, and landslides—the several armed forces combine their efforts to bring aid and comfort to the victims. At such times, they transport food, clothing, and medicines to the scene; set up temporary shelters and hospitals; and guard against looting.

Moreover, on a day-to-day basis, the military carries out myriads of social services. The air force often flies food and clothing into depressed areas and the police force maintains first-aid stations throughout the republic where everything from inoculations to maternity care is provided—in many places this being the only medical attention available.

The military also is very much committed to upgrading technical

[6] See Waldo Retamal González, *El servicio militar del trabajo.*

skills. Technical training has been emphasized for a long time, though the facilities for such training were greatly expanded in the 1960's. For example, the army cooperates with the Technical Cooperation Service (an affiliate of the Chilean Development Corporation) to offer courses to its enlisted men and noncommissioned officers in such trades as carpentry, electricity, masonry, automobile mechanics, and plumbing. By 1966, it was scheduled to impart these skills to four thousand men.[7] Furthermore, the army maintains a railroad running some sixty miles up into the cordillera on which it teaches every aspect of the operation of a train. Many of its firemen, conductors, and the like find comparable employment in the state railroad system upon completion of military service.

Moreover, the army, navy, air force, and police all devote considerable attention to literacy education. The army takes in approximately 5 per cent of its recruits as illiterates, distributes them throughout a number of units, and then teaches them to read and write.[8] The navy has been the most active in establishing literacy instructional centers for adult civilians in the cities, while, since 1964, the *carabineros* have collaborated with the Ministry of Education to provide literacy training and mobile libraries for the rural population.

As a direct consequence of these educational endeavors, men acquire skills and functional literacy that enlarge their opportunities for economic mobility. The training also acts as an important medium of political socialization inasmuch as thousands of enlisted men from every corner of the nation are brought into the services every year and inculcated in national values. This includes concepts of the proper role of the military in society as well as elements of patriotism. It also promotes a national outlook, a view the armed forces attempt to impart to civilians (e.g., the air force regularly flies a number of youths from outlying regions to Santiago) as well as to recruits. Finally, civic education is implemented during elections when the army acts as a watchdog over the voting process; by being called upon to ensure that voters are free from untoward pressures at the voting place, soldiers also learn the meaning of honest voting procedures.

[7] *El Mercurio* (Santiago), February 29, 1964.

[8] Interview with Colonel Dan S. McMillan.

Several authors have viewed these types of role substitutability (i.e., the military performing what are primarily nonmilitary functions) in a dim light. George Blanksten has observed that evidence exists to show that, "as economic development progresses, the function of the military becomes increasingly specific and differentiated until it reaches the point at which it is limited virtually exclusively to the specialized military task of defending the community."[9] It is obvious from the foregoing discussion that Chile has not reached the stage where it simply defends the community. Kenneth Johnson, in an insightful treatise on causal factors of instability in Latin America, also sees dangers in the multifunctional military: "The prevailing lack of role specialization and interdependence among performance entities in Latin America is a continuing invitation to armies and government bureaucracies to usurp each other in a power grab."[10] Nevertheless, this has not been the case in Chile. Indeed, there is a contrary opinion that, at least in the Chilean situation, the workings of role substitution actually encourage many military personnel to anticipate civilian life and opportunities for advancement with their newly acquired skills. Thus, it may be true, as Professor Johan Galtung believes, that, by splitting loyalties between military and civilian roles, multifunctionalism obstructs the growth of an "entrenched military psychology."[11] Whatever the case, there exist many positive factors for the perpetuation of multifunctionalism in the military and very few instances to suggest that such a system is breeding political activism.

Societal Inhibitions to Military Adventurism. The third major reason for the military's generally apolitical stature can be found in the larger political community. Chile stands out as one of the very few Latin American states where a rule of law prevails and where a respect for the constitutional process is at the root of the political value system.

[9] George Blanksten, "The Aspiration for Economic Development," *Annals of the American Academy of Political and Social Science* no. 334 (March 1961): 17.

[10] Kenneth Johnson, "Causal Factors in Latin American Political Instability," *Western Political Quarterly* 17, no. 3 (September 1964): 438.

[11] Conversation with Johan Galtung, associate professor of sociology at the University of Oslo and visiting member of the Facultad Latino Americana de Ciencias Sociales, in Santiago, November 8, 1963.

In other words, Chile is a nation where the Constitution is regarded as the supreme law of the land and not just a temporary expedient to underwrite a momentary regime. Article 22 of the Constitution of 1925 proclaims civilian supremacy over the military. Significantly, this concept is reinforced by the customary attitude of most Chileans, who possess a strong distaste for military intrusion in politics. This became manifest in 1924 following Ibáñez' brief seizure of political power. Then, even though the military had had a long tradition of staying out of politics, this single act caused people to spit on officers who appeared in public and to leave local establishments when officers entered. As a result, officers were prohibited from wearing their uniforms outside encampments for a time.[12]

By 1932, after several years of military rule, competing power groups and the populace in general had become so angered at what they considered the ineptness of government by the army that they pushed the military from politics. Undoubtedly, this was a tremendously important lesson to the armed forces; in the next years younger officers, who looked with disdain at their senior officers' political adventurism and who bowed to civilian antipathy to military involvement in politics, rose to command positions and reinforced professional attitudes in the generation of officers who followed them.

Actually, both the Penal Code and the Code of Military Justice explicitly prohibit politicizing the armed forces. The Code of Military Justice demands that "the military man must not become involved in politics. He is forbidden to belong to associations of a political character and to participate in acts of a political nature."[13] Early in 1964, a retired first sergeant was caught circulating political pamphlets and discoursing on current politics among a group of air force personnel. Immediately, he was detained and the news media labeled his act one of great gravity.[14]

Finally, an important ingredient in military-civil relations is a virtually guaranteed percentage of the national budget going to the armed

[12] Próspero, *Visión espectral de Chile*, pp. 55–58.

[13] "Reglamento de disciplina para las fuerzas armadas," in República de Chile, *Código de justicia militar*, p. 184.

[14] See *La Tercera de la Hora* (Santiago), April 17, 1964.

forces. This amounts to slightly more than a fifth of the total and usually constitutes the largest single budgetary item. Of course, this is a serious drain on the economy and, since all military hardware must be purchased abroad, adversely affects the already serious problem of balance of payments. On the other side of the ledger, the armed forces do provide a number of valuable nonmilitary services to the nation and the large slice of the budget is one way to keep the military satisfied and out of active political maneuvering.

Military and Society in the Contemporary Scene

All this is not to suggest that the Chilean armed forces are completely divorced from governmental matters or that there never exist threats to their largely nonpolitical posture. Intraservice rivalries between junior and senior officers occasionally break the surface—for example in the middle 1920's, contention between reformist junior officers and conservative senior officers spewed forth into the political system. And, once in a while, secret clubs with political orientation pop up in the officer class. Los Pumas and La Línea Recta were organized early in the 1950's among a few junior officers who were attracted to the Argentine army's ascendancy to political power and strove for a commensurate preeminence for themselves in the Chilean government. Their basic plan centered on the 1952 elections when they aspired to lift Ibáñez into the presidency and then to aid him in acquiring dictatorial powers.[15]

What, then, is the present state of the armed forces? To all intents and purposes, they operate autonomously, generally leaving politics alone though bargaining with the government to keep their existing perquisites and periodically pushing for improved benefits. Edwin Lieuwin sums up their ties with government as follows: "The military's representative in the government, the defense minister, makes it understood that the armed forces' customary 20–25 per cent of the national budget must not be revised downward. A sort of gentleman's agreement exists. If the government allows the armed forces to function unmolested and to look after their own affairs, it need have no

[15] John J. Johnson, *Military and Society*, p. 125; Próspero, *Visión espectral de Chile*, pp. 58–61.

fear they will seize control."[16] In other words, they can be classified as a "veto group" insofar as governmental policy affecting them is concerned; but they do not actually try to govern.[17]

As has been noted, the armed forces' public image generally is excellent. Officers are well trained and highly disciplined. By and large, enlisted men are conscripted for one year at the age of nineteen. All social classes contribute men to the military and the Chilean armed forces are free from the record of brutality and oppressiveness that characterizes the military in many Latin American nations. Even the police are exceptionally well disciplined—probably the best in all Latin America—and attend various training programs that teach them social and economic subjects as well as police science.[18] They certainly cannot be accused of the rampant corruption and ubiquitous bribery so prevalent among their counterparts in many other Latin American countries. From time to time, Marxists express dissatisfaction about the fact that the *carabineros* represent the oligarchy (despite the fact that overwhelmingly the police come from the lower classes) and that it is not fair to locate so many of them in the poor sections (though that is where the crime rate soars and where they perform needed services) rather than scattering them among the neighborhoods of all social classes.

Actually, the police are remarkably adept in their jobs and generally reluctant to turn to their coercive powers in dealing with the citizenry. Political rallies and street demonstrations proceed unhindered by police curtailment unless a clear threat to order develops. Should a possibility for disorder or violence seem imminent, the police are deployed in troop carriers at strategic points several blocks away from the source of the potential trouble. The *carabineros'* special weapons for mob control are tear gas and armored trucks, or *guanacos* (llamalike animals known for their habit of spitting), which shoot streams of water under high pressure. The army performs a back-up role to the police if they cannot resolve the problem themselves. However, in most instances

[16] Lieuwin, *Arms and Politics*, p. 169.

[17] Gil, *Political System of Chile*, p. 296.

[18] Interview with Moisés Poblete Troncoso, professor of law and social sciences at the Universidad de Chile, in Santiago, January 29, 1964.

only a handful of *carabineros* are present at rallies and then they attempt to do little more than ensure an orderly flow of traffic and pedestrians.

The outcome of the presidential election of 1964 seemed critical to many Chileans as an indicator of the military's ability to keep clear of political involvements. As commonly transpires in Chilean elections, all the political parties made friendly gestures toward the military. Both of the main candidates, Frei and Allende, promised that if he were elected the military could look forward to salary boosts, an improved pension plan, and access to public housing on retirement.[19] The two presidential nominees tended to correlate closely in their general promises, but differed somewhat in specific details. Allende favored a reorganization of the armed forces along the most modern lines—including the organization of paratroop and air-transport units, more armored components, and a greater attention to technical and literacy training. Frei also called for the modernizing of the military services. His program recognized that the military would continue to receive its fair share of the national budget, while suggesting that the branches of service should look for ways to reduce red tape and overcome "bureaucratic asphyxia." In order to alleviate the balance-of-payments crises, Frei proposed that attention be given to the possibility of manufacturing some military hardware in Chile. Frei and Allende alike formed veterans' political-action groups as means of catering to the interests of the military in active service.

To a large degree, the candidates' proposals to upgrade the armed forces represented efforts to placate the military, to encourage them to remain politically aloof, and to minimize the military's anxieties about what would happen to them after the outcome of the election. In fact, Frei undoubtedly faced the lesser difficulty of the two nominees in terms of arousing the military's concern about his presidency. True, there was some talk about whether the army would back up his agrarian reform program if it came down to the necessity of running large landholders off their estates; but this was a modest ripple on the waters of

[19] Frei's program was extensively reported in *El Mercurio* (Santiago), May 21, 1964; Allende's obtained major coverage in *Vistazo* (Santiago), May 18, 1964.

civil-military relations compared to Allende's situation. It was widely recognized that, although the military remained mute on domestic politics, for the most part the officer class held views that were sympathetic toward the United States on international matters. They favored the U.S. position in the Cuban missile crisis and appeared sympathetic to the United States' situation in its controversy with Panama over the Canal Zone. Many had studied in special military schools in the United States or in Fort Gulick in the Canal Zone.[20]

In short, the Allende camp increasingly feared that the military would seize government in a coup d'état in order to keep the Socialist-Communist coalition out of government. Rumors went so far as to suggest that the Central Intelligence Agency had gained control of the Argentine army, which was posed on the Chilean border ready to sweep over the Andes and seize the Chilean government if Allende should win. Of course, this could have been a ploy by the Allendistas to rally support to their side on the basis of nationalistic feelings. Anti-Allendistas carefully pointed out that the entire military system would be endangered in the event of Allende's electoral triumph. They insisted that Allende was soft on communism and, should he become President, would appoint a chief of staff subservient to his will. Colonels considered disloyal to the government's interest would be sent abroad on special missions or as attachés. Then, pro-Allendistas could be moved up into staff ranks. This would be accomplished by passing over lieutenant colonels who were considered unsympathetic to the government in favor of those with less seniority, but who were loyal to Allende. Since the custom was for officers to resign who have been denied promotion in preference for those farther down the seniority ladder, in short order Allende would gain control of command positions.[21]

In all events, the Allende forces carefully avoided any action that might serve as an excuse for a military takeover. Whether from a genuine fear that he would not be permitted to assume the presidency if elected or as a propaganda device (or a combination of both), Allende

[20] Interview with Colonel Dan McMillan.

[21] Interview with General (retired) Alfonso Cañas Ruíz Tagle, in Valdivia, March 9, 1964.

met with President Jorge Alessandri a week before the election to gain the chief executive's assurance that he would employ every power of his office to bring about an orderly transfer of the presidency. President Alessandri did maintain an atmosphere of complete impartiality; Frei won the election by an absolute majority and the military kept its silence.

It remains a moot question as to what the armed forces would have done if Allende had walked away from the 1964 election as the victor. Indeed, it is hazardous to attempt to define too closely any possible combination of circumstances that would propel the armed forces into a political posture. Several times during his presidency, Jorge Alessandri (1958–1964) pumped for an end to the arms race in the Americas and became known as a leading spokesman for arms reductions in the Latin American nations. Throughout the discussions, the Chilean military generally remained silent—at least in public. On the other hand, late in 1966 President Frei announced that Chile had ordered twenty-one jet fighters from Great Britain at a time when the government was engaged in a costly program of economic reform. Since Chile could hardly be considered threatened militarily by another nation, it raised a question as to the efficacy of so expensive an outlay. (Frei reasoned that, since the air force trained many pilots who eventually would be employed by the Chilean national airlines, they needed experience with more up-to-date equipment.)

Nevertheless, permitting the military periodically to modernize its hardware seems part and parcel of the agreement between the armed forces and the civilians. As long as the armed services are granted their autonomy, they will not bring pressure to bear on the other decision-making levels of government. Excepting for some cataclysmic event, such as a severe economic reversal, there appears to be little likelihood that Chile's military will break its customary professional and nonpolitical tradition.

Clergy

Chile, like all the Latin American countries, can be classified as a Roman Catholic nation. The Catholic church has held a preeminent place in Chile's history and Roman Catholicism continues to dominate the religious attitudes of most Chileans. Its priests generally constitute as well-trained and urbane a lot as are to be found in Latin America and the number of Catholics per priest (2,750 to one) is in quantitative terms one of the most favorable ratios in all Latin America.[22]

However, by themselves these comments present an incomplete picture of the relative position of Chilean Catholicism in the hemisphere, for in many ways Chile is probably the least Catholic of Latin American societies. First of all, 88 per cent of Chileans at best can be considered Catholics in any sense.[23] Even in raw statistics this is one of the lowest percentage rates in Latin America. In educational background, this ranges from 90 per cent of those completing an elementary education down to 67 per cent of college-educated people.[24] Moreover, adults are notoriously lax about fulfilling devotional obligations. It is estimated that only about 13 per cent of Chilean women and 7 per cent of the men actually attend Sunday mass.[25]

In addition to the high percentage of nominal Catholics, many of whom have little or no contact with the Catholic religion between baptism and the last rites, Chile contains within its borders the largest proportion of Protestants of any Latin American country. They amount to a minimum of 11 per cent of the population and include both Protestant immigrants from central and northern Europe and a much more sizable element of Chilean nationals who converted to Protestantism. Most of the latter joined Pentecostal sects, which constitute close to three-quarters of the more than 800,000 total number of Protestants.[26] Protestantism has been expanding at a consistent pace. The earliest census that recorded religious affiliations listed only 1 per cent of the nation with a Protestant preference in 1907; but the percentage reached 4.1 per cent in 1952 and jumped to more than 11 per cent in

22 This is in measurable contrast to such traditionalist Catholic nations as Colombia and Ecuador, which average about 3,500 Catholics per priest, or, say, to Honduras, which falls to some 10,000 Catholics to one priest (Gary MacEoin, *Latin America: The Eleventh Hour*, pp. 205–215).

23 Alexander T. Edelmann, *Latin American Government and Politics*, p. 170.

24 François Houtart and Emile Pin, *The Church and the Latin American Revolution*, pp. 170–172.

25 J. Lloyd Mecham, *Church and State in Latin America*, p. 222.

26 *Ibid.*

the late 1950's.[27] To a large degree, successful Protestant proselytism coincides with the increase in alienation, particularly among poorer segments, with the established order. Rightly or wrongly, the poor relate the Catholic church to that system, whereas the Protestant congregational environment presents a sharp contrast to the traditional ways:

> Contrasting with the rigidity of the Latin American class system, its emphasis on feudalistic and paternalistic tutelage over the lower classes, the following structural principles of the Protestant congregations may be pointed out: (1) the assumption of ethical equality of the members of a community regardless of family, wealth, educational background, and occupation; (2) the assumption that the individual members of a community are morally and intellectually capable of solving their common problems in a responsible fashion; and (3) the assumption that leadership does not imply restriction of freedom of expression and judgment.[28]

The religious situation in Chile is made still more complex by the presence of a noticeably persistent strain of anticlericalism. Much of this derived from the nineteenth century when, because of its opposition to democratic precepts, the Church was associated with reactionary colonial institutions that carried over into the republican era. Its reputation was not enhanced by the great economic wealth it allegedly possessed nor by the fact that it always seemed to stand shoulder to shoulder with forces opposing social change. Francisco Bilbao equated the Catholic church to slavery and Domingo Arteaga Alemparte exclaimed: "So deplorable has been the record of the Church in regard to political interference that it is impossible for a Catholic to be a good citizen."[29] Much of this anti-Catholic sentiment found its home in the Radical party, which also sheltered most of Chilean Masonry, and later in the Marxist parties as well. Instead of being a passing phase, there are indications that anticlericalism actually has been increasing in recent years. This was the prevailing viewpoint, for example, of a large sam-

[27] Emilio Willems, "Protestantism and Culture Change in Brazil and Chile," in *Religion, Revolution, and Reform*, ed. William V. D'Antonio and Fredrick B. Pike, pp. 94–96.

[28] *Ibid.*, pp. 103–108.

[29] Bilbao's views are summarized in William R. Crawford, *A Century of Latin-American Thought*, pp. 69–74. Arteaga is quoted in *The Conflict between Church and State in Latin America*, ed., Fredrick B. Pike, p. 16.

ple of Catholic clergymen and laymen whose views were solicited by a Catholic University research team in the early 1960's.[30]

The multifaceted nature of attitudes toward religion has been an outgrowth of and a contribution to significant shifts in values and power relationships that have transpired over a century or so. In the traditional period, Catholicism enjoyed dominance as the established Church and as the principal arbiter of social values. But, beginning in the 1920's, this dualistic hegemony fell apart under the onslaught of attacks from new leftist movements and from evangelical elements. According to Ivan Vallier, both groups "preach a new reward system, assume a militant posture against the existing social order, and articulate a cohesive set of anti-Catholic values."[31] As a consequence of the inroads made by the leftists and the Protestants, "for the first time, a line was cut between a value system fused with Catholicism and a non-Catholic value system."[32] Of all the Latin American republics, this process has probably reached its apogee in Chile where, especially among the poorer societal strata, Marxists and Pentecostals own a large and continuously broadening base of adherents.

Church-State Relations

Another important manifestation of the changing state of Catholicism in Chile resides in the domain of Church-State relations. Unlike most Latin American republics, Chile disestablished the Church peacefully. However, this achievement did not arrive before a long struggle between forces supporting and opposing the Church had run its course.

In fact, Chile entered the nineteenth century extremely intolerant of non-Catholics and "the influence of the Church weighed on society and its customs with all the intensity of a slab of lead."[33] The colonial

[30] The survey found that 47.5 per cent of the 1,000-person sample believed anticlericalism to be on the rise; only 20.5 per cent evaluated it as declining, and the remaining 32 per cent noticed no change (Joseph H. Fichter, *Cambio social en Chile: Un estudio de actitudes*, p. 30).

[31] Ivan Vallier has written brilliantly on this and other aspects of the Latin American church in his study, "Religious Elites: Differentiations and Developments in Roman Catholicism," in *Elites in Latin America*, ed. Lipset and Solari, pp. 190–232. The quotation is from p. 195.

[32] *Ibid.*

[33] Ricardo Donoso, *Las ideas políticas en Chile*, p. 175.

Church had imposed an enormous obligation upon its parishioners —demanding a strong religious faith and repeated expressions of devotion to the single Church. Not surprisingly, the early Chilean constitutions mirrored this situation. The Constitution of 1818 stated unreservedly that "[the] Roman, Apostolic, Catholic religion is the single and exclusive one of the State of Chile. Its protection, conservation, purity and inviolability will be one of the primary duties of the heads of society, who will never permit any other public cult nor any doctrine contrary to that of Jesus Christ."[34]

Quite simply, Chile was Catholic and few saw fit to question the single religion concept. Perhaps the writings of Juan Engaña most accurately echoed the prevailing views of his day when he opposed the presence of two religions in one society as a dangerous precedent that would only bring about irreligion as well as internal strife. Such a situation would ultimately heap destruction upon the State. It should be obvious to everyone, then, that only societies committed to one religious faith (meaning Catholicism in Chile) could expect to achieve unity and order.[35]

Chile experienced several turbulent years before the order Engaña called for could be safely established. Then, in 1831, stability was ushered in with the implantation of the Autocratic Republic, a conservative regime that was to last thirty years. Guidelines on religious matters were laid out in the Constitution of 1833, which recognized Roman Catholicism as the state religion and as the only faith that could be professed publicly. It granted power to the President to appoint high clergy, to control Church patronage, to pass on the applicability of official Church documents to Chile, and to negotiate and maintain formal relations with the Papacy.[36]

All this implied a very rigid, inflexible system. In practice, however, good sense carried the day and non-Catholics were permitted the free exercise of their religion as long as they did so privately and away from public view. At one point, *El Mercurio* of Valparaíso had the temerity to favor additional toleration, though its suggestion fell on

[34] *Ibid.*, p. 176.
[35] *Ibid.*, pp. 182–186.
[36] Mecham, *Church and State in Latin America*, pp. 206–207.

thoroughly unappreciative clerical ears and, in 1843, Santiago's archbishopric brought out a new publication, *La Revista Católica*, to counter such untoward statements.[37]

During the long rule of the Autocratic Republic the Church was generally protected by the government; periodic outbursts of anticlericalism were shunted aside and even the excitement engendered by such a firebrand as Francisco Bilbao could be dealt with simply by exiling the perpetrator of unorthodox concepts. Nevertheless, the clergy gradually weakened somewhat in its ability to influence the decision-making process and more and more it depended upon the good graces of powerful presidents. Simultaneously, a rising tide of liberalism finally spilled over into an armed insurrection and, in 1861, inaugurated a new political era, the Liberal Republic, that survived the next three decades.

Now, slowly but certainly, alterations were made in the Church's position in society. In 1865, Congress passed the Ley Interpretiva, which permitted Protestants to erect their own church buildings—something they had been doing illegally for several years—and to enjoy genuine freedom of worship therein. Also, they acquired the right to found schools for the purpose of teaching their religious beliefs to their children. In 1874, Church courts were abolished, priests were subjected to ordinary criminal law, compulsory tithing was ended, and Protestants gained permission to be buried in Catholic cemeteries. A decade later, civil marriage and a civil registry of vital statistics further reduced the authority of the Church.[38]

From 1892 until 1925, known as the period of the Parliamentary Republic, no important new legal enactments appeared that affected the religious question. Still, the mood of the country was changing and so was the Church.[39] Liberal encyclicals issued by Pope Leo XIII suggested new directions for the Church in terms of social policy. These in turn stimulated a reconsideration by many Chilean clergymen

[37] Galdames, *History of Chile*, p. 284.

[38] Church-State relations are extensively discussed in Donoso, *Las ideas políticas en Chile*, Chap. VII.

[39] This period is summarized in John J. Johnson, *Political Change in Latin America*, pp. 68–69.

of their proper function in society. In 1899, Enrique Concha Subercaseaux offered his proposals for "social Catholicism" in *Cuestiones Obreras* and a year later brought a number of local unions together into a central organization. The Reverend Julio Restat set up the Federación de Obras Católicas, and somewhat later the legendary Jesuit priest Alberto Hurtado Cruchaga created El Hogar de Cristo to care for poor children and the aged and was instrumental in establishing the Acción Sindical Chilena (ASICH), a central grouping of industrial workers.

Thus, a rapidly expanding segment of the Chilean clergy came to challenge the premises upon which conservative clerics had stood for so long. But the liberal adherents to social action would have to wait a while before their views gained general hierarchical approval and many projects fell to the wayside as a result. As late as 1926, the archbishop of Santiago suppressed a liberal periodical, *El Sindicalista* and ordered the dissolution of a labor grouping, La Casa del Pueblo—both founded by Monsignor Guillermo Viviani.[40]

Paralleling the appearance of liberal currents within the Catholic church, the anticlericals continued their unceasing efforts to break the ties between Catholicism and the State. Secularists finally carried the day in 1925 with the constitutional division of Church and State. Despite the immense animosity this issue engendered in earlier years, the act of separation transpired peacefully and almost amicably. Certainly, it was a very popular move at the time and the Church, apparently realizing this fact, offered no obstacles to its fruition. The determinance of the question, probably worked out directly between President Arturo Alessandri and the Vatican's Cardinal Gasparri,[41] disestablished the Church and granted to it full control of its organization and properties and the right to establish its own schools at all levels. In addition, the Church enjoyed the unimpaired right to accept bequests; it obtained a freedom from taxation on nonincome-producing properties; it continued to receive subventions to underwrite its schools; and it was subsidized with a small allocation from the government over the next five

40 Carlos D. Hamilton, "Contemporary Social Developments in Latin America," in *Church and Society*, ed. Joseph N. Moody, pp. 774–783.

41 Mario Bernaschina González, *Manual de derecho constitucional*, p. 33.

years to help the Church put its financial house in order. In short, it was a "dignified solution to a delicate problem in which both sides showed great prudence and moderation."[42]

The contemporary status of Chilean Church-State relations seems to be a satisfactory one for virtually all elements in society. True, some conservatives bemoan the absence of religious instruction in the public schools and from time to time leftists grumble about insidious Church influence in public policy formation; but the 1925 solution is a definitive one in so far as the law is concerned and there is no doubt but that the Catholic hierarchy favors the present arrangement. Joseph Fichter's survey of attitudes among Catholic clergymen and laymen revealed total agreement that the Church is able to operate far more effectively without close bonds to government. Fewer than one in twenty sampled were even sympathetic to a government subvention to the Church.[43]

The present political position of the Church as an institution can probably best be categorized as a veto group in politics. That is, it exerts no continuing pressure on the decision-making process, though it periodically expresses itself on matters of immediate concern to Roman Catholic beliefs (e.g., birth-control measures, divorce, and so on). On those occasions when the Church deems an expression of its position necessary, it customarily chooses informal and indirect contacts with public agencies by means of Catholic lay groups.[44]

Clergy and the Political Process

Although the Church-State controversy has been settled for decades and the Church only rarely intervenes in governmental matters, at times priests perform in ways that touch upon the political process. Of course, the clergy's techniques and goals have varied depending upon the time and circumstances.

Until recent years, conservatives dominated the organization and the thinking of most of the Church; they stood alongside the most aristocratic elements in society, acting as a brake on social progress.[45] This

[42] Raúl Cereceda, *Las instituciones políticas en América Latina*, p. 214.
[43] Fichter, *Cambio social en Chile*, p. 39.
[44] Gil, *Political System of Chile*, pp. 295–296.
[45] See Richard Pattee, *Catholicism in Latin America*.

status quo orientation, which opposed any social legislation threatening the oligarchy, pushed fledgling labor groups—even those initially founded by priests—into the hands of the secular left. In essence, societal elements over whom the Church exercised the least control moved even farther away from the Church because of the actions of reactionary clerics. By the 1920's, clerical authority diminished measurably with the rise of middle sectors, whose secularization of much of education, disestablishment of the Church, and related measures reduced the Church's operative sphere of influence.[46]

Naturally, some Catholic leaders still find themselves more comfortable in the conservative camp. One of these, Jorge Iván Hübner Gallo, vigorously condemns Christian Democracy, for example, as being inspired by the French Revolution, a movement whose teachings are covered with a thin veneer of Christianity, but which in no sense represents the true beliefs of Roman Catholicism. Indeed, the Christian Democrats' entire history demonstrates an unfortunate liaison with "democratic idolatry," that is, the profession of "liberty and human rights."[47] Accordingly, it repeatedly has entered into pacts with the Communists. In this regard, it perpetrated one of the greatest crimes ever committed against the Chilean republic when, in 1958, it voted to repeal the Laws for the Defense of Democracy (which had proscribed the Communist party). Hübner is an open admirer of Franco's Spain, which he lauds as the first regime to fight communism. He admits that Spain is not a liberal democracy, created to the likes of Masons and Christian Democrats; what it is, though, is "an authentic State of Law, a bastion of Catholicism, where more than in any other country of the world one can find respect for the dignity of man as a spiritual being and [attention to] the unremitting demands of the Common Good."[48]

Hübner's concept of the twentieth century's ideal state constitutes an anachronism in the major thinking of the modern Chilean church. No other clergy in Latin America today possesses so many liberals, so

46 Luis Ratinoff, "The New Urban Groups: The Middle Classes," in *Elites in Latin America*, ed. Lipset and Solari, p. 66.

47 Jorge Iván Hübner Gallo, *Los católicos en la política*, p. 67.

48 *Ibid.*, pp. 77–78.

much dynamism; nor can one locate a hierarchy in any Latin American church that has stepped forth as a force for social change to the same degree as has the Chilean leadership. The earlier groundwork laid by Concha, Hurtado, and others was significantly strengthened by the admission of foreign priests into Chilean clerical ranks. Particularly influential, priests from France and the Low Countries imbued the Chilean church with a Gallican flavor and a reformist tone in marked contradistinction to the conservative primacy, say, of Spaniards in the Colombian church and of Italians in Argentina.[49]

The Chilean clergy's generally progressive views can be detected from several angles. Fichter's study (to turn to it one more time) is quite revealing on this score. Overwhelmingly, the 328 priests who were sampled favored increased salaries for workers as a necessary prerequisite to economic prosperity (77.4% for, 8.5% neutral, and 14.1% against the proposition). Of more interest, because of its controversial nature, a strong majority also supported land redistribution as an essential concomitant of a healthy economic system (56.7% in favor of redistributing farm properties, 16.8% being neutral, and 26.5% antagonistic to the idea). Almost the same major proportion considered the rate of social change in Chile to be too slow (57.3%), whereas only 18.3 per cent appraised the rate of change to be too fast (another 22.9% felt it to be going along at an adequate pace and the rest, 1.5%, expressed no opinion).[50]

Moreover, the writings and public statements of a number of outstanding prelates and priests have attracted formidable attention internationally, while fortifying reformist movements at home. The Belgian-born Jesuit Roger E. Vekemans, founder and director of the School of Research and Social Action and of the Catholic University's School of Sociology (both in Santiago), is a renowned commentator on social and economic matters and a leading intellectual light in the

[49] A few priests from the United States have reached Chile and carried out some important projects, though their influence has not been as considerable as the Europeans'. One of the problems has been the more conservative posture of so many U.S. prelates (conversation with Roger Vekemans, in Santiago, November 8, 1963).

[50] Fichter, *Cambio social en Chile*, pp. 46, 57.

Christian Democratic movement. His commitment to deep structural changes in society is unequivocal: "Without thorough and quick social change on a truly revolutionary scale, it will not be possible to achieve authentic and rapid economic development in Latin America; and without really starting economic expansion, there is no possibility of responding adequately to the revolutionary crisis that obtains in the region."[51] Father Vekemans pulls no punches in condemning the Latin American church itself for being so slow to realize this situation: "Since Hispanic Catholicism doesn't seem to be able to make the continent suitable for normal human life and since, despite the papal encyclicals, the social situation in Latin America is one of the worst in the world, it is obvious that the people of Latin America look for other solutions."[52]

A similar line of thought was enunciated by the late Monsignor Manuel Larraín, bishop of Talca, one of the giants of Catholic social action. Larraín saw the roots of Latin America's social difficulties in the appalling differences in social status existing between rich and poor, in the subhuman way of life of peasants, Indians, and "subproletarian masses," and in the unbelievably rapid technological growth occurring throughout the continent. All this is "aggravated by the lack of strong traditions of family life, social cohesion, and respect for labor."[53] Among a number of pastoral letters that call for sweeping reforms to meet these problems head on, Larraín went so far as to advocate the government's expropriation of property, without repaying the landowners, when this would be for the good of the community.[54] Such views, and the fact that he actually worked to implement the liberal currents of thought in the Church (e.g., he was the first bishop in Chile to voluntarily turn over Church lands to peasants), provoked strong

[51] Roger E. Vekemans, "Economic Development, Social Change, and Cultural Mutation in Latin America," in *Religion, Revolution, and Reform*, ed. D'Antonio and Pike, p. 132.

[52] Quoted in Edelmann, *Latin American Government and Politics*, p. 177.

[53] Manuel Larraín, "Lo que espera de la acción católica la América Latina de hoy," reprinted in part in Lewis Hanke, *South America*, p. 153.

[54] *Pastoral*. For an interesting earlier liberal statement from another Chilean priest, see Jorge Fernández Pradel, *Hacia un nuevo orden por un catolicismo social auténtico*.

responses. On the one side, many of his students from the days when Larraín was vice-rector of the Catholic University in Santiago went on to organize what eventually evolved as the Christian Democratic party. Others, however, equated Larraín's policies with unbridled radicalism and some went so far as to name them "Black Communism."[55]

Undoubtedly one of the most exceptional documents to come forth in the annals of the Catholic church in Latin America was the Chilean bishops' Pastoral Letter on Social Reform and the Common Good.[56] Issued in 1962 under the signatures of all twenty-four Catholic bishops after months of intensive research and study, it drew upon sources that ranged from government statistics to Communist publications. The Pastoral Letter begins with an explanation of the Church's "right and duty" to speak out on the condition of life in the nation and then it factually delineates the multitudinous social and economic ills besetting the nation: rural poverty, inadequate housing, insufficient employment opportunities, disparate income distribution, low levels of education, and undernourishment. Moreover, it rails against a situation in which it has become less and less possible for people to make requests of public officials and then to expect solutions to their problems.

The Pastoral Letter exhorts all Christians to remember their obligations to their fellow men and to participate in aiding them by constructive social action:

> To be a true Christian, one must take up a position regarding these reforms, for the purpose of obtaining social structures that will permit those in the lower income levels to gain greater participation in the fruits of the productive process. . . .
>
> To do this the Christian must favor the institutions of social claim and, if it corresponds to him, take part in them. He will also have to support institutional changes, such as true agrarian reform, reform of corporations, taxation reform, administrative or governmental and other similar reforms.

[55] Mecham, *Church and State in Latin America*, pp. 223–224.

[56] The following references to the Pastoral Letter, as well as the quotations, are taken from *New York Times*, November 5, 1962; reprinted in the *Congressional Record*, Vol. 109, Part 9, 88th Cong. (July 9, 1963), pp. 12278–12282. Also, see "Pastoral Plan of the Bishops of Chile," in *Recent Church Documents from Latin America*, pp. 1–12.

Every bit of energy must be devoted to bringing about these structural changes, though they will be insufficient unless a vastly augmented supply of goods and services in the national economy can also be created. In this regard, it "is contrary to the social doctrine of the Church to use means of production without taking their contribution to the common good as the guiding principle."

Ultimately, social and economic progress depends upon the political process for its effectuation. However, this cannot be accomplished through a Communist formula and the bishops go on to detail why Marxism fails to offer an appropriate antidote to the nation's ills. At the same time, the bishops take a swipe at rightist political groups by reminding the voters "to bear in mind the real intentions and the concrete possibilities of the political parties, and consider them also together with their principles, programs, and promises." After all, their "Christianity cannot be judged merely by statements." The letter does not hesitate to spell out its distaste for dual standards in those who faithfully comply with the strictest religious performances, but who live a scandalously contradictory life in their businesses and professions.

The bishops' Pastoral Letter stepped on many toes. Leftists objected that it did not specifically name the culprits responsible for the nation's economic and social backwardness and, additionally, condemned the Church's interference in secular matters. Rightists either interpreted it to be a full-scale attack on Communism or, somewhat curiously, as a slap at the Christian Democrats for cooperating with the Communists on several congressional votes. For their part, the Christian Democrats accepted the letter as an excellent summary of their own doctrine and goals. Theirs was probably the most accurate evaluation of the letter's meaning inasmuch as one of their own idealogues, Father Vekemans, seemed to have played a major role in drawing up the document.[57]

Amplification of the bishops' Pastoral Letter followed in a number of publications. For one, the scholarly Catholic journal *Mensaje* came out a year later with an issue, "Revolutionary Reforms in Latin America," which solidly backed up the letter with two hundred pages of statistical and interpretive treatises on social, economic, and political

[57] A summary of press responses to the Pastoral Letter can be found in *Hispanic American Report* 15, no. 9 (September 1962): 839–840.

reforms. But most significantly of all, the Chilean prelates—led by Cardinal Silva Henríquez, the archbishop of Santiago—earnestly sought to implement their proposals by concrete action. Beginning in 1962, the Church moved to divest itself of some of its ecclesiastical properties by turning these over to individual farm families. (Nevertheless, not all Church holdings were put under this program and some return was expected from those that were dispersed to peasants.)[58] Institutes were established to impart skills and leadership training to rural people.[59] Priests moved into the urban slums to work and live with the impoverished found there and to aid them in setting up production and credit cooperatives. In short, a half century of efforts to install Catholic social action in the Chilean church reached fruition in the 1960's with the hierarchy's proclamation of open warfare on society's ailments.

Any analysis of the chain of events that brought the Chilean church to its present progressiveness must include at least brief mention of the types of religious elites observable among the Latin American clergy. Ivan Vallier discovers four such types.[60] The traditionalists, or what Vallier labels the "politicians," affiliate with secular power elements in society. They survive with backing from these outside groups and enter into momentary arrangements that serve their purposes; they associate closely with the upper class, perform their ritualistic functions perfunctorily, and ignore the laity. Poverty, disease, and so forth are viewed simply as a natural part of human existence.

Besides the politicians, there are three new elites that have appeared in recent years. The "papists" stand for a "militant, modern Catholicism aimed toward 're-Christianizing the world.' "[61] They reject any and all political involvements in favor of creating self-sufficiency within the Church. Toward this end, they emphasize internal reorgani-

[58] See William C. Thiesenhusen, *Chile's Experiments in Agrarian Reform*, pp. 65–68.

[59] For an extensive treatment of Church involvement in the rural areas of Chile, see Oscar Domínguez C., *El campesino chileno y la acción católica rural.*

[60] Vallier, "Religious Elites," pp. 203–226.

[61] *Ibid.*, p. 204.

zation and strengthening and they seek to forge links with the working classes.

The second of the new elites, the "pastors," define their principal "task as that of building up strong, worship-centered congregations."[62] Thus, priests move more widely among the people, laymen perform directly in the liturgy, and liturgical matters are stressed over religious symbolism and pietistic behavior. The pastors' intention is to bring clerics and laymen together with the sacraments in a "religiously based social bond."[63]

Finally, the "pluralists" recognize that Roman Catholicism is but one of several religious postures extant in Latin America; it should cooperate with the others in order to be better able to carry out its basic religious obligations—to work for social and economic development and, especially, to pursue programs that lift up the destitute members of society. The Church, then, must strive for social revolution—"not as a 'political party,' nor as an anxious guardian of social privilege, but as a differentiated, grass-roots agency of moral and social influence."[64]

It seems quite clear that Chile stands as one of two or three nations (Vallier cites similar happenings in Brazil and Venezuela and to some degree in certain dioceses of a few other countries) where the pastors and pluralists exercise pervasive influence in the Church. This has great political import with the rise of Christian Democracy, for it enables the pastors and pluralists to dedicate themselves to religious values and actions while the Christian Democratic party carries their wider objectives into the political system.

Concluding on the Church, then, what actually is the nature of Catholicism's political influence and what are its political ties in contemporary Chile? In fact, it is hazardous to try to assess the specific political impact of Church influence. To the degree that Catholic values permeate elements of society, a conditioning has occurred that may hold some sway over individuals' attitudes toward politics. For example, women

[62] *Ibid.*, p. 205.
[63] *Ibid.*
[64] *Ibid.*, p. 206.

tend to vote in far greater percentages for political parties friendly to the Church than do men. Furthermore, it can safely be assumed that the Church reinforces attitudinal patterns among some people by means of its programs of leadership training, adult literacy work, and formal education (though a word of caution is necessary here in that a number of graduates of Catholic educational institutions went on to become leaders of the extreme left). The priest who lives and works in the slums and the bishop who hands the title for ecclesiastical land to a peasant may also be imparting political views.

But there also have existed and, in some ways, do persist more direct relationships between the clergy and politics. Historically of course, the Conservative party was a confessional grouping, with strong and open ties to the hierarchy. In another era the Conservatives regularly received electoral help from local priests who, by encouraging their parishioners to vote the "right way" and by other acts, supported their Conservative friends. The Liberals were slightly anticlerical by the standards of the time, but included many members faithful to the Church; whereas the Radicals and Marxists were clearly anti-Church. Inevitably, the growth of progressive features in the Chilean church and liberalism among its laity isolated the Conservatives on the right of the political spectrum and, at the same time, shifted the base of national political power to the reformist side of the center.[65]

As has been mentioned, the growth of Christian Democracy alongside the increasingly strengthened position of the pastors and pluralists among the clergy, permitted the clergy largely to withdraw from politics (except perhaps for its condemnations of communism) and to stick more closely to religious concerns. Of course, the religious realm is interpreted quite freely to encompass a wide latitude of social and economic questions. Nevertheless, the present Chilean church emphatically disavows political activism by priests. Indeed, in both the 1958 and 1964 presidential elections, the hierarchy's official position was one of absolute political neutrality.

Sometimes, however, the Church's dicta on what political alliances

[65] Johnson, *Political Change in Latin America*, pp. 68–69.

are proper for its laity seem like direct intervention in the political process. Thus, the Church admonishes its flock not to support political parties that violate the precepts of the Church or that are antagonistic to God. In saying this, the Church sets itself off against several political elements: "The parties which embody false principles in any form, like those of Marxism, of doctrinaire liberalism, of antireligious laicism are, at the same time, contrary to the Christian conscience and they compromise the common good."[66]

This proved somewhat awkward in the campaign leading to the 1964 presidential election. First, when a few priests encouraged their parishioners to vote "God's way," it occurred to some that they were questioning the qualifications of Julio Durán, a long-time leader and presidential nominee of the avowedly anticlerical Radical party. The Primate's office countered with the issuance of a statement specifying that (1) the Church is above politics and thus no one can claim its political approval, (2) the Church does not favor any specific political candidate, leaving its followers to vote according to their own Christian conscience, (3) no one is to try to mix the Church in the electoral struggle—all members of the Church being exhorted to strictly follow this norm, and (4) the hierarchy reiterates its call to everyone to make every effort to maintain peace and harmony, respecting the thoughts of others and not interfering in the inalienable rights of the individual.[67]

Next, because of its strong stand against Marxism, it seemed that the Church in effect opposed the candidacy of the Socialist-Communist presidential candidate, Salvador Allende. Once again, the Cardinal's office spoke out, noting that the Cardinal and all his bishops already had categorically opposed any clerical intrusion in the electoral campaign and that all priests must remain completely apolitical.

Eduardo Frei, the Christian Democratic standard-bearer in 1958 and 1964, insisted that he had no awareness of any bishop or priest recommending a vote for the Christian Democrats or for any other party. And then he concluded that if "the Church were to say, 'Vote for the

[66] Julián Rentería Uralde, ed., *La iglesia y la política*, p. 58.
[67] *Las Ultimas Noticias* (Santiago), November 9, 1963.

party that we recommend,' it would be a catastrophe because the people do not want to see the Church playing the political game."[68]

Obviously, the political party that maintains the closest ties with the clergy today is the Christian Democratic movement. It inherited these relationships at its founding, though it has faced substantial clerical opposition on occasion. In 1948, to cite one instance, a group of priests berated the radical nature of the party and went so far as to urge that Christian Democrats be expelled from Church councils.[69] For their part, the Christian Democrats, while accepting such intellectuals as Father Vekemans in advisory capacities, endeavor to banish any image of Christian Democracy as the exclusive domain of Roman Catholicism.

In brief, the Roman Catholic church in Chile accepted its disestablishment in 1925 and went on to become one of the most progressive churches in the hemisphere. And while it speaks out forthrightly in behalf of reforms, it has withdrawn to the background in terms of political activism—relying mostly on lay elements to carry its occasional messages into the political system.

Students

The university student in Latin America knows a long-established tradition of political activism, and his institutions of higher learning usually operate as autonomous agencies when they are not fettered by governmental oppression. Universities serve both as centers for planning political action and as refuges for those escaping police pursuit.

The reasons for politicized students in Latin America are varied.[70] Certainly the fact that so miniscule a percentage of youths are fortunate enough to reach the university (one to three per thousand in one generation) makes them a special breed—looked up to by the uneducated for ideas and leadership and sought out by the older generation of societal leaders as their heirs. In short, they are the achievers and they

[68] In D'Antonio and Pike, eds., *Religion, Revolution, and Reform*, pp. 112–113.

[69] Gil, *Political System of Chile*, p. 269.

[70] Kalman H. Silvert, "The University Student," in *Continuity and Change in Latin America*, ed. John J. Johnson, pp. 217–221; S. Walter Washington, "The Political Activity of Latin American Students," in *Latin American Politics: Studies of the Contemporary Scene*, ed. Robert Tomasek, pp. 116–118.

hold in their grasp the greatest chance for power and position.[71] Being privileged they assume responsibility early in life. When still a child by U.S. standards, a boy of ten years or so "no longer takes orders from his mother or his nurse but bosses all the women in the household . . ." and he is "encouraged to assert his ego in every way possible, especially in politics."[72] Ordinarily pushed into political dialogue early in life and being one of the few in society to move up the educational ladder, the student assails his nation's social ills, and his education provides him with the theoretical tools to propose grandiose schemes (fewer practical ones) to resolve society's dilemmas. A similar pattern of activism develops among the few youths of working-class backgrounds who reach the university and who find in social action their own surest path to status.

In their tactical grab bag, the students often pull out techniques of violence as their stylistic preference. This author has witnessed Mexican students viciously destroying buses and Venezuelans demonstrating angrily against a proposed rule that would limit the number of times a person could fail and then repeat a class at the university. On a Saturday morning in Bogotá, he was unable to enter his hotel because high-school students rushed the hotel entrances demanding free bullfight tickets from the clientele inside; senselessly, the students clashed with police and many youths were hauled away unconscious and wounded. An hour later, he was trapped in a taxi while rampaging university students, remonstrating against unpopular university procedures, hurled missiles and sought to overturn vehicles in the downtown streets.

While not unknown for such disorderly actions, the contemporary Chilean student is more likely to express himself with ardor, but to avoid unrestrained militance. Occasionally his vigorous protests incite others to turbulence and then, in distaste for the disorder, he will earnestly seek to quell the disturbance. The Chilean's customarily peaceful expression of protest contrasts sharply, for example, with his Bolivian counterpart, many of whom have studied in Chile under an

[71] Darcy Ribeiro, "Universities and Social Development," in *Elites in Latin America*, ed. Lipset and Solari, p. 368.

[72] Washington, "The Political Activity of Latin American Students," p. 117.

arrangement between the governments of the two nations. An anecdote may assist in pointing up the comparison: On one occasion, Chilean engineering students staged a grievance demonstration with the usual panoply of placards and signs—and in complete orderliness. The Bolivians were shocked at the absence of guns and the altogether too quiet nature of the proceedings; this certainly was not the way in which they were accustomed to issuing their demands. From then on the Chileans referred to the Bolivians as "RPM's" (or, "revolutions per minute") in order to symbolize their stylistic differences.[73]

The University System

The role of the university in Chile's national life has evolved through several stages, though higher education always has performed importantly. Out of its professorial ranks have come countless political leaders and, from Manuel Montt to Eduardo Frei, many of the nation's presidents. One of the most far-reaching developments in the history of the university grew out of the University Reform Movement, which first erupted in Argentina's University of Córdoba in 1918 and then reverberated throughout Latin America.

Until that time, the Latin American university remained primarily the preserve of the oligarchy and it held to largely archaic educational practices.[74] The Córdoba Movement called for a clear break with the past and proposed (1) to democratize the university, freeing it from restrictions based upon class, race, or family; (2) to open opportunities for the needy to enter the university by permitting flexible attendance; (3) to insist on student participation in governing the university, thus ending control by a closed corporation of professors; (4) to regularly review professors' qualifications to ensure that they kept up with their subject specialties; (5) to promote group discussions as a counterforce to the static nature of the educational system; (6) to establish "popular universities" for adults, and especially for workers and peasants, wherein university students would take it upon themselves to teach the less fortunate; (7) to tie the university more closely to the problems

[73] Related by Malte Crasemann, in Santiago, October, 1963.

[74] For a discussion of the nature of the traditional university, see Rudolph P. Acton, *The Latin American University*.

of community and nation; and (8) to forge stronger bonds among Latin American universities.[75]

The impact of these proposals on Chilean education was great. The old orientations that were long established from colonial times suffered an onslaught of demands for change that brought a level of student-administrative-faculty co-government in the university, the installation of a host of new curricula, and a stronger check on the professors' effectiveness and competence. In the early 1920's, students became more politicized and a general excitement about educational levels and goals stimulated widespread discussion in the country. However, not all of the Córdoba reforms were achieved. A principal impediment to their full implementation in Chile has derived from that nation's chronic defects in the economic system, which have inhibited the allocation of revenues to the universities sufficiently substantial for badly needed improvements in facilities and personnel. As a consequence, academic energies often have been diverted away from attention to internal university problems and over into activism in national politics as the only focus for problem resolution.[76]

Although several institutions of higher learning appeared in the colonial period, the most venerable being the University of San Felipe, the nation's oldest existing institution only dates from 1842 when the University of Chile was founded in Santiago. Nevertheless, ever since its formation, the University of Chile has enjoyed a preeminent position in the nation's educational system.[77] Thus, it has exerted a direct influence on the other universities through its power to determine admission and curriculum standards. Moreover, in 1954 it assumed the major burden for creating a new university in Valdivia, the Universidad Austral, which continues to be closely associated with the parent institution; beginning in 1960, it brought forth a number of two-year regional colleges, somewhat resembling California's junior colleges;

[75] Luis Alberto Sánchez, "The University in Latin America: The University Reform Movement," *Américas* 14, no. 1 (January 1962): 13–16.

[76] John P. Harrison, "The Role of the Intellectual in Fomenting Change," in *Explosive Forces in Latin America*, ed. John TePaske and Sydney N. Fisher, pp. 32–33.

[77] Máximo Pacheco Gómez, *La Universidad de Chile.*

and for years the University of Chile has offered university-level classes in various cities outside the capital.

Besides the University of Chile and the Southern University in Valdivia, Chile's other universities are the University of Concepción, a private university tracing its primary origins to 1921 and depending heavily for its financial resources upon a national lottery; the State Technical University, established in 1931 under a private bequest to provide free education to qualified youths from poor families; and the Church-related institutions—the Pontifical Catholic University of Chile, located in Santiago since 1888, and the Catholic University of Valparaíso (formed in 1924), which initiated a branch, the University of the North, in Antofagasta in 1956.[78] Despite the fact that only three of the universities (the University of Chile, the Southern University, and the State Technical University) are public establishments, the private as well as the public institutions receive revenues from the national government. The University of Chile, which enrolls roughly as many students as the other universities combined, by law receives 10/18 of the total allocation; the University of Concepción and Catholic University at Santiago each obtains 2/18; and the remaining institutions (the Catholic universities at Valparaíso and Antofagasta being lumped together) receive 1/18 each.[79]

Professor Luis Scherz-García of Santiago's Catholic University has outlined three stages through which the Latin American universities have been evolving. These are the "static," "critical," and "dynamic-dualistic" phases.[80] The static stage is a relatively quiescent period in which the university (ordinarily a state institution) is adapted to a static society or in which the university remains inactive despite some initial changes in the social system. In this stage, the university's main role is simply to turn out trained professionals in the traditional fields. At the same time, a few student elements move to the forefront in attacking the inequities of the existing society and in demanding altera-

[78] For an overview of the Chilean educational system, see Clark C. Gill, *Education and Social Change in Chile.*

[79] Luis Scherz-García, "Relations between Public and Private Universities," in *Elites in Latin America,* ed. Lipset and Solari, pp. 406–407.

[80] *Ibid.,* pp. 383–396.

tions of the social system. The student leaders' principal attribute in this period is their oratorical ability.

The critical phase finds the university responding to deep changes in the social system by expanding its curriculum into new subject fields and offering educational and cultural services to wider sections of the community. Moreover, the university enjoys greater autonomy from the government, though authoritative forces still may impose financial sanctions upon politically recalcitrant institutions; and there is a growth in the number and security of private universities, which often begin to receive financial support from the government. Now interest groups outside the university assume the primary role of leading the fight for social reforms, thus reducing student groups to a less significant, more agitational position. Also, students tend to slide out from under the control of the ideologically extreme left in favor of more moderate leftists, while student leaders shift from their earlier oratorical stance to an increasing emphasis on organizational matters.

In the final or dynamic-dualistic stage, the university itself now serves as an instrument of social change and society has reached the point when it is ready to accept a new kind of university institution, one that is closely coordinated with the community. Within the university, a subsystem of pure science has become firmly entrenched and it acts as a catalyst for the replacement of old institutional forms with radically modernized new university arrangements. The minority of student activists, reflecting the modernizing influences from the subsystem of scientific research, carry their denunciation of social ills into the society at large as well as entertaining especial concern for the refurbishment of the university from top to bottom. In this regard, they have moved into a visionary stage of leadership development.

With the exception of the Universidad de Concepción, which appears to have moved into the final phase, the Chilean universities seem to be nearing the end of the critical phase. Accordingly, many of their endemic problems as well as transitional ones have been pushed into the open. This has been pointed out by Clark C. Gill, who suggests that "[in] spite of its many handicaps (such as a scattered campus, a loose administrative organization, and a lack of resources, facilities, and qualified staff) the University of Chile gives the impression of an ambivalent institution, anxious to explore and experiment yet reluctant to cut itself away from the safe moorings of the past."[81]

Such ambivalence is manifested in many ways. For example, the University of Chile's pioneering efforts to respond to a critical need for greatly augmented educational opportunities by launching the regional colleges, in effect was diminished by its reluctance to accept class work as transferable from the new colleges. Furthermore, the universities rely upon a highly criticized, antiquated system of comprehensive examinations for admission to study in the universities. The examination system compels the high schools to devote such an excessive amount of time in the last years to factual knowledge in order to qualify students for the examinations that other educational goals are often ignored.[82] That something in this process is amiss is exemplified in the fact that approximately 50 per cent of those who take the entrance examination fail to pass and that, of those fortunate enough to gain admission to the university, more than one-third leave by the end of their first year.[83] The gravity of the situation is exemplified in Chile's serious shortage of professional expertise, partially the result of a "brain drain" to other countries, but largely a consequence of the universities' failure to produce enough qualified professional people. (One study projected a deficit for 1970 of 73 forestry engineers, 123 agronomists, 265 architects, 871 dentists, and 2,058 physicians.)[84]

Another aspect of this problem impinges upon the relative ability of qualified youths from all economic classes to realistically aspire to a university education. Superficially, Chile is fortunate in this regard in that it ranks along with Argentina, Cuba, and Panama in being one of the few nations in all Latin America where "there is a sufficiently broad base of persons with primary education to provide some social heterogeneity to the student body passing through secondary education

[81] Gill, *Education and Social Change in Chile*, p. 88.

[82] Alfonso Asenjo, "La universidad y el trabajo," *Anales de la Universidad de Chile* 121, no. 127 (May–August 1963): 42–69.

[83] Hernán Ramírez Necochea, *El Partido Comunista y la universidad*, pp. 95–100.

[84] Jorge Riquelme Pérez *et al.*, *Estudio de recursos humanos de nivel universitario en Chile.*

into the university."[85] Despite this comparative advantage, probably no more than 3 per cent of the nation's entire university-age stratum enter a university and very few of this small number come from working-class homes, totalling only about 1.5 per cent in the University of Chile and 0.6 per cent in the Catholic University of Santiago.[86] The origins of this unfortunate situation are not to be located in any purposeful discrimination on the part of the university system, but in the desperate economic condition of a large proportion of the population, which, in the absence of a sufficient amount of scholarship aid, simply cannot afford to underwrite so many years of education.[87] This is statistically observable in Santiago where investigations show that of upper-class students who begin elementary school, 73 per cent complete one year of high school; of middle-income groups, 32 per cent finish one year of high school; and of low-income students, only 14 per cent remain at the end of the first year of high school.[88] This tendency continues on through the educational system and, by the same token, restricts the few students of working-class background who do reach the university to subject fields with a shorter curriculum. Almost none ever complete the minimum seven years necessary to get through medical school. Professor Osvaldo Sunkel of the University of Chile pinpoints all this as "a bias in favour of the children of high-income families, who attend better schools for a longer time and therefore receive better education."[89]

Some hopeful signs for improvement have occurred in recent years. In 1954, a law was enacted to establish the Council of Rectors. Comprising the presidents of all the nation's universities, the council endeavors to cooperate in stimulating research, developing physical facilities, and finding means to upgrade other features of higher education. Internal disagreements do persist, mostly stemming from some

[85] Kalman H. Silvert, *Chile*, p. 209.

[86] Asenjo, "La universidad y el trabajo," p. 48.

[87] Juan Gómez Millas, *Tradición y tarea universitaria*, pp. 88–89.

[88] Osvaldo Sunkel, "Change and Frustration in Chile," in *Obstacles to Change in Latin America*, ed. Claudio Véliz, p. 137.

[89] *Ibid.*, p. 138.

inherent differences in purpose between the public and private institutions and from the University of Chile's unusual power in higher education.[90] But the council is an important beginning and its formation augurs well for necessary reforms in the future.

Another salutary event was the installation in 1964 of a political regime under Eduardo Frei that promised to do more than just talk about socioeconomic reforms. Despite enormous obstacles in his way, Frei succeeded in stimulating economic growth (moving along at better than 6% annually) and at first in slowing the devastating inflation (down from 47% in 1964 to 17% in 1966).[91] The somewhat broadened income distribution that resulted from the government's economic policy together with a heightened emphasis on education, pushed pre-university enrollment from 1.8 million in 1964 to 2.3 million in 1966 and university enrollment from 35,027 students to 48,700 during the same years.[92]

In the mid-1960's, Chile boasted a state university and a private university as good as any in Latin America as well as some improvements in opening the educational system to a larger cross section of population. Nevertheless, many of the shortcomings persisting for decades remained and countless new difficulties were being created as the Chilean universities slowly moved from the critical to the dynamic-dualistic stage of development. Student groups continued to perform their decades-old function of questioning procedures and objectives in the university and in society. In the process they frequently aired their grievances publicly and sought recourse from the political system.

The Students' Political Role

Political activism among Chilean university students has been apparent for many decades, though the intensity of political involvement has fluctuated measurably. The one major student group that has registered any real mark in the history of such activism is the Federación de Estudiantes de Chile or FECH, founded in 1906 as the students'

[90] Scherz-García, "Relations between Public and Private Universities," pp. 392–396; Gill, *Education and Social Change in Chile*, pp. 76–77.

[91] *Christian Science Monitor*, May 31, 1967.

[92] *Ibid.*

voice at the University of Chile. Although its early years were noted primarily for the cultural activities it provided its members, FECH did enter into relationships with the fledgling labor movement by offering some basic literacy and medical-legal services to workers. Occasionally the students protested against university and governmental practices, but these were sporadic acts at best and they typified a general lack of coordinated policy or over-all goals on the part of the students.[93]

However, in the period following World War I, FECH leaped into political prominence. The Córdoba Movement for educational reforms excited Chilean students to challenge their own educational environment. Furthermore, they assumed a far more political stance because of their close attachment to the ideological left—the Anarcho-Syndicalists and the Marxists—who controlled the main current of organized labor. This doctrinal orientation emerged in various reports that FECH issued in the early 1920's. On one occasion, its Social Action Committee called for the creation of a new national confederation uniting workers and intellectuals, for the replacement of capitalist competition by economic cooperation, and for the socialization of the means of production.[94] Somewhat earlier, FECH won the ire of many people for its opposition to bellicose Chilean gestures toward Peru, an unpopular stand that provoked an attack on its offices by angered citizens.

In 1931, students could take credit for initiating a strike that ultimately brought down the dictatorial government of Carlos Ibáñez, and, from the 1930's on, partisan politics became inextricably interwoven with student government. Candidates for student offices have run their campaigns as members of national political groupings and, for the most part, they have allied themselves with the stands on issues taken by the political parties with which they were affiliated.

Leftist coalitions officered the student federations during most of the last thirty years. Still, in 1946, a conservative coalition halted a decade of left-wing directorates and by the middle 1960's, with the meteoric rise of Christian Democratic strength nationally, the Christian

[93] Frank Bonilla, "The Student Federation of Chile: 50 Years of Political Action," *Journal of Inter-American Studies* 2, no. 3 (July 1960): 311–334.

[94] Carlos Vicuña Fuentes, *La cuestión social ante la Federación de Estudiantes de Chile*, pp. 79–88.

Democrats held hegemony not only in the University of Chile, but also in all the other universities except the leftist stronghold in Concepción.

The students in each of the universities establish their own federations, though they rather closely parallel the structural pattern prevailing at the University of Chile.[95] Membership is open to everyone enrolled in the university and continues to be in effect until two years after a person has left the university. Each federation is governed by three principal organs: a convention, an assembly, and an executive committee. FECH's convention comprises all students at the University of Chile and is supposed to gather every two years. More important, the assembly (*consejo directivo*) brings together the elected presidents and delegates of each of the schools that make up the university—the number of delegates being proportionate to the school's enrollment (from a minimum of two in a school with less than two hundred students up to five in a school with more than five hundred, plus one more delegate for each additional three hundred students). Their regular meetings, to be held every fifteen days, are open to all members of FECH and commonly involve partisan debates. Finally, the eleven-member executive committee (*comité ejecutivo*) constitutes the most powerful single group of officers in the FECH hierarchy. Both the assembly and the executive committee serve one-year terms, but are eligible for reelection.[96]

As has been noted, FECH is far and away the most significant of the Chilean student federations and the only one that periodically has exerted substantial pressure on the national political scene. (On the other hand, the Federation of Students of Concepción at times has been influential in regional politics.) Much less political persuasion and activity is attributable to the other universities. Silvert believes that this is true in Latin America generally because the "state universities, leading in the modernization of the traditional academic disciplines along with a growing dedication to the physical sciences and empiricism, at-

[95] For example, the principal organs of the students' federation at the University of Concepción are the congress, assembly, directorate, and executive committee (see "Estatutos de la Federación de Estudiantes de Concepción," mimeographed, Title III).

[96] "Estatutos de la Federación de Estudiantes de Chile," mimeographed, Titles II and III.

tract the innovators—and thus the nationalists."[97] It should be noted, however, that even at the University of Chile not all the members of FECH actively participate in its activities. Bonilla observed that in 1956 and 1957, while 55 to 60 per cent of the student body voted for officers, fewer than sixty out of thirteen thousand students took part in organizational matters on a regularized basis and less than 5 per cent of those enrolled at the university belonged to political party youth groups.[98] In a more recent study, Myron Glazer conducted an extensive investigation of students in the Schools of Engineering, History, Medicine, and Physics at the University of Chile. Among these specific groups sampled, student membership in political parties totaled 18 per cent, with more enrolled in party lists who were in their second and third years at the university than in their first year.[99]

Thus, students fall into several categories regarding the level of politicization. Student officers at the University of Concepción appraised themselves and their fellow students as being one of three types.[100] At the apex of involvement are the militants, who carry the heaviest burden for managing the student organizations and who actually enter actively into local or national politics; idealists constitute a second element and they are noted more for talking than for action; the third segment comprises those students who by and large remain indifferent to political activity, but who may go along with friends on specific points of contention. From another standpoint, students also differ in the types of issues that concern them. Some students prefer to devote organizational attention almost exclusively to university affairs and to divest themselves of partisan affiliation; a more powerful element insists upon full participation in the political life of the nation and in "the nature of things the latter must win, for it takes politicking to move to the forefront of the FECH in the first place."[101]

[97] Silvert, *Chile*, p. 224.

[98] Bonilla, "The Student Federation of Chile," p. 316.

[99] Myron Glazer, "The Professional and Political Attitudes of Chilean University Students," Ph.D. dissertation, Chapter V, Table III.

[100] Interview with the Executive Committee, Federation of Students of Concepción, in Concepción, March 5 and 6, 1964.

[101] Kalman H. Silvert, *The Conflict Society: Reaction and Revolution in Latin America*, p. 185.

Although only a minority of students ever become very firm in their political commitment, virtually all students are subjected to pressure to commit themselves to a political party. This is inherent in a system where aspirants to student offices cater for votes along political party lines and where student militants solicit partisan support for a great variety of causes. Consequently, on entering the university a student is likely to be approached by several activist colleagues. The new student almost certainly will encounter a representative of the Christian Democrats, the best organized of university political groups, and probably he will meet someone from the Marxist student coalition, the Leftist University Movement (Movimiento Universitario Izquierdista or MUI). Party members try to help the new student find his way through university procedures and they also put him in touch with the issues dividing the various political elements at that time.[102]

In many ways, the political process in the university is a microcosm of national politics. As noted, most students seek offices with political party labels and campaign as vigorously, and sometimes as bitterly, as occurs in national politics. Indeed, university questions commonly take a back seat to those governing the national scene. If a national electoral campaign is under way, students expand their activities through the university and out into the community, always pumping on behalf of their favored political parties.

Ideologically, Chilean students fall into a center-left category. Leftist groups controlled FECH during most of its history and in the mid-1960's the Christian Democrats became dominant in all the universities except for the Socialist-Communist command of the University of Concepción. Glazer's sample found that close to two-thirds of the students interviewed classified themselves as somewhere in the center-left spectrum, whereas only from 2 to 6 per cent of the students interviewed at each of the four schools specified their political leanings to be to the right.[103] In fact, this rather closely paralleled the political posture of Chileans generally who voted heavily for the cen-

[102] Based on the author's observations in 1963 and 1964. Also see Glazer, "Professional and Political Attitudes," Chap. V.

[103] *Ibid.*, Chap. V, Table XII.

ter-left political parties in the presidential election of 1964 and in the congressional election of 1965.

Glazer's study also is revealing in sorting out factors that influence students' political activity and attitudes. Among his conclusions, Glazer observes that there is a strong correlation between the amount of political awareness expressed in the home and the students' entrance into political activity in high school (i.e., the presence in the family of political discussion or at least political interest is a major influence in inducing youths to engage in early political experiences) and subsequently into university politics; that a proportionately large number of students from lower-middle and working-class backgrounds tend to be politically motivated, probably because student politics offers them an opportunity to play a stronger social role than they had known in their earlier environment and to participate more fully in bringing about social change; and that the strongest single moulder of the students' political attitudes was the political views of their fathers.[104] The last point helps to explain the rather moderate and reformist style of most student actions as well as the presence of the bridges that exist between student and other social leaders. Moreover, as students approach graduation and entrance into professional life, their styles may moderate even further: "Thus, in their student days they take part in all the working-class struggles which are noteworthy for the social generosity of their aims—and indeed, often initiate campaigns which subsequently attract other sections of the population. Once they have graduated, however, they become equally involved—inherent in marriage—in a working discipline which prompts them to a more conformist and conservative attitude."[105] During an interview in 1964,[106] student leaders at the University of Concepción (all of whom were Marxists and mostly enrolled in the medical school) decried the tendency of those who had graduated before them to become more moderate in their political styles and middle class in their values. They

[104] *Ibid.*, Chap. V.

[105] Ribeiro, "Universities and Social Development," p. 369.

[106] Interview with the Executive Committee, Federation of Students of Concepción.

believed this to occur even among professionals from working-class backgrounds. At the same time, they somewhat guiltily projected a similar future for themselves unless the Socialist-Communist coalition would come to power and revamp aspects of the university and the social system generally.

The Concepción student leaders' views are interesting in the way they reflect the fact that they are in the only Chilean university to have moved from the last phase of the critical stage in university development into the final, or dynamic-dualistic, stage. Then, as Scherz-García suggests, students tend to be more visionary and not only attack endemic social ailments but also demand an overhaul of the university in all its aspects.[107]

The student officers interviewed by this writer had become politically active and affiliated with either the Communist or the Socialist party when they were between the ages of thirteen and sixteen. Despite the rigorous course of study they pursued, all of them shared their energies and time in community service projects and in grass-roots political activities along with carrying out their responsibilities as student leaders.

They all held a firm view of the existing condition of the university and of the role the university should play in transforming society. To cite just one line of their thinking, though a very important one, the Concepción student officers considered the greatest failing in the university to be lack of planning—a high priority item of the Frapistas generally. They believed this should be a realistic type of planning that would cater to Chile's specific needs and not to some outsider's concept of what the ideal university's relationship to society should be. Since Chile desperately needed more specialists in certain fields, a great many more students from lower economic classes should be admitted and financially underwritten to complete their professional training. The university should work to push its graduates into regions of the country where they are most needed—as by sending physicians into the rural areas and small towns. By the same token, the best professors should be allocated throughout all the nation's universities in-

107 Ribeiro, "Universities and Social Development," p. 387.

stead of the bulk of them being concentrated in Santiago. Part of every university student's obligation should be to spend a portion of his time serving the needs of the poor. All in all, the students carefully tried to delineate national needs and then to define the university's responsibility in meeting those needs.

The issues that attract student attention are multitudinous in number and types. Chilean students express themselves on matters that affect them directly, such as items relating to university reform or an effort to raise bus fares (of great concern to students, since they are so dependent upon public transporation). But in addition, they have attacked everything from unpopular governmental measures that seemed to infringe on basic freedoms (e.g., the repressive Laws for the Defense of Democracy and the "Gag Law" on news media) to such economic problems as inflationary tendencies and the plight of underpaid workers.

Moreover, in their effort to communicate their views, students have utilized several techniques. These take the form of actions by both unofficial and official structures. Unofficial measures stem from clusters of students espousing a particular viewpoint—whether Christian Democratic, MUI, or other—who do not speak from elected positions in student councils. At various times, either singly or in debate with each other, they issue proclamations and demands that claim to be the will of great numbers of students. Official actions, however, are the province of the *directorio* of the student federation and have the power of being authoritative resolutions. Although one may doubt the representativeness of the *directorio*'s decisions at given times, the *directorio* is empowered with the authority to act on behalf of all the students in articulating on a particular question and in sanctioning street demonstrations and university-wide strikes in order to strengthen its bargaining position and to press for the acceptance of its demands. Resolutions produced by the *directorio*, in practice usually worked out in advance by the executive committee, are considered to carry great force. Indeed, they are "believed to have a greater impact on the public than a statement by the youth of any single political group."[108]

[108] Bonilla, "The Student Federation of Chile," p. 329.

Resolutions, proclamations, conventions, deputations, street demonstrations, and strikes are all among the students' stock in trade. In fact, some manifestation of student associational or political action seems to reach the public eye almost weekly. For example, in one six-month period a partial tally of some of the types of activities in which university students participated included street demonstrations in support of a number of different labor strikes; elections for new student officers, whose views received wide press circulation; numerous public manifestations against the government's proposed law to impose restrictions on the news media; a meeting of a deputation of student leaders from all the Santiago-based university federations with the minister of foreign relations to review the current boundary dispute with Argentina; trips abroad by several student delegations for professional or political purposes; a dispute among Socialists, Communists, and Christian Democrats regarding an event in the School of Veterinary Medicine; and the holding by Christian Democrats of their national student congress in Valparaíso and by Marxists of the second annual Latin American Youth Congress in Santiago. And throughout all this time a steady stream of every imaginable kind of political action engulfed student activists in the forthcoming national elections.[109]

Of course, in the process of their regular pursuits student organizations come into contact with nonuniversity structures. Student militants undoubtedly hold their most regularized ties with the political parties, which do not just solicit their support in elections, but which institutionalize student representation in high party councils. Furthermore, political parties make a great deal of student federation elections that go in their favor and often view the outcome as a boost, if not a bellwether, to party fortunes.

Trade unions form the other type of organization with which students most frequently find common cause. Bonds between students and labor characterize much of the history of FECH and the contemporary dominance of students of a center-left orientation in all the universities ensures a probable continuance of friendly relationships. At times, student leaders stand at the rostrum of labor gatherings, and

[109] Observed by the author between September, 1963, and March, 1964, during part of his stay in Chile.

trade unionists regularly show up at meetings of student political groups. Students frequently back national labor efforts with demonstrations and, for their part, union officials from time to time express sympathy for student demands.

Nonetheless, despite friendly institutional ties, the coming together of students and labor is sporadic at best. The vast majority of student militants and labor leaders hold to strong political convictions and, whatever the hegemony that one political party possesses over a particular federation at one time, opposing political elements fragment the organizations. Thus, Chile's central labor confederation (CUT) has been led in recent years by Marxists, though non-Marxists make up at least as large a grouping in the central; many unions remain outside CUT and also encompass a variety of political beliefs. The same thing transpires in student structures. Thus, Christian Democrats gained a majority of student posts in FECH in 1963 with 5,601 votes; but the Marxists obtained 3,881 votes, the Liberals 1,060, and the Radicals 703.[110] For these reasons, whatever the sympathetic views that exist between students and labor generally, they entertain highly informal relationships and join together only very irregularly toward a common objective.[111]

It is difficult to evaluate the over-all impact of student influence in the political system. Certainly it has been uneven and, as Bonilla concludes, student political pressure appears to reach its high-water marks during times of political crisis, especially in response to repressive governmental measures or when the opposition political parties are in disarray, and in moments of economic disorder.[112] At such moments students may prove to be a decisive force in national politics, as they were in 1931 when they contributed significantly in bringing down Chile's single sufferance of dictatorship in this century; often, though, they have been ignored or pushed aside, as transpired in the govern-

[110] *El Mercurio* (Santiago), October 28, 1963.

[111] Almost without exception, the leaders of labor federations and confederations interviewed by the author indicated an unwillingness to admit students into their consideration of associational matters. However, when labor issues became an item of public record, they did welcome fraternal expressions of sympathy from the students.

[112] Bonilla, "The Student Federation of Chile," p. 334.

ment's passage of the Laws for the Defense of Democracy (1948) and the "Gag Law" (1964) over strenuous student protests. In large measure the explanation for this state of affairs probably lies in the existence in Chile of a number of competing interest groups (especially of the economic variety) and of a highly stratified class system that gets in the way of student claims upon the decision-making process.[113] In crisis periods, when some of the other interest groups or political parties lie in a weakened condition, students tend to move into the power void and seem more able to articulate their demands with confidence that attention will be given to them.

In comparison to student groups in many Latin American countries, perhaps the most nearly unique feature of the Chilean students is their style of operation. That is to say, while the Chilean youths overwhelmingly adhere to reformist or radical doctrines in their political attitudes, customarily their tactics are moderate. Or to put it another way, even when students call for sweeping structural changes in the social system, they are the first to express horror if the zeal of their oratory inflames others to violence—for their obvious preference is for utilizing electoral and legal means to achieve political ends.[114]

[113] Silvert, "The University Student," pp. 223–224.

[114] Both Glazer and Bonilla subscribe to this view. Also, the author came to the same conclusion from observations and interviews at the University of Chile, the Catholic universities in Santiago and Valparaíso, the University of Concepción, and the Southern University.

CHAPTER FOUR

Interest Groups: Management and Labor

It goes without saying that in the developing nations of the world there is a tendency for the political styles and the nature of group involvements in politics to change as societies modernize. On the one hand, certain groups that earlier exercised a predominate sway over the political system move to a more differentiated role-playing position—periodically expressing themselves on political matters that bear importantly upon their immediate interests, but not actually controlling the decision-making process.

As the previous chapter suggested, the Chilean military boasts a high level of professionalization and rarely intrudes in the political process; most of the high clergy constitute a vital force on behalf of social and economic reform and rely mostly upon lay groups for political expression; and the students, who certainly include highly politicized elements in their ranks, generally adhere to moderate, nonviolent approaches in their political activism.

On the other hand, economic interest groups were thrust into the political system from the time of their formation and vigorously compete in the political process to this day. Managerial elements formed part of the oligarchy that ruled Chile during much of the period since independence. As a consequence, when trade unions emerged at the turn of the century, they not only contended with employers' groups in the economic sphere—usually viewing management as labor's class enemies—but they also struggled against the coercive power that a management-dominated government turned upon labor. Thus, economic power and political power were inextricably intermeshed and economic issues were inevitably fought out on political battlegrounds.

Nevertheless, as Chile began to experience modernization, the economic interest groups' political styles were transformed along with broader social metamorphoses. Informal and personalized approaches were augmented with more formalized and continuous ones; goals acquired a larger scope as the process of modernization called upon government to foster the expansion of economic and social services. The growth in size and power of new social groups (e.g., the new middle sectors and organized labor) also brought about the need for rules to govern the political and economic actions of these interest groups. Thus, the state additionally intervened in society to regulate group relations and to circumscribe what it considered abusive practices or untoward activities.

All this led to a more complex social system and to an increasingly complex decision-making process, which was forced to respond to more varied and forceful group pressures. The growing complexity of government in turn necessitated an alteration in group styles; thus, whereas in the premodern era, group activity was "inclined to be more personalized, episodic, private, local, and diffuse," in the modern epoch it tends to be more "systematically organized, relatively impersonal in style, continuous, public, and focused on larger targets."[1]

[1] Robert E. Ward and Roy C. Macridis, eds., *Modern Political Systems: Asia*, p. 80.

The following discussion analyzes the internal organization, associational needs, and structural methods of both management and labor as they relate to the political system. Without doubt, the struggle between these two elements represents what is far and away the most significant aspect of interest group politics in modern Chile.[2]

EMPLOYERS' GROUPS

Organization

Knowledge of organizational make-up provides several elementary insights into the nature of an interest group. To begin with, the mere existence of formal organization ordinarily suggests some degree of cohesion and interaction as well as the likelihood that it will last for a while. In addition, the presence of organization implies that the membership has agreed to some division of labor and that they, at least at the time of their establishment as a group, agreed to certain common values.[3] When considered together, these factors offer a collective key to comprehending the relative permanence and the power of interest associations.

Managerial groups in Chile have their principal origins in the nineteenth century. The essentially agrarian nature of the economy led to the early formation, in 1838, of the National Society of Agriculture; a commerce central was organized in 1858 and peak associations for industry and mining appeared in 1883 and 1884.

Today, four powerful structures articulate the needs of agriculture (Sociedad Nacional de Agricultura), commerce (Cámara Central de Comercio de Chile), manufacturing (Sociedad de Fomento Fabril), and mining (Sociedad Nacional de Minería). All headquartered in Santiago, they combine to form the Confederation of Production and Commerce (Confederación de la Producción y del Comercio).

All four associations are similarly organized with three basic organs

[2] This is in major distinction to many Latin American nations where labor usually is not a significant competitor and where such elites as the economic oligarchy, the military, clergy, and maybe students dominate interest group politics. For a general discussion of interest groups in Latin America, see Robert Alexander, *Latin American Politics and Government*, pp. 84–137.

[3] David B. Truman, *The Governmental Process*, pp. 112–115.

—an assembly, a directorate, and an executive committee.[4] The assembly comprises all members of the organization and meets annually. Those unable to be present may pass their voting rights on to an attending member. Among its functions, the assembly approves the annual report and budget proposed by the directorate, elects directorial and administrative officers, deliberates on matters of general interest to the organization, and submits items affecting the association in the nation's economy to the directorate for study.[5]

Supreme authority for interim decision making rests with the directorate, a much smaller body than the assembly, but representative of the entire membership. Agriculture's directorate contains sixty members, the manufacturers' association sixty-four, mining eighty, and commerce more than a hundred. The directors serve for two- or three-year terms and may be reelected.

Customarily, sessions are called at least once a month. The directorate's scope of authority is as wide as the interests and activities of the association itself. It directs all phases of the organization through its departments; sets general and specific policy; intervenes in any conflict between members; dictates a code of ethics for component groups; accepts and cancels memberships; fills directorial and administrative vacancies; establishes ordinary annual dues as well as special quotas; administers all the organization's assets; enters contracts or any negotiations necessary for the welfare of the association; acts on behalf of the association judicially or extrajudicially; proposes changes in the bylaws; presents the annual report and budget; creates or alters depart-

[4] The actual names vary among the associations. The assembly is known as the *asamblea general* or *junta general*; the directorate is called *consejo directivo, directorio*, or *consejo general*; and the executive committee is referred to as *comité ejecutivo* or *comisión ejecutivo*. An outstanding study of organizational and other associational aspects of these management groups is Constantine C. Menges, "Public Policy and Organized Business in Chile: A Preliminary Analysis," *Journal of International Affairs* 20, no. 2 (1966): 343–365.

[5] Structural and other aspects of these central organizations are set out in their bylaws, or *estatutos*. As of early 1964, the specific *estatutos* in force for the Sociedad Nacional de Minería were approved in 1939; for the Cámara Central de Comercio, 1948; for the Sociedad de Fomento Fabril, 1956; and for the Sociedad Nacional de Agricultura, 1963.

ments and committees; and selects individuals to represent the association on public and private agencies. In fact, the directorate's power is virtually unlimited in so far as the association is concerned.

All the day-to-day housekeeping and supervisory work falls upon the shoulders of the executive committee, which ranges in size from five to ten officials among the four groups. Agriculture and mining limit membership on their executive committees to the board of directors (*mesa directiva*)—the president, vice-presidents, secretary general, and, in the case of mining, its manager as well. The manufacturers' executive committee encompasses the board of directors, two representatives of the directorate, and four department heads; commerce's directorate elects nine members to the executive committee who in turn select a board of directors from their own group. In each case, these committees assemble frequently, usually on a weekly or biweekly basis.

The four management societies hold to similar criteria for admission to membership. All allow for individual and group memberships and permit foreigners as well as Chileans to join; both voting and nonvoting members are provided for in the bylaws. Of the 4,500 adherents to the National Society of Agriculture, the dominant three-quarters comprise individual landowners engaged in commercial farming and regional agricultural organizations; the remaining one-quarter represents smaller farm interests. Consequently, the Society's membership pervades virtually the entire nation and most of the varied categories of agriculture, though big agriculture predominates. Only one major farm organization, the Consorcio Agrícola del Sur, prefers exclusion. Located in six southern provinces (Bío Bío, Cautín, Malleco, Valdivia, Osorno, and Llanquihue), this consortium finds that the peculiar nature of farming in that area demands a stress on regional efforts to articulate its needs. But it does send a representative to the SNA's assembly and both associations collaborate periodically for common ends.[6]

Among the various segments of agriculture, the wine industry falls into a special category. The wine growers', manufacturers', and distributors' associations all join together into the Corporación Vitiviní-

[6] Interview with César Sepúlveda Latapiat, secretary general of the Sociedad Nacional de Agricultura, in Santiago, March 31, 1964.

cola. At the same time, the growers' Asociación de Viticultores holds membership in the Sociedad Nacional de Agricultura, forming a useful bridge between the two powerful central structures.

Upwards of 80 per cent of all Chile's manufacturing firms belong to the Sociedad de Fomento Fabril. And, as is the case with the other managerial groups, membership derives from regional associations and individual enterprises. In 1964, only one important structure remained outside the SFF, the regional manufacturers' organization of Concepción. Many of the Concepción directorate had held office for several decades and, while alterations in provincial and national economic life had occurred, the SFF felt that the provincial leaders in Concepción had remained rather stuffy, old-fashioned, and impervious to contemporary challenges. Cleavage led to an outright rupture between the two. Despite this development, however, all manufacturing enterprises in the area maintained their membership in the SFF, undoubtedly pointing up the transitory nature of the severance.[7]

Chile's national Chamber of Commerce contains local chambers of commerce and individual commercial firms as members; the Mining Association includes regional groups, producing companies, and mining engineers. In these and in the other management groups special affiliations are permitted for sympathetic and interested individuals and organizations abroad; for Chileans not directly engaged in agriculture, commerce, manufacturing, or mining but whose proclivities place them in related currents (such as university students and professional people); and for a few honorary members having demonstrated extraordinary merit or who have given exceptional service in the association's cause.

Finances

To secure their financial bases, the management societies depend heavily upon quotas assigned by the executive committees to component members.[8] Two formulae determine the precise amount due. One

[7] Interview with Jorge Dávila Saxton, administrative manager of the Sociedad de Fomento Fabril, in Santiago, March 30, 1964.

[8] In addition, a major source of financial support derives from investments. For example, the Chamber of Commerce in its annual report for 1963 listed

approach, most widely favored, defines quotas on an ability to pay that is based upon either assets or productivity. For example, the Manufacturers' Association adheres to a ratio based on total capital and reserves, with payable quotas ranging from a minimum of forty-five to eight thousand escudos annually (or in 1964 terms, from about $14 to $250). Mining used to establish quotas from tonnage of ore produced by copper and coal companies and then specified given amounts for other types of mining enterprises. Recently, it changed its formula. Now contributions derive from the relative need that each member group has of the central—certainly a more intangible approach, but one that permits continuing involvement in the association by firms not overly desirous of help and reluctant to be assessed too high a quota.[9] At any rate, the trade associations appear to be sufficiently affluent to satisfy a wide range of component wants and to discharge diverse and continuing functions.

Functions

The functions performed by the managerial centrals are extremely varied; some of these are diffuse in nature and seek a wide result in society, while others are specific and are aimed directly at the welfare of the organization and its components. At the societal level, all the associations engage in countless efforts to promote their economic interests throughout the nation. Each insists, with good cause, that by the development of its particular field of endeavor the nation at large must necessarily reap the benefits, though the employers' groups are careful to avoid any inference that they put themselves before the nation. In other words, there is nothing of the dictum that "what is good for manufacturing, commerce, and so forth is good for Chile." Still, as will be noted in the following section on labor, trade unionists frequently assert that the practical application of management's general

assets of more than 8,800 escudos from shares of stock and about 7,800 escudos coming from dues (Cámara Central de Comercio de Chile, *Memoria y balance*, pp. 32–33).

[9] Interview with Jerónimo Pérez Zañartu, manager of the Sociedad Nacional de Minería, in Santiago, February 18, 1964.

ideals often seems remarkably self-oriented and to the disadvantage of the rest of society.

Not surprisingly, the housekeeping activities and services that the centrals offer to their component groups are much more explicit in definition and more regularized in effectuation. For it is in their internal maintenance and development that employers' associations have found one of their greatest strengths: cohesion built upon a high degree of satisfaction of components' needs. Machinery exists for the resolution of internal conflicts through conciliation or arbitration and rules of the game have long been recognized. This conduces to generally harmonious dealings among associates and a resultant discipline that keeps such bickerings or power struggles as may infrequently erupt mostly away from the public's notice. Such a situation occurred in early 1964 among leaders of the Corporación Vitivinícola de Chile. Despite a serious schism among the top leadership, there never was any indication to this effect in the media of information and it seemed to be little known outside the disputants themselves.

Further, considerable effort is made to minister to the members' particular wants. At one level, this means providing some of the benefits of a mutual-aid group. Sociedad Nacional de Minería recognizes its function to "organize means of mutual aid among its associates against risks of sickness, accidents or death, as well as providing other forms of mutual help."[10] At another level, as with the National Society of Agriculture, it means offering countless technical services. In fact, most of the facilities of SNA's large central headquarters are made up of offices for the purveying of technical agricultural information and of a commercial section that procures seeds, fertilizers, machinery, and other needed items for the farmer.

In addition, all the associations provide their clientele with a myriad of legal, informational, and other aids on a day-by-day basis. For example, the manufacturers' group is in constant contact with all its affiliates elaborating on the latest statutory enactments and executive ordinances, carefully delineating the application of such new rulings

[10] Chapter 1, Article 3 of the *Estatutos*.

in matters affecting taxation, import duties, investment capital, and the like. The manufacturers' central also cooperates closely with a recent phenomenon in Chilean management organization, the Instituto Chileno de Racionalización de Empresas (ICARE). Founded in 1953, ICARE was the first management consultant firm to appear in Chile. Given over to time-and-motion studies and questions of human relations in industry, it has been a great boon to a reappraisal of management procedures and has received the support of most of industry.[11]

A related function of employers' groups is that of collecting and circulating the results of research investigations with an end to upgrading technical procedures. Perhaps this is most important to agriculture and mining, but it has great applicability to other management structures as well. The evidence seems to indicate a stress upon tapping the resources of scientific institutions, universities, and the government more than underwriting much research within the management association proper. Nonetheless, an outpouring of vital technical materials through a central clearinghouse serves component groups well.

In addition, all four associations are fully cognizant of the importance of projecting a favorable image upon the general public. Each association maintains a public-relations department that issues news releases regularly and publishes a trade journal. The Sociedad de Fomento Fabril releases its monthly journal, *Industria*, and a host of other publications. Among its regularly issued publications are the annual report, or *Memoria*, and the *Hoja de Información Económica*; other bulletins, such as *¿Qué es la Sociedad de Fomento Fabril?* and *¿Qué es la Industria Chilena?*, appear more sporadically. All these are packed with statistics and economic information that focus on business trends and other items related to manufacturing. Similarly, the Sociedad Nacional de Agricultura comes out with its monthly, *El Campesino*, and Sociedad Nacional de Minería with *Boletín Minero*. During the span of a year, the Cámara Central de Comercio de Chile sends approximately two dozen copies of *Circular Informativa* to its members. These appear periodically and each spotlights a single theme,

[11] The workings of ICARE are explained more fully in Robert J. Alexander, *Labor Relations in Argentina, Brazil, and Chile*, pp. 310–311.

such as taxes, monetary policy, customs, labor costs, and new government programs.

A large portion of the managerial groups' public-relations function is directed particularly to educational institutions. From elementary schools on up to the universities, special programs and relationships are developed. Agriculture tries to inculcate an interest in farming in the elementary schools, while mining is more closely tied to scientific studies in the universities. Perhaps commerce sums up the attitude of all when it says that it seeks the "study of all problems and matters which affect commerce in its several branches" and to diffuse the results of "these studies among members of the Institution and other interested people, with an end to forming a clear national conscience about the needs of commerce, its own problems, and the policy required for its prosperity, expansion, and better service."[12]

Two final functions, relations with labor and a representational function on governmental agencies, will be developed more fully at the end of this chapter. For now, it should be noted that the management centrals claim to stand shoulder to shoulder in their insistence upon implanting ideal working conditions for their labor force. SFF states as one of its ends the promoting of "conditions necessary for obtaining a climate of just and cordial treatment and understanding with intellectual and manual co-workers, which will permit these to better their material and spiritual living conditions within the possibilities of the industry."[13] The structure that most frequently is accused of failing to provide minimum satisfactory working and living conditions, Big Agriculture, piously aspires to "foment the culture and well-being of agricultural workers for the improvement of their habits of hygiene in their living conditions, the custom of athletic sports, and of other adequate entertainment."[14] To any agricultural worker who might read such a statement (if he were literate) while sitting on the earthen floor of his shack-home next to a pigsty or manure pile, this must take some award for the epitome of absurdity. Still, despite the

[12] Title II of the *Estatutos*.
[13] Title I of the *Estatutos*.
[14] Title I of the *Estatutos*.

unevenness of employers' treatment of workers on the job, certainly in the urban areas there has been a decline in the paternalism implied in the previous statements, as workers are paid straight salaries out of which they seek to provide for their own necessities of life.[15]

Effectiveness of Goal Satisfaction

When comparing the relative ability of labor and employers' groups to penetrate the political system for the satisfactory resolution of their problems, it would be natural to remark on the apparent superiority of management. But this would be an oversimplification; for, while employers' groups clearly have enjoyed greater ingress to the decision-making process, it should not be assumed that the road has always been an easy one. Periodically, political regimes have withheld favors from management, and, very importantly, government cannot always aid management even if it should be inclined to do so.

In fact, employers' associations and the economic interests they represent have been saddled with the debilitating effect of decades of inflation as well as with a general deterioration of economic production. Savings that could strengthen the nation's ability for capital reinvestment slip into private safes or into foreign banks as a hedge against the side effects of the economic muddle. Because of the general economic malaise of the economy, government has been forced to impose high customs duties on machinery and other finished goods imported from abroad in order to try to compensate for chronic imbalance of payments. Further, the government sets maximum prices on many goods, especially agricultural products, that delimit normal profit margins.[16]

In short, managerial groups are confronted with countless government actions that affect them vitally in matters from taxation and currency exchange policies to customs and investment procedures. All this necessitates management pressure on a broad front to protect what

[15] W. Paul Strassmann, "The Industrialist," in *Continuity and Change in Latin America*, ed. John J. Johnson, p. 181.

[16] For a very insightful elaboration of these problems, see Markos Mamalakis and Clark W. Reynolds, *Essays on the Chilean Economy*.

it considers its legitimate rights. In essence, management requires regularized channels to the policy-making and policy-effectuation agencies of the government for the recognition of its claims.

Labor Groups

Origins

The great historical continuity enjoyed by employers' associations finds almost no equivalent in Chile's organized labor movement. Some federations and locals boast considerable viability over a relatively long time, but the rise of confederal structures and of trade unionism generally is fraught with vicissitudes that have periodically reduced labor to a severely crippled state.

As occurred in most of Latin America, the first labor organizations to appear in Chile were mutual-benefit societies.[17] These mainly comprised skilled artisans of a single trade and endeavored to protect members against risks of job and life. The earliest of these appeared in the middle of the nineteenth century; they were La Igualdad (1850), Sociedad "Unión de los Tipógrafos" (1853), and Sociedad de Artesanos (1858). The value of such an organization was proved repeatedly and became the popular wave of its day as the 13 societies that held legal recognition in 1870 rose to more than 150 in 1900.[18] By 1964, the total number of mutualist groups affiliated with the Confederación Mutualista de Chile reached 300, though by then other organizational forms dominated the labor movement and so total membership was not large. Nevertheless, they still performed those mutual aids which had served their components so well in the past. On the 110th anniversary of the founding of the Sociedad "Unión de los Tipógrafos," Luis Ramírez Sanz outlined the work of the Confederación Mutualista as "mutual aid which is undertaken among its thousands of

[17] There exist many useful studies of the history of Chilean trade unionism. A few of them are Julio César Jobet, *Recabarren: Los orígenes del movimiento obrero y del socialismo chilenos*, and "Movimiento Social Obrero" in *Desarrollo de Chile en la primera mitad del siglo XX*, I, 51–106; Moisés Poblete Troncoso, *La organización sindical en Chile*; and Hernán Ramírez Necochea, *Historia del movimiento obrero en Chile—antecedentes—siglo XIX*.

[18] Moisés Poblete Troncoso and Ben G. Burnett, *The Rise of the Latin American Labor Movement*, p. 58.

members in case of sickness and death; its collective preoccupation on behalf of procuring employment for the member who has lost it; the maintenance of private clinics within their respective social centers—in the majority their own, given the correct investment of their social funds; the creation of night schools and of libraries with the support of private individuals who know how to appreciate a better cultural standard in our working classes."[19]

Despite their long history, mutual-aid societies never incorporated more than a small percentage of the entire working class and virtually all these were of highly skilled trades who enjoyed a far greater financial security than the bulk of Chilean rural and urban laborers. Today they are quite conservative, rarely constitute anything of a threat to employers, and rather assiduously avoid political involvements. In fact, it is the official policy of the Confederación Mutualista that it and all its affiliates "maintain and must observe absolute aloofness in all political and electoral campaigns."[20]

The first substantial organized opposition to management came in the 1890's when Anarcho-Syndicalists formed a host of "societies of resistance." At first leaping into prominence in northern Chile where life in the nitrate mines was particularly brutal, they subsequently spread southward through Antofagasta to Santiago and Valparaíso. Few of the resistance societies ever knew more than an ephemeral existence. The shortage of trained leaders weakened them and a coalition of management and government coerced and fought them. Hundreds of people were killed in clashes involving maritime workers at Valparaíso in 1903 and laborers protesting the cost of living in Santiago in 1905, and in disputes affecting railroad workers in Antofagasta and nitrate workers at Iquique in 1907.

All this activity set the stage for the appearance of Chile's first nationwide labor central. Formed out of the chaos of the early 1900's, the Gran Federación Obrera Chilena (in 1917 the "Gran" was dropped and afterward it was known simply as FOCH) early took a leftist turn. At first dominated by moderates, it was seized during World War I by Socialists, and in 1919 a major reorganization at

[19] *El Mercurio* (Santiago), October 4, 1963.
[20] *Ibid.*

Concepción placed it under Communist hegemony. From that point it was just a short hop to affiliation in 1921 with the Red Trade Union International (labor's arm of the Communist International) and a year later to negotiating cooperative arrangements with the Chilean Communist party. At its height late in the 1920's, FOCH claimed more than 100,000 members.[21]

The authoritarian presidency of Carlos Ibáñez del Campo (1925–1931) ushered in a second principal phase in the history of Chilean trade unionism that would last for the next two decades. Ibáñez' conservative administration lent governmental support to moderate unionism to the detriment of the dominant leftist leadership. New centrals were founded, older ones declined, and repeated efforts at regrouping occurred. FOCH and an affiliate of the Industrial Workers of the World from the United States, which had been established during World War I, languished in the face of a hostile officialdom. Meanwhile, in 1925, Catholic elements sought to merge into the Confederation of White Unions, and rightists, reflecting certain governmental tendencies, formed the profascist Republican Confederation of Civic Union. Neither survived the Ibáñez era.

The challenges of the depression, governmental opposition to labor, and the resultant proliferation and weakening of trade unionism fostered repeated attempts at consolidation. Then, in the mid-1930's, these efforts at last reached fruition in the form of a new central, the Confederación de Trabajadores de Chile (CTCH). CTCH evolved out of core elements from FOCH, dominated by Stalinists who reconstituted the old central following Ibáñez' fall from power; from the Confederación Nacional de Sindicatos Legales, a Socialist-controlled amalgamation of most of the legally recognized unions; and from the Confederación General del Trabajo (CGT), an Anarcho-Syndicalist group founded in 1930. Soon afterward, the Anarcho-Syndicalists withdrew from CTCH and went on their own way, leaving CTCH in Marxist hands.[22]

[21] U.S. Department of Labor, *Labor in Chile*, p. 35.

[22] For the nature of its program, see CTCH, *II Congreso Nacional de la Confederación de Trabajadores de Chile.*

These were among the more successful years in labor's struggle for expansion and status. The Popular Front government of Pedro Aguirre Cerda (1939–1941) evinced a sympathy to trade unionism and initiated major economic and social reform.[23] Then, competition between Socialists and Communists for leadership of organized labor marked the World War II years. A slim Socialist lead was narrowed and finally reversed in 1946 when, in January of that year, the Communists called for a general strike, boycotted by the Socialists, which enjoyed general popularity among the working classes. This, along with their support of Gabriel González Videla, the victorious presidential candidate in the 1946 elections, swung trade-unionist control to the Communists.

But beginning in August, 1947, most of labor suffered a serious setback as a result of President González Videla's change of attitude toward the Communists. Then, at the President's urging, Congress enacted the infamous Laws for the Defense of Democracy. Aimed at dumping Communists from labor leadership, its application hindered moderates as well as Marxists and pushed the labor movement into a tailspin. A schism erupted in the CTCH and Chilean trade unionism generally fragmented hopelessly in the wake of the governmental onslaught.

After several years of drift and with the return of Carlos Ibáñez to political prominence—what seemed to trade unionists to be the ultimate threat to their survival—renewed efforts for the consolidation of the labor movement ended up in 1952 with the convening of a National Constituent Congress for a Single Central Organization of Chilean Workers. Out of the conference emerged a new confederation, the Central Unica de Trabajadores de Chile (CUT), which combined the Communist and Socialist wings of the CTCH with the all-but-disintegrated CGT and several other small groups. CUT's executive board contained a broad representation of political colorations, though its doctrine reflected the more radical composition by placing CUT in direct opposition to the traditional capitalist order: "The present cap-

[23] John R. Stevenson, *The Chilean Popular Front.*

italist regime, founded on private property of the land, of the instruments and means of production and on the exploitation of man by man, which divides society into antagonistic classes: exploited and exploiters, must be substituted by an economic-social regime which will liquidate private property in order to achieve a society without classes, in which man and humanity are assured their full development."[24] Furthermore, it declared itself independent of any specific political partisanship or government. This did not mean that it was apolitical, but rather that it cut across all political views with an end to furthering the interests of the total working mass. Toward this goal, it regarded the strike as "the maximum expression of the struggle of the salaried classes," and it rejected any supposed distinctions between "legal" and "illegal" strikes in favor of utilizing all methods that would bring justice to the working classes.[25]

Although CUT encompassed far and away the largest number of organized workers, several centrals and federations preferred to stay outside its organization. The Confederación Nacional de Trabajadores (CNT) appeared in 1958 when Anarchist-dominated locals pulled out of CUT and endeavored to establish a direct counterforce. Espousing a strongly anti-Communist line, CNT joined with ORIT, the Inter-American Regional Labor Organization, but has failed to cut into CUT's power. Christian Democrats also sought to break CUT's preponderant position in Chilean labor by founding the Movimiento Unitario de Trabajadores de Chile (MUTCH) in 1961. An amalgamation of several older organizations, of which the most important was Acción Sindical Chilena, the Christian Democrats experienced a very limited success in attracting members. One large and tremendously important federation has kept its independence from CUT, though occasionally the two break bread together in a common cause. This is the powerful maritime workers' union, the Confederación Marítima de Chile (COMACH). The Confederación de Empleados Particulares de Chile (CEPCH), founded at Valparaíso in 1948, tried to maintain an apolitical stance, but finally affiliated with CUT in 1969.

[24] Quoted in Jorge Barría Serón, *Trayectoria y estructura del movimiento sindical chileno, 1946–1962*, p. 54.

[25] *Ibid.*

Organization

Despite the disruptive and chaotic nature of the history of Chilean central organizations, each of the principal centrals has built upon the structural foundations and earlier experiences of its predecessors. Such was the case also with CUT, which borrowed from CTCH's organizational format and learned lessons from the bitter internal rivalry that ultimately caused CTCH to fall apart.

In large measure CUT's organizational make-up has been determined by the nature of its basis of membership. There are three general categories of membership—active, fraternal, and sympathetic. The last two types of groups maintain their autonomy, but send observers to national congresses and periodically join CUT in actions of mutual advantage. Perhaps the most important of fraternal structures is CEPCH, which operates independently in behalf of white-collar employees while keeping friendly relations with CUT. Sympathetic groups include a wide range of social organizations that tend to fall outside the usual definition of trade unions (e.g., the Federation of Students of Chile, or FECH), but that for a variety of reasons share CUT's goals.

The bulk of active membership is composed of workers who are members of federations that in turn affiliate with CUT. However, there are in addition local groups—commonly with less than twenty-five workers who are inhibited by law from enjoying full union rights—that join CUT under its very informal and open admission policy.[26]

Many of the federations are quite large in membership and enjoy a relative independence of action that frequently militates against stands taken by CUT leadership. As will be seen, this constitutes an on-going threat to cohesion and necessitates the issuing of most directives as suggestions rather than orders. Thus, the call for a general strike will ordinarily be requested of components and only rarely will all respond fully to the action recommended.

It is extremely hazardous to estimate membership figures for the federations and other national unions that comprise CUT, due to the

[26] Interview with Luis Figueroa Mazuela, secretary general of CUT, in Santiago, February 18, 1964.

tendency to inflate the number of organized workers contained in a given structure and, also, to the fact that occasionally a worker possesses dual membership. The national Department of Labor counts a person twice who belongs to both an industrial and a professional union; but it does not even consider such unions as that of government workers, which are not supposed to exist under the law.[27] Thus, while CUT leadership occasionally lapses into a euphoric claim of one million, total membership certainly is much less and probably stands at under a third of a million. One of the best recent studies of the Chilean labor movement lists the following federations with their probable membership as of CUT's Third National Congress in August, 1962:

Federation	Membership
Federación Nacional Minera (miners)	30,000
Federación Nacional de Trabajadores de Metal (metal workers)	12,000
Federación Nacional de Trabajadores de la Edificación, Madera y Materiales Construcción (construction workers)	6,500
Federación Nacional de Curtidores (tanners)	1,000
Federación Nacional de Panificadores (bakers)	6,000
Federación Nacional de Química y Farmacia (chemical and pharmaceutical workers and employees)	3,500
Federación Nacional Obrera Vitivinícola (wine workers)	1,500
Confederación de Trabajadores del Cobre (copper workers and employees)	16,000
Federación Obrera Nacional del Cuero y Calzado (leather and shoe workers)	8,000
Confederación de Obreros Molineros y Fideeros de Chile (millers)	3,500
Confederación de Obreros Cerveceros de Chile (brewery workers)	2,000
Federación Nacional de Campesinos Indígenas (agricultural workers)	10,000

27 Interviews with Hernán Troncoso, professor of law at the Pontifical Catholic University, in Santiago, February 19 and 26, 1964.

Federación Nacional de Trabajadores de Utilidad Pública (public utility workers and employees)	6,000
Federación Nacional de Empleados de Compañías de Seguros (insurance employees)	1,200
Federación Nacional de Trabajadores Hoteleros (hotel workers)	4,000
Federación Industrial Ferroviaria de Chile (railroad workers)	24,000
Agrupación Nacional de Empleados Fiscales (governmental employees)	22,000
Asociación Nacional de Empleados Semi-fiscales (quasi-government employees)	4,500
Federación Nacional de Trabajadores de Salud (health workers)	26,000
Unión Nacional de Obreros Camineros Fiscales (government highway workers)	3,000
Federación de Educadores de Chile (teachers)	30,000
Asociación Nacional de Empleados Administrativos y de Servicio del Ministerio de Educación (government employees)	3,500
Asociación de Profesores y Empleados de la Universidad de Chile (professors and employees of the University of Chile)	5,000
Asociación Nacional de Empleados y Obreros de la Empresa de Transportes Colectivos del Estado (public transportation workers and employees)	5,000
Comando Nacional de Obreros Portuarios Fiscales (government port workers)	1,500
Junta Nacional de Obreros Municipales de Chile (municipal government workers)	10,000
Asociación Nacional de Empleados Municipales (municipal government employees)	4,500
Federación Nacional de Suplementeros (newspaper venders)	3,000
Federación Nacional de Comerciantes de Ferias Libres (shopkeepers)	3,000[28]

[28] Adapted from Barría, *Trayectoria y estructura del movimiento sindical chileno*, pp. 387–389.

In addition to these twenty-nine federations and other nationally organized groups, CUT claims thirty thousand members from local unions and associations that directly affiliate.

Thus, two types of organizational bases form CUT—the industrial and professional federations, each with its own internal organization, and countless local groups dispersed throughout Chile that are consolidated by CUT itself. Local groups combine in hierarchical fashion through communal, departmental, provincial, and regional (or zonal) directive councils and congresses, whereas each federation maintains its own type of structure. At the top of CUT's organizational chart are the Assembly of National Federations and Associations (Pleno de Federaciones y Asociaciones Nacionales), National Congress (Congreso Nacional), and the National Conference (Conferencia Nacional). (See Chart 1.)

The National Directive Council serves as CUT's functioning executive between congresses. This means that it makes most of the decisions relating to daily matters and represents CUT before the government as well as in other formal capacities. The bylaws specify its duties as being:

a) To comply with the Bylaws, the Declaration of Principles, and the Work Programs and to make certain that they are carried out.

b) To put into practice the Resolutions of the Ordinary and Extraordinary National Congresses and the Recommendations of the Assemblies of National Federations and Associations and of the National Conferences.

c) To represent CUT before government organs and before International Organizations.

d) To convoke Ordinary and Extraordinary National Congresses.

e) To convoke Assemblies of National Federations and Associations and National Conferences.

f) To give account of its activities before the Ordinary National Congress.

g) To draw up the Annual Budget of Cash Receipts and Expenses and to inform the National Federations and Associations and the Provincial, Zonal, and Regional Councils of it.

h) To promote international solidarity with the workers' struggles; and,

i) To publish the Conclusions of Congresses and Conferences and to

CHART I

Central Unica de Trabajadores de Chile, Structure as of Third Congress (1962)

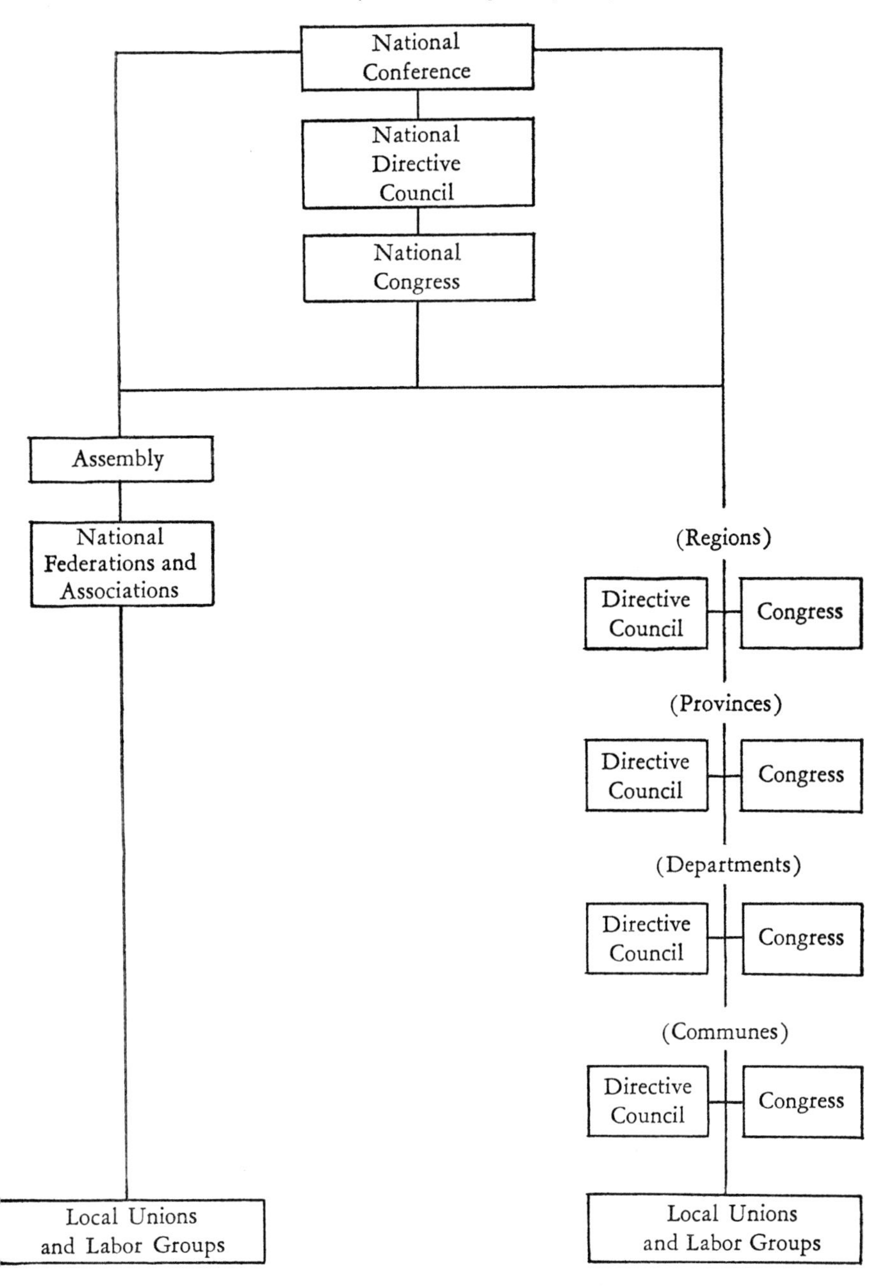

edit a newspaper or official magazine which will help to keep the bases informed of the activities of CUT.[29]

The number sitting on the National Directive Council has varied because of attrition between congresses and as a result of alterations in composition imposed by the congresses themselves. Hence, the constituent convention that founded CUT in 1953 set the total at twenty-five; after 1957, however, the integration of several new federations caused it to jump to thirty, though by 1959 it had dropped to twenty-one. The Third Congress, which convened in 1962, invoked a new formula that called for the council to be made up of a fifteen-member Executive Secretariat plus one representative from each of the national federations affiliated with CUT. The federations' councilors each held from one to three votes depending upon the size of his organization.[30]

The Pleno, or Assembly, never achieved clarity of purpose or much operational meaning. It pulled together the National Directive Council and all the federations' executive councils, as well as an additional three delegates from the Santiago regional organization, thus recognizing the tremendous concentration of unionism in the nation's capital. Ostensibly, the Pleno was to assemble at least once every three months in order to consider those subjects for discussion proposed by the National Directive Council. It seems to have been the intention of CUT's founders to provide for a body, the Pleno, that could advise the National Directive Council in decision making and, at the same time, ensure that such policies would filter down through the federations' hierarchies to the bases. Apparently, there never developed any reason to commend the Pleno on either score, leading CUT's president on one occasion to complain that the umbilical cord that "ought to unite the National Directive Council permanently with its bases, the so-called National Council of Federations [or Pleno], has failed lamentably. An organism without a life of its own and without personality cannot subsist; sooner or later it must succumb. In general, the sessions of the National Council of Federations are very poorly at-

[29] Article 27 of the 1962 bylaws. See CUT, *Chile necesita cambios de fondo*, p. 13.

[30] Article 16 of the 1962 bylaws.

tended or are not held because of a lack of people. As a general rule, the agents representing the Federations and Labor Centrals do not give account of the agreements, resolutions, and orientation of CUT's National Directive Council to their bases."[31]

While the Pleno, or Assembly, fell short of the specifications set out for it when CUT's hierarchy first was molded, the National Conference has assumed somewhat more importance. Broader based than the Pleno, it not only draws its membership from the National Directive Council and the federations (three representatives from each) but also admits three delegates from each of the regional organs. Although the bylaws dictate that it should be consultative in nature and convoked on the bid of the National Directive Council, happenstance has given the National Conference a more vital role to play. This derives from the infrequency of congresses and the consequent need to assemble as broad a cross section of CUT as possible for interim consultations. The National Conference fit the bill and became an important sounding board for labor problems and internal partisan differences and a significant channel of communication between the Directive Council and the rest of CUT's hierarchy.[32]

Of the several national organs, the bylaws grant ultimate authority to the National Congress. A large body, the congress includes the entire National Directive Council, three representatives from each of the federations, national associations, provincial councils, and regional councils, as well as a varying number of delegates from component unions.[33] Although all the delegates were to be elected by secret ballot, the inner workings of each labor group actually determined the selection process—sometimes by secret ballot, at other times by open voting,

[31] CUT, "Informe del Presidente," *Segundo Congreso Nacional Ordinario*, p. 7.

[32] Interview with Oscar Núñez, president of CUT, in Santiago, February 20, 1964. For a lengthy discussion of CUT's Organization, see Barría, *Trayectoria y estructura del movimiento sindical chileno*, pp. 219–285.

[33] The formula for the Third Convention was one delegate for a labor group of 25 to 100 members, two for 101 to 300, three for 301 to 500, five for 501 to 1,000, seven for 1,001 to 1,500, and ten for 1,501 to 2,500. Larger groups were allocated an additional delegate for each fraction of 500 members over 2,500 (CUT, *Tercer Congreso Nacional Ordinario, Convocatoria*).

and in some instances by delegates being chosen by the executive councils. A curious problem grew out of this laxity of controls over choosing delegates in that a few skeletal groups—constituted by no more than a "president," "secretary," and a paper organization—showed up at national congresses as voting participants. The Organization Committee of the Third Congress (1962) denounced this procedure and evinced a willingness to draw up a more standardized and verifiable selection method.[34]

Originally, the bylaws suggested that regular meetings of the National Congress should be convoked every two years. But financial and organizational problems postponed the first regular Congress twice that long, to 1957; the Second Congress met on schedule in 1959; but the Third Congress did not convene until 1962. Then, recognizing the seeming futility of aspiring to biennial meetings, the Third National Congress set the whole decision in the hands of the National Directive Council with the suggestion that it try to assemble congresses every three years.

Furthermore, the presence at the Third Congress of seventy fraternal organizations—including such important ones as CEPCH, Federación Bancaria, and Sindicato Profesional de Empleados de la Compañía de Teléfonos de Chile—appeared to serve notice that these would continue to maintain close relations with CUT and "persevere in unity of action."[35] Moreover, delegations were in attendance that represented several international labor organizations and a dozen foreign trade-union centrals—all the latter being from Communist countries or from Communist-controlled Latin American labor confederations. Not unexpectedly, not a single labor group in the United States sent either a delegation or fraternal greetings.[36]

During its five days of deliberations, the Third Congress ranged

[34] Barría, *Trayectoria y estructura del movimiento sindical chileno*, p. 167.

[35] CUT, *Chile necesita cambios de fondo*, p. 4.

[36] The international organizations represented were the Communists' World Federation of Trade Unions and the Christian Democrats' Latin American Confederation of Christian Trade Unionists; foreign trade unionists came from East Germany, Red China, North Korea, Cuba, Czechoslovakia, Hungary, Rumania, North Vietnam, and the Soviet Union as well as from Communist-controlled unions in Panama, El Salvador, and Uruguay (*ibid.*, pp. 36–38).

over a variety of subjects and actions. Besides performing such housekeeping functions as electing officers and revising the bylaws, the congress gave consideration to methods of strategy. In this regard, CUT cited its principal tasks to be enlarging its bases, strengthening union organization, coordinating workers' actions, freeing workers from exploitation, and "confronting and defeating, in this historical epoch, imperialism and its allies, the big bourgeoisie and the landowning and feudal oligarchy."[37] Resolutions were passed dealing with numerous aspects of the economic and social conditions of Chilean workers, while deep antagonism was expressed toward "North American Imperialism" and the landowning and financial oligarchies.

Many observers of the 1962 Third Congress averred that it was stacked to favor the Socialist-Communist cause despite a much wider ideological range among CUT's total membership. In part, this could be laid to the zeal of Marxists compared with an alleged laxness among many moderates and the inherent radical nature of labor leadership, which carried down from the origins of Chilean trade unionism. Whatever the case, the Marxists' control of vital committees and the management of the convention assured them a major voice in the proceedings. One prominent labor leader asserted that, although democrats constituted an actual majority of the delegates, the Socialist-Communist coalition by controlling such key position as the Credentials Committee rejected nominations of moderate representatives and, instead, placed their own people in commanding positions.[38] Allegedly, many of the latter spoke for organizations that simply did not exist in fact. Antipathy between the two elements was reflected in the hall being literally split physically by an aisle—on the one side sitting the Marxists and their followers and on the other democratic groups. The Cuban representative was give an hour to speak to the assemblage, whereas José Goldsack, president of the Latin American Confederation of Christian Trade Unionists (CLASC), was granted only five minutes—though he survived for eight. Whenever Goldsack would make a point, the Marxists ridiculed him with a chorus of "amen." On the

[37] *Ibid.*, pp. 16–17.

[38] Interview with José Goldsack, president of the Confederación Latinoamericana de Sindicalistas Cristianos, in Santiago, February 12, 1964.

other hand, when the Soviet Union's delegate sought to deliver his address, the moderates yelled him down. Throughout this episode the atmosphere was tense as both sides hurled accusations across the aisle.[39]

Despite the dominant role played by the extreme left in CUT's national congresses, there is a certain amount of give and take present; also it seems probable that the leadership's attitudes as well as the resolutions of the convention correspond well with the views of much of the membership: "[The] National Congress is the maximum representational expression of CUT as its bylaws indicate, it is an index of the degree of organization, of the attraction which it exercises over its affiliates and sympathizers, it is an assembly where the major problems that afflict the salaried workers of the country are debated and a tribunal so that the different ideological groups which function in it can express their points of view."[40]

Finally, a few words seem in order regarding the structural form of some of the more important remaining federations and centrals that lie outside the organizational framework of CUT. Undoubtedly, the two most significant independent federations are those of the maritime workers and the white-collar workers. The maritime workers' central, the Confederación Marítima de Chile (COMACH), heads up four subsidiary structures belonging to several types of port workers as well as to ships' crews.[41] In all, 102 local unions totalling approximately forty thousand blue- and white-collar workers hold membership. The biggest of these, the stevedores' federation (FEMACH), is based upon three zonal councils that encompass virtually all the Chilean ports. The First Zonal Council is located in Antofagasta and coordinates labor matters for the northern ports; the Second Zone, at Val-

[39] Interviews with José Goldsack and with Alfredo di Pacce, executive secretary for the Atlantic Region of the Confederación Latinoamericana de Sindicalistas Cristianos, in Santiago, January 21, 1964. Referring to this situation, Goldsack related that "we yelled back and forth at each other and we were ready to fight—we wanted to fight!"

[40] Barría, *Trayectoria y estructura del movimiento sindical chileno*, pp. 217–218.

[41] The four are the Federación de Estibadores de Chile, Federación de Empleados de Bahía de Chile, Federación de Tripulantes, and the Federación de Marineros Auxiliares de Bahía.

paraíso, resides in the most significant shipping region and serves as headquarters for both FEMACH and COMACH; the Third Zone covers southern Chile and is centered at Concepción's port of Talcahuano. National organization is highly simplified and permits rapid decision making as well as a high degree of policy effectuation.[42] Much of this derives from the power and organizational competence of the existing president, Wenceslao Moreno, one of Chile's authentic and most effective labor leaders.

Practically all of Chile's organized white-collar employees in private industry affiliate with the Confederación de Empleados Particulares de Chile (CEPCH). CEPCH builds upon nine main component bases—employees in industry and commerce, metallurgy, telephone, copper and steel, insurance, transportation, and public utilities as well as salesmen and chauffeurs and conductors. Its national organization consists of the National Congress (Congreso Nacional), granted maximum authority by the bylaws; the National Executive Directorate (Directorio Ejecutivo Nacional), a nine-member board that coordinates the daily operations of the Confederation; and the National Council (Consejo Nacional), an advisory group made up of the directorate, executive officers of the affiliated federations, and two members from each of CEPCH's provincial councils. Although CEPCH has proved successful in attracting most of the organized white-collar workers in private enterprises—some 40,000 of 50,000 employees—it continues to have great difficulty breaking down barriers between itself and the remaining 150,000 or so still outside union organizations.[43]

Finally, two national centrals persist that rather unsuccessfully have tried to challenge the power of CUT as the single nationwide voice of

[42] Interview with Wenceslao Moreno, president, and Juan Lubiano, administrative secretary, of the Confederación Marítima de Chile, in Valparaíso, January 30, 1964.

[43] A series of interviews with Enrique Sánchez, secretary general of the Confederación de Empleados Particulares de Industria y Comercio, a component of CEPCH, in Santiago, between October, 1963, and June, 1964. Also, interviews with Antonio Carrozana, administrative secretary of the Confederación de Empleados Particulares de Industria y Comercio, in Santiago, November 3, 1963; and with Federico Mujica, vice-president of the Confederación de Empleados Particulares de Chile, in Santiago, February 5, 1964.

labor. In 1958, the Inter-American Regional Labor Organization sponsored the establishment of the Confederación Nacional de Trabajadores (CNT) and continues to provide a modest financial infusion, which keeps CNT going. Its principal constituent groups are the Confederación de Chóferes, with whom it shares offices, the Federación de Industrias de Materiales Eléctricas, the Asociación Nacional Pensionados de Seguro Social, and the Confederación Regional del Norte. Its leadership claims 126 unions with a total of 80,000 members,[44] though other estimates suggest that 35 directly affiliated unions and 20,000 adherents may be closer to the truth.[45] At least two of its components also have membership in CEPCH. According to its founding principles, CNT is militantly anti-Communist, democratic, and nonpolitical. Its future seems dim unless it can find common ground with a far greater number of federations; but to date, CNT has been stalemated in its overtures to other structures.

The Christian Democrats' Acción Sindical Chilena (ASICH), a component of Movimiento Unitario de Trabajadores de Chile (MUTCH), also suffers from an enigmatic position in the Chilean labor movement. Originally founded in 1947 by a number of workers inspired by Father Alberto Hurtado, ASICH had as its principal goal the training of labor leaders. It was reconstituted in 1956 and again in 1961 to try to upgrade it into an authentic labor central—in the latter year adding the name Confederación Cristiana de Trabajadores (thus, ASICH-CCT). Part of its development problems derived from an apparent lack of clarity as to its ideological position. For it defined itself as manifestly devoted to the establishment of a "social Christian order," which would provide its members with an "ideological unity."[46] On the other hand, this ideological basis did not mean either "a determined political position or an obligatory religious creed for its members."[47] To many this suggested nothing less than purposeful

44 Interviews with Carlos Ibáñez King, president, Luis Lavín Céspedes, secretary general, and Héctor Durán Cacenes, director of publications, of the Confederación Nacional de Trabajadores, in Santiago, January 23, 1964.

45 U.S. Department of Labor, *Labor in Chile*, pp. 39–40.

46 *Movimiento Unitario de Trabajadores de Chile*, p. 17.

47 *Ibid.*

ambiguity, while in fact tying itself to the Church. Indeed, the head of CNT wondered if ASICH and its affiliation with the hemispheric Christian Democratic group, Confederación Latinoamericana de Sindicalistas Cristianos (CLASC), did not cause it to be "too involved with Germany, Rome, and the clergy."[48] Whatever the case, as Eduardo Frei delineated his program during the 1964 presidential campaign, ASICH's doctrinal position acquired a somewhat clearer position as well.

These, then, were the major forces of organized trade unionism in Chile in the 1960's. CUT loosely held together the bulk of organized labor in Chile and periodically attracted fraternal support from the more important unaffiliated federations, such as COMACH and CEPCH. CNT and ASICH sought to break CUT's confederational predominance, but they encountered strong opposition from CUT and failed to expand their membership appreciably among unorganized workers. Although membership estimates are very sketchy and uncertain, in the early 1960's all of organized labor probably included no more than 20 per cent of the laboring classes of Chile.[49] This figure was kept especially low because of the almost total absence of unions among agricultural workers—of whom probably considerably less than 1 per cent held union cards. In addition, much of urban labor remained unorganized and 90 per cent of those in unions were to be found in the metropolitan areas of Santiago, Valparaíso, Concepción, and Antofagasta.[50]

Effectiveness of Goal Identification and Satisfaction

Whatever the magnitude of management's need for satisfactions from the political system—and they were sizable in the early 1960's—at least it was not hamstrung by the multitudinous laws, regulations, and informal sanctions that inhibited the legitimate activities of labor and that usually made it a weak competitor in pressure politics. And yet, from the early republican period basic freedoms were built into the constitutional framework that should have accrued to labor's ad-

48 Interview with Carlos Ibáñez King.
49 U.S. Department of Labor, *Labor in Chile*, p. 38.
50 *Ibid.*

vantage once trade unionism became relatively pervasive. Thus, from the Constitution of 1883 until the presently operative Constitution of 1925, guarantee of the "right of association without previous permission" has been a mainstay of group protections. In addition, protective labor legislation came into force as early as 1924, though a complete labor code was not enacted until 1931. Nonetheless, the code's beginnings, based upon the recommendations of Professor Moisés Poblete Troncoso of the University of Chile and its passage stimulated by President Arturo Alessandri, in fact predated any major labor movement. Thus, both constitutional and statutory protections provided the legal atmosphere (if in fact not the most ample defense) of trade unionism prior to its actual attainment of organizational viability.[51]

The Labor Code. Probably more than any Latin American republic, Chile maintains a high regard for legality. Unfortunately, the deep-seated rule of law that characterizes the political system generally, in some instances has been used to the detriment of specific societal elements. Relevant here has been the apparent earliness and liberality of labor laws in Chile, whereas the Labor Code actually has been used to delimit trade unionism's organizational growth.

At the outset, several special features of the Chilean Labor Code must be explained. The code recognizes the right to join or form a union as residing with men and women over eighteen years of age who work in the same enterprise or who are of the same or similar occupations. Consequently, unions may be either professional (craft) or industrial (plant-wide). In plants, factories, or other economic enterprises where 55 per cent of the workers vote to join a union and the union gains legal recognition, then all the workers in that enterprise will be considered members of the union. Professional unions come about when a minimum of twenty-five workers in the same or a similar occupation wish to unite.[52]

[51] Conversations with Moisés Poblete Troncoso, professor of law and director of the Institute of Social and Economic Sciences at the University of Chile, in Santiago and Viña del Mar, between October, 1963, and June, 1964.

[52] These stipulations are to be found in Book III, "On Union Organizations," of the Labor Code. Title One deals with general rights and duties of union members, while Titles II and III treat industrial and professional unions spe-

A curious feature of the code is its insistence upon drawing a distinction between manual workers, or *obreros*, and white-collar workers, or *empleados*. Francisco Walker Linares, professor of labor law at the University of Chile, argues that this is a perfectly natural method of demarcation: "The ideal of social law probably is that there should not be legal differences between employees and workers, inasmuch as the existence of classes among the salaried is contrary to its ends; however, such an ideal is difficult to realize if one considers the diverse nature of the functions which workers and employees perform, and the differences of cultural level and of education between both, especially in the countries of Latin America."[53]

Be that as it may, such a distinction caused an uneven distribution of benefits to the two sectors at different moments in labor's history. Originally, the code permitted provisions for certain special benefits for the *empleados* (e.g., family allowances), which *obreros* did not procure until after the Second World War. This transpired in the 1920's when Arturo Alessandri's favors fell upon the middle class, and blue-collar laborers searched around for the scraps left over.[54]

Contrariwise, when manual workers acquired more stamina in their associational endeavors and their trade unions performed more strongly as bargaining agents, *obreros* registered advances that did not automatically spill over onto *empleados*. For example, white-collar groups have complained bitterly about their inability under the law to secure a closed or union shop, a right enjoyed by *obreros* if 55 per cent of a plant's workers subscribe to union membership. There seems to be no earthly reason for the disparity and *empleados* seem justified in branding it as discrimination; but the point remains that the blue-collar unions pushed through the change in the code and the white-collar groups did not.

A final point regarding more or less unique aspects of the Labor Code relates to incongruities between legal enactments and what pre-

---

cifically. The entire code is indexed and summarized in Juan Díaz Salas, *Legislación social: Código del trabajo*, Vol. X.

[53] Francisco Walker Linares, *Nociones elementales de derecho del trabajo*, p. 249.

[54] Alexander, *Labor Relations in Argentina, Brazil, and Chile*, p. 269.

vails in practice. Theoretically, unions must obtain legal recognition (*personería jurídica*) in order to bargain collectively with employers. In fact, many unions that do not have this legal status deal with management. Even more curious is the sanction against both government workers and employees forming their own unions;[55] yet they constitute one of the largest "associated" elements in Chile and are among the most active in employing the strike and other trade-unionist techniques to improve working and living conditions. This fact points up a discrepancy that hinders appropriate trade-union activities and clouds the whole picture of labor performance in Chile.

At the same time that the Labor Code was set up to give official recognition to the rights and privileges of organized labor, it has actually inhibited the development of trade unionism by forbidding unions to pay salaries to their officers (except for the special case of the copper workers),[56] thus largely ruling out the possibility of full-time union leaders; by limiting the use of a checkoff of membership dues to *obreros*; by discouraging the widest possible operation of central organizations; and by severely restricting the use of union funds (e.g., unions are not *legally* allowed to create strike funds).

Under the code the government has wide supervisory powers over union organization, elections, and finances. From one point of view this seems desirable and helpful. The General Directorate of Labor (Dirección General del Trabajo), under whose aegis all labor matters reside, can be considered a protector of labor rights, ensuring legality in union operations to the benefit of members, seeing to it that workers participate in their just right to regulate rest, have healthful and safe working conditions, and are properly informed of their privileges. The Dirección acts as an adviser, and arbitrator, and a facilitator and simplifier of legal processes.[57]

But many labor leaders claim that in practice it militates against the growth of trade unionism, especially in situations where a strong antipathy of management toward organized labor prevails. For exam-

[55] Article 368 of the Labor Code, Díaz S., *Legislación social*, pp. 134–135.
[56] Article 377 of the code, *ibid.*, p. 136.
[57] Ivan Ríos Ladrón de Guevara, *La dirección general del trabajo*, pp. 16–20.

ple, in the initial phase of attempting to establish a union, many feel that reform in customary procedures is essential. As constituted, the code requires that a would-be union notify the local labor inspector of its intent. This information is then forwarded to the Dirección General del Trabajo for review as well as to the laborers' employers. After much paper work and probably a considerable time lag, the Dirección sends an inspector to make a final appraisal on the capability of the union to exist under the law. Until that occurs, union leaders may be harassed by their employers and workers coerced into withdrawing from membership on the threat of losing their jobs. Of course, when it works well this process can protect innocent workers from improprieties by unprincipled labor officials. But all too often it only cancels a legitimate associational effort.[58]

Once a union is formally established the code tries to protect certain labor officials from management's opposition. Thus, union directors are covered by an immunity (*fuero sindical*) and may not be dismissed from their jobs until at least six months after they have left office unless the employer obtains permission to do so from the labor tribunal in his district. Nevertheless, this proviso protects only leaders of local unions possessing legal recognition; it does not cover leaders of federations or confederations—whether or not they are legally recognized—nor does it protect officials of local unions that have failed to acquire recognition. At best, the six-month rule may only delay the inevitable firing of union leaders. Robert Alexander chronicles such an occurrence in the case of the Yarur textile factory in Santiago.[59] In 1939, a company union was established under the control of Communists. After a short time, the Communists were replaced by a slate of pro-management union leaders who held almost continuous hegemony during the following years and rarely inconvenienced Yarur with re-

[58] This problem was discussed by many interviewees, especially among white-collar elements. One who experienced this directly and witnessed his union crumble was Antonio Carrozana, former president of the Sindicato Profesional de Empleados de INDAC, interviewed in Santiago, November 3, 1963.

[59] Alexander, *Labor Relations in Argentina, Brazil, and Chile*, p. 299.

quests for salary increases or other improvements in their work situation. Meanwhile, the Communists who had originally led the union were discharged as soon as the six months' protective period had transpired.

The foregoing discussion for the most part refers to the urban worker who wanders a perilous path between the day-to-day controls of his employer and the circumscriptions imposed by an archaic Labor Code, which permits the government a wide range of intrusions into union matters with insufficient care for precious labor needs. Of the two evils, probably most union officials believe the code is the more serious transgression, for, if it could be improved so as to operate more to labor's advantage, it would at least ameliorate the uneven struggle they feel they presently experience vis-à-vis management.[60] An interesting study run by the Department of Labor Relations of the University of Chile concluded, however, that, despite the presence of a number of labor leaders who considered management unfriendly to unions and workers, an even larger segment characterized the atmosphere in which they dealt with employers as good. When the question was posed, "In general, how does management treat the directorate of your union?" 58 per cent described the relationship as friendly and courteous, 33 per cent as courteous but cold, and only 9 per cent defined the relationship as discourteous and arbitrary. The same union presidents when asked about management's attitude toward their unions proved somewhat less enthusiastic; 18 per cent believed that management would like to destroy the union as undesirable; 27 per cent did not believe that employers would seek to eliminate the union, but that they would try to keep it from becoming any stronger; 7 per cent considered employers unconcerned with the union; 31 per cent believed they would help the union within certain limitations; and only 17 per cent felt that management would cooperate with the union as much as possible.[61]

[60] Without exception, every labor leader interviewed by this writer expressed some disturbance about the Labor Code, even though some indicated that relationships with management were relatively good.

[61] This survey reached almost all presidents of local unions with more than five hundred members in Santiago, Valparaíso, and Concepción and about

It is extremely doubtful that a similar survey would finish with comparable data if agricultural workers were polled. For prior to 1965, the agricultural laborer lived and worked under especially destitute circumstances that could only be labeled feudal. His unsanitary home, insufficient caloric intake, and miserable working conditions have been widely documented and lay at the feet of the *latifundista*, who in addition made certain that the worker possessed no means of self-defense. Discriminatory legislation all but destroyed his opportunity to unionize. The Labor Code required that, in order to organize, a given farm had to have at least twenty workers over eighteen years of age who had worked at least one year on that farm.[62] Inasmuch as the worker's entire family must serve the landowner, a high percentage of the labor force falls under the eighteen-year-old requirement. One Chilean congressional study found that out of some 14,500 farms, only 1,500 contained more than twenty workers. Consequently, less than 10 per cent of the farms could meet this basic prerequisite.[63] Another stipulation of the code demanded that ten laborers on the farm seeking unionization had to be able to read and write,[64] a provision that reduced the number of eligible workers even more considerably, since illiteracy rates run so high in the countryside.

Now, should he try to establish a union, the worker encountered all the coercive powers that rest in the hands of the landowner. As with the urban workers, the farm laborer had to apprise the government labor inspector of the intent to organize.[65] During the sixty days the law permitted him to complete the process many things often happened.[66] Thus, when this information reached the landowner, the union organizer ran the distinct likelihood of acquiring the stigma of being an "agitator" and he usually was dismissed from his employment. Homeless and jobless he then sought sustenance for himself

half of those locals smaller than five hundred (Henry Landsberger, Manuel Barrera, and Abel Toro, *El pensamiento del dirigente sindical chileno*).

[62] Article 433, Díaz S., *Legislación social*, pp. 151–152.

[63] Interview with Professor Hernán Troncoso.

[64] Article 431, Díaz S., *Legislación social*, p. 151.

[65] Article 435, *ibid.*, p. 152.

[66] Article 438, *ibid.*, p. 153.

and his large family by searching for work on other farms only to be refused, thanks to his erstwhile employer who contacted other landowners in the area and branded him as a "troublemaker," unsuitable for work.

If by some incredible good fortune, workers should organize a union the Labor Code continued to harass them. They were not permitted to federate with other unions in order to strengthen their bargaining position.[67] Even worse, labor conflicts were outlawed during planting or harvesting,[68] events occurring several times a year in much of Chile's agricultural zone. Of course, these were the only moments when workers held any bargaining weapon at all. In short, the landowners who wrote the Labor Code announced to their workers that they were extending their collective rights, when in fact they made organization all but impossible: by 1960, of more than 300,000 farm workers in Chile, fewer than 2,000 possessed union membership.[69]

Organized labor's over-all condition in the early 1960's was not as strong as in some earlier periods and, as has been indicated, a large proportion of potentially organizable workers still remained outside labor associations. Labor's organizational vicissitudes can be shown by the fluctuations in total number of unions and in total membership.[70] The decade of the 1930's was one of rapid expansion for Chilean trade unionism. From the final adoption of the entire Labor Code until the beginning of World War II, the number of unions increased almost continuously—from 421 in 1932 to 1,977 in 1941. Then the total number dipped during the 1940's (the low point being in 1945 when there were only 1,581 unions); but gradually the associational process picked up again, reaching a high point in 1956 when 2,382 unions existed. Afterward, the downward trend reappeared.

A similar, though not the same, pattern marked statistics on the

67 Articles 426 and 431, *ibid.*, pp. 150–151.

68 Article 470, *ibid.*, p. 160.

69 Actually, most estimates placed the total at less than 1,500. For example, see U.S. Department of Labor, *Labor in Chile*, p. 38.

70 The following labor statistics can be verified in several sources. One of the most useful of these is James O. Morris, Roberto Oyaneder C., *et al.*, *Afiliación y finanzas sindicales en Chile, 1932–1959*, pp. 17–34.

total number of organized workers: from 55,000 in 1932, up to 209,000 union members in 1941, down to 194,000 in the following year, and then a fairly steady growth to 1957 with more than 300,000 organized workers, followed by a subsequent decline to the early 1960's. The most compelling reason for the decline of both union and membership totals hinges upon changes in government policy.

A further breakdown of these statistics shows that in recent years professional unions constituted a little under two-thirds of all unions, industrial structures somewhat more than one-third, and agricultural groups about 1 per cent of the total. On the other hand, the percentage of members falling into the professional and industrial union categories is not the same, since approximately 57 per cent are in industrial groupings and 42 per cent in professional unions. Thus, there are almost twice as many professional as industrial unions (some 1,116 to 616), but the average membership in professional unions, averaging less than 100, is very much lower than for the industrial unions, which average somewhat more than 240 to a unit.

Something also should be said regarding the proportion of organized workers relative to the total active population in Chile. As has been mentioned before, many obstacles lie in the path of attempts at such statistical analysis. For example, the number of workers and employees who belong to two unions may range from one-sixth to one-third of the total number of union members listed by official statisticians.[71] This double listing, of course, obscures any efforts to determine the absolute number of organized workers. Furthermore, the government does not include public employees in its labor censuses, because they are not allowed to organize, yet almost 140,000 of them are "associated," most being tied to CUT or to one of the other centrals and they perform very much like any union. Nor do official statistics consider unions not enjoying legal recognition, though "free" unions represent some important working-class elements. In any event, most observers place the unionized percentage of the active working population at no more than 20 per cent. This figure is strengthened by heavy

[71] Interview with Professor Hernán Troncoso.

union membership in some economic pursuits, which range from 50 to 90 per cent in coal and copper mining and in the maritime and steel industries, and weakened by the presence of few organized workers in agriculture and the textile and service industries.

Internal Organizational Problems. In addition to such raw data that demonstrate that organized labor could stand buttressing in the several areas specified, there are other indications to suggest that Chilean trade unionism needs internal refurbishing as well. Four especially problematic aspects persist and they have to do with leadership and goals. To no small extent they derive from restrictions embodied in the Labor Code and the resulting government regulation of union activities as well as to coercion employed by given managerial elements in their dealings with workers. But full blame certainly must not be heaped upon the code and the employers; for, despite these exogenous intrusions, labor itself could do a great deal more to put its own house in order.

The lack of internal cohesion subsists at two levels—in the labor movement, generally, where no single central speaks for all the organized workers, and in CUT, specifically, which suffers from considerable internal dissidence. Both of these maladies result from weaknesses in the basic makeup of trade unionism as well as from outside influences.

As was pointed out earlier, no single central speaks for all Chilean trade unionism. In part this stems from a vagueness in the code as to the position of federations and confederations; the former are not specifically named and confederations are ascribed rather uncertain roles. Industrial confederations may only deal with educational, assistance, and welfare matters and may foster cooperatives.[72] Professional confederations are supposed to have the same rights as the constituent locals—including the "study, development and legitimate defense of their common interests"—but they must have legal recognition before they can act on their affiliates' behalf.[73] This has created a definite ambiguity in that no government to date has granted *personalidad jurídica* to a confederation, though several regimes, especially in the 1930's

[72] Article 386, Díaz S., *Legislación social*, p. 141.
[73] Article 414, *ibid.*, p. 147.

and early 1940's, unofficially accepted the existence of centrals and invited them to select representatives to sit on government boards.[74] CUT, however, never has been so generously treated and only obtained representation on one official agency, the governing board of the Central Bank, by a technicality in the law.[75]

But the main factor contributing to a lack of labor unity owes its origins to the long-time politicization of most of the Chilean labor movement. Anarcho-Syndicalists, Socialists, Communists, Christian Democrats, Radicals, and others compete for control. The history of Chilean trade unionism is replete with mergers and then divisions as a falling out between opposing political ideologies took place. This was exemplified in the 1960's by the presence of CNT, of Anarcho-Syndicalist origins and a member of ORIT, and of ASICH, the Christian Democratic central—both operating separately from the Marxist-dominated CUT. Moreover, some groups have tired of the political struggle and attempted to turn their organizations into purely economic institutions devoid of political involvements. In earlier years, the private employees' CEPCH used to support political parties; but they did not receive reciprocal aid from the parties and so broke off these relationships. They have stayed outside CUT for much the same reason—that is, their disenchantment with political causes.[76] The powerful maritime workers' central, COMACH, also follows this line. Though, in addition, the dominant personal position held by Wenceslao Moreno, head of COMACH and one of Chile's most able labor officials, and the customarily good working relations between COMACH and management might be threatened if COMACH merged with CUT.

Oscar Núñez, president of CUT, contended in 1964 that his central really represented practically all organized labor in Chile and that such groups as ASICH and CNT were only minor irritations. Nevertheless, Núñez admitted that "in these difficult times when the government

[74] Alexander, *Labor Relations in Argentina, Brazil, and Chile*, pp. 303–304.
[75] Interview with Oscar Núñez.
[76] Interviews with Enrique Sánchez and Federico Mujica.

wants to destroy CUT we need labor unity and the presence of ASICH and CNT give the appearance of disunity."[77]

Another dimension of the problem of factionalism resides within CUT where two types of centrifugal forces compete. First, there is not always close harmony among the component federations or between some federations and CUT's national leadership. It must be remembered that the federations themselves are very unevenly matched in their size, resources, and internal discipline. A wealthy and powerful group like the Copper Workers' Federation, which benefits from special legal privileges, can go its own way and achieve a high ratio of success, whereas the Health Workers' Federation, though a fairly large group, possesses virtually no financial resources, is discriminated against by the code, and requires fraternal support from many other unions if it is to have any opportunity to see its demands converted into policy changes. All this militates against the combined efforts of CUT when performing as a single entity. Indeed, CUT is such a heterogeneous grouping that it requires exceptional leadership talents to coordinate the disparate interests of factory workers, white-collar employees, agricultural laborers, and retired persons—all of whom rely upon structures of such varying strength. And since this leadership is almost entirely working on a part-time schedule, bargaining procedures are left to federations and their locals and only very rarely does CUT dare to try to assemble a united front on economic issues.

Because of its inability to act forcefully at all times on economic questions, CUT, like its predecessors, seems to compensate by stressing political functions. But more than this, it is almost compelled to act politically because of the highly politicized nature of most of its leadership. And here rests the second major force creating dissension within the organization itself. Among the officials of the thirty or so affiliated federations and of the local unions that directly adhere to CUT are to be found virtually every shade of the political spectrum; a large proportion of these same leaders are militantly involved in the machinations of their respective political parties. This is true to such

[77] Interview with Oscar Núñez.

a high degree with some that it is difficult to identify their prior loyalty, whether it belongs to the union or to the political party.

The composition of CUT's congresses attests to its partisan nature. As can be seen in Table 1, delegates ran the full gamut of political

TABLE 1

Composition of CUT Congresses by Political Parties

Political Party	1953[a]		1957[b]		1959[b]		1962[b]	
	No.	%	No.	%	No.	%	No.	%
Communists	503	21.3	514	39.9	645	44.7	751	31.1
Socialists	600[c]	25.3	352[c]	25.9	405	28.1	686	28.4
Christian Democrats	150	6.3	200	14.7	211	14.6	433	17.9
Radicals	150	6.3	122	9.0	60	4.1	150	6.2
Anarchists	188	7.9	30	2.2	30	2.0	50	2.0
Trotskyites	18	0.7	18	1.3	17	1.1	20	0.8
Independents	157	6.6	—	—	—	—	12	0.5
Nonparticipants	589	25.6	188	8.8	72	5.0	312	12.9
Total delegates	2,355		1,424		1,440		2,414	

[a]This was the constituent congress that created CUT.
[b]These were the regular congresses.
[c]At both of these congresses the Socialists were split. In 1953, there were three groups (the Partido Socialista Popular, the Partido Socialista Chile, and the Partido Socialista Disidente); in 1957, there were two (the Partido Socialista and the Partido Socialista Disidente).

SOURCE: Adapted from Jorge Barría, *Trayectoria y estructura del movimiento sindical chileno, 1946–1962*, pp. 332–333.

preferences from the middle to the far left and even those labeled "independent" included many with vigorous political, though not party, loyalties. (The classification "nonparticipants" refers to delegates who failed to appear, attended only briefly, arrived too late, or who for some reason never performed actively in the convention. It was not possible to define their political inclinations.)[78]

In the few years between the assembling of the Constituent Congress in 1953, until the Third Congress in 1962, several political developments stood out, though the Communists remained dominant.

[78] Barría, *Trayectoria y estructura del movimiento sindical chileno*, pp. 332–338.

Anarchists almost completely withdrew in 1957 when they reestablished their own central. In many ways they never quite belonged to CUT anyway, since they were a union-oriented group without political party ties. The Trotskyites remained a feeble, propagandistic segment with a negligible influence. The schisms that plagued the Socialists in the first two congresses were finally bridged after the 1957 meetings, and while they continued to bicker within themselves they did present a united front in CUT. The fortunes of both the Radicals and the Christian Democrats seemed indicative of the political as well as the labor scene —the former experiencing ups and downs and the latter steadily expanding.[79]

Since the Congress selects the National Directive Council, it follows that a cross section of political interests more or less commensurate with those found in the Congress should be found on the Council. The possibility for surprises in the selection process, or of any disruption in the proportional representation of parties in Congress being reflected in Council membership, is very unlikely because of voting arrangements worked out ahead of time—particularly between the Communists and Socialists—and for the simple reason that the board must be politically representative of the components if the central is to hold together. After the Third National Congress, held in August, 1962, the new council contained six Communists, five Socialists, three Christian Democrats, and one Radical. The specific allocation of the offices was as follows: president, Oscar Núñez (Socialist); secretary general, Luis Figueroa (Communist); vice-presidents, Humberto Elgueta (Radical) and Emiliano Caballero (Christian Democrat); secretaries of organization, Luis Quiroga (Christian Democrat), Juan Vargas Puebla (Communist), and Isidoro Godoy (Socialist); secretary of international relations, Julio Benítez (Socialist); secretary of finances, Juan Campos (Communist); secretaries of conflicts, Carlos Cortez (Socialist) and Roberto Lara (Communist); secretaries of farm matters, Carlos Bustos (Christian Democrat) and Amador Díaz (Socialist); women's secretary, Mireya Baltra (Communist); and secretary of education and culture, Julio González (Communist).[80]

[79] Robert Alexander, *Organized Labor in Latin America*, pp. 96–100.
[80] Interview with Luis Figueroa M.

In large measure, CUT gives the appearance of an enigma with the pervasive threats to its cohesion and yet with an ability to survive. The most perplexing riddle, however, is why non-Marxist elements—who constitute a majority of all organized labor in Chile—do not wrest control of CUT away from the Marxists or, failing that, why they do not move over into one of the democratic centrals already extant? Answers to these questions go to the heart of the nature of Chilean trade unionism. To begin with, it must be understood that, while it is true that the Marxists, and especially the Communists, control unions all out of proportion to their actual membership in those structures (it is widely held that the total number of Communists in the labor movement is not over 10%), they possess strengths that generally help them to overwhelm their opposition. The fact that they have been around almost from the beginning of trade-union activities gives them superb contacts with workers. The average laborer, of limited literacy, has only the barest idea of what "communism" is, but he does know that the Communists are pleasant fellows who talk in terms of what the worker wants. Loyalties build up that tend to remain constant. This was demonstrated in the 1964 presidential election campaigns in Concepción, where a massive, modern housing development constructed largely from Alliance for Progress monies still was saturated with FRAP posters and FRAP supporters—the residents' fealty to the Communists carrying over from their tawdry earlier days of living, despite the obviously non-Communist help that provided their new homes.

Furthermore, the Communists have never been quite so riddled with the internecine warfare that debilitated the Socialists. True, there has been a tiny Trotskyite faction and more recently a pro-Peking element, but neither has created a power struggle at the movement's top level. The strengths developing from cohesion and great internal discipline have been augmented by a relatively strong financial base, highly dedicated and active leaders (whereas democratic trade unionists are most generally characterized, even by themselves, as "lazy"),[81] a solid basis

[81] However, in fairness to the moderates, it should be noted that many Communists, being financially supported by the Communist party, are the first to arrive at union meetings and the last to leave; whereas, the moderate lead-

of operation in several large unions (as, the coal miners), and a coherent program of revolution that caters to the central attitudes of the depressed working classes.

Christian Democracy forms the first impressive opposition in recent times to Communist power (buttressed with the Socialist alliance). But it still is new and has not brought forth the most dynamic leaders in labor circles, so its development relies to a high degree upon its relationship with the Frei regime. When Frei assumed the presidency, that relationship was ambiguous, and in the earlier presidential campaign the Labor Department of the Christian Democratic party contained both politicians and labor leaders who vied for power. The political leaders, in particular, were jealous of the trade unionists and suspicious of the many Christian Democratic labor leaders who did not directly attach themselves to the campaign organization.

This is not to suggest that ASICH did not make overtures to their counterparts in CUT to withdraw, for several efforts did occur. They set up MUTCH (Movimiento Unitario de Trabajadores de Chile) in 1961 for this very purpose. But Christian Democrats remained in CUT, which was far and away the biggest central—an important psychological attraction to the rank and file—and MUTCH continued to be only a large uncertainty. Also, Christian Democratic leaders were fearful of being destroyed by CUT propaganda as "divisionists" if they endeavored to split away from the parent group. In the meantime, Christian Democrats in CUT have cooperated with their colleagues in ASICH when convenient. Thus, when CUT appointed several of its leaders from the various political parties represented in its central organization to attend the Congreso de Unidad Sindical de los Trabajadores de América Latina held in Brazil during December, 1963, and January, 1964, CUT's Christian Democratic delegates boycotted the conference in line with policy dictated by the Christian Democratic hemispheric organization.[82]

Despite CUT's obvious problems of pulling together the diverse

ers have other responsibilities that delimit the amount of time and energy they can give to union activities.

[82] Interviews with Luis Figueroa M. and José Goldsack.

partisan backgrounds of its membership and coordinating activities to which a substantial number (if not all) of the affiliates will subscribe, many consider CUT with all its weaknesses to be extremely valuable. Edmundo Polanco, a Socialist and national president of the big railroad workers federation, is one of those who suggests that CUT is essential to the Chilean labor movement: "The major value of CUT is that when there are conflicts among labor groups, they can go to CUT where they have facilities and techniques to act as a sounding board and help to resolve interunion disagreements. CUT is also important in working across the board for all union needs, with all political expressions participating in doing this."[83] Polanco also points out that unions need to know what employers can actually do in the way of providing salary increases and other benefits to organized labor. Obviously, a central like CUT can more easily obtain a clear idea as to just what industry can afford in a given moment and situation.

Roberto Lara, head of the Communists' coal miners' federation, admits that frictions erupt from time to time because of the many political colors contained by CUT; but he considers them to be relatively unimportant. Even in a presidential campaign year political differences do not tear the organization apart. This is because the partisan feelings that exist in the political sphere do not prevent all political groups from working together for labor needs. Moreover, "they have learned of the need for unity in order to survive."[84] This was exemplified by the struggle that labor experienced during the period of the Laws for the Defense of Democracy. Ostensibly an attack on Communists, in fact it caused all kinds of labor leaders to experience persecution. This convinced most of labor that the oligarchy responsible for the Laws for the Defense of Democracy (and later the "Gag Law") were not just seeking to break the back of Communism, but of all labor.

Finances. Besides the problems surrounding efforts to secure cohe-

[83] Interview with Edmundo Polanco, president of the Federación Industrial Ferroviaria de Chile, in Santiago, November 4, 1963.

[84] Interview with Roberto Lara Olate, secretary general, and Pedro Véliz Araya, secretary of conflicts, of the Federación Industrial Nacional Minera, in Santiago, February 10, 1964.

sion in the labor movement, another challenge to organized labor in Chile is in the realm of finances. But just as variations exist in the levels of cohesion attained by the various labor groups, so, too, diversity marks the ability of federations and confederations—and the political elements within them—to implant a sound financial base.

A University of Chile study categorized the sources of revenue tapped by local unions as (1) profit sharing, (2) donations, (3) dues (being of three kinds—initiation fees, regular monthly dues, and special assessments), (4) fines, (5) income (a nebulous classification including profit, interest, dividends, rent, and the like), (6) loans, (7) surplus (left over from the previous year's budget or money acquired through the sale of assets), and (8) unexplained revenues (i.e., those which could not be labeled because of a lack of definition by the unions or inability to peruse the union's books).[85]

Table 2 demonstrates the importance to industrial unions of revenue from profit sharing, a financial resource that ranges roughly between 30 and 70 per cent of total revenues. Chile was one of the pioneers in Latin America to provide for profit sharing and, in general, it is based upon 10 per cent of a firm's net profits less 10 per cent held by the company. Dues, the only other major revenue source (surplus is too ambiguous a category to include here and usually means little more than a carry-over in the treasury from the previous year's holdings), ranks much lower in importance and contributes only from about 5 to 30 per cent of over-all revenues.

Since profit sharing is restricted to industrial unions, professional or craft unions must rely completely upon other financial sources. Consequently, dues are overwhelmingly vital to their economic viability and constitute from almost half to 90 per cent of total revenue. At first glance, industrial unions would seem to be greatly advantaged by an almost certain return from profit sharing. Nonetheless, only about half of all the industrial unions actually gain revenue in this manner, and, unfortunately, the real return from profit sharing has fluctuated markedly over the years with a distinctly downward trend being registered in the last two decades. On the other hand, the professional

[85] Morris and Oyaneder, *Afiliación y finanzas sindicales en Chile*, pp. 58–60.

TABLE 2

Relative Percentage of Types of Revenue Accruing to Professional and Industrial Unions (1959)
(Detail does not necessarily add to one hundred, due to rounding)

Unions by Number of Members	Profit Sharing		Donations		Dues		Fines		Income		Loans		Surplus		Unexplained	
	Pro.	Ind.	Pro.	Ind.	Pro.	Ind.	Pro.	Ind.	Pro.	Ind.	Pro.	Ind.	Pro.	Ind.	Pro.	Ind.
25–49	—	69	—	—	70	5	—	—	a	a	—	—	29	25	—	a
50–74	—	51	—	—	49	5	—	—	23	3	—	—	21	40	7	a
75–99	—	51	—	—	80	5	—	—	a	1	—	—	18	42	1	1
100–174	—	61	—	—	72	8	—	a	3	a	—	—	25	30	a	a
175–324	—	24	—	16	78	28	—	—	a	a	—	a	21	31	a	a
325–524	—	46	a	2	89	11	—	a	a	8	3	4	6	28	1	a
525–1,024	—	30	—	a	90	24	—	—	—	4	—	6	10	35	a	2
1,025 & more	—	48	5	—	80	12	—	—	a	6	4	30	11	3	a	a

[a]Less than 1 per cent.

Source: Adapted from James O. Morris, Roberto Oyaneder C., *et al.*, *Afiliación y finanzas sindicales en Chile, 1932–1959*, pp. 65–66.

unions have held rather firmly in absolute terms and even increased somewhat the total return acquired from dues.[86]

Of course, all these revenue sources are ones that can be identified from accessible records and thus represent unions that are legally recognized and that must file annual financial statements with the General Directorate of Labor. They do not apply to the "free" unions, though revenues aside from profit-sharing income are similar, and they fail to take into account other fund-raising methods. For example, there is well-substantiated evidence to the effect that Communists of the miners' union in Lota for a time maintained a "protection racket" to augment their funds. Apparently, they hired a number of private police to visit local businessmen and threatened to boycott their shops if they refused to "donate" to the Communist union. This was a powerful form of coercion, since approximately 40,000 people were attached to the mines out of a city of about 52,000. Parenthetically, it should be noted that this was a period when labor in Lota was faced with a great deal of intimidation from management, who employed their own private detectives to act as informers and strike breakers. Consequently, the miners' union sought every possible channel of help for its own preservation.[87]

Besides the customary contributions of component structures, Chile's three central labor organizations each seems to have access to financial aid from abroad. In 1964, it was widely believed that CUT received assistance from the Soviet Union and Cuba, though its Communist and Socialist leaders denied this fact.[88] CNT, sponsored by ORIT, admittedly received money from the United States, but claimed that it was in small amounts and insufficient for the most minimal needs of the organization.[89]

As has been indicated, the Christian Democrats only began as a labor group in 1947 and then with humble origins. Father Alberto Hurtado, who had been underwriting a number of charitable activities,

[86] *Ibid.*, pp. 35–67.

[87] Interview with Professor Hernán Troncoso.

[88] Interviews with Oscar Núñez, Luis Figueroa, Roberto Lara, and Edmundo Polanco.

[89] Interviews with Carlos Ibáñez King and Luis Lavín Céspedes.

wrote to several thousand people asking for financial assistance for his work. Among the enterprises he outlined in his appeal was the new Christian Democratic labor group, ASICH. The returns were modest and permitted him to continue his undertakings for only a few weeks. Next, he set up a foundation (later named after Father Hurtado) to formalize money-raising programs and to channel the allocation of funds. The foundation, headed by one trade unionist and four outsiders, for the most part was able to keep the names of contributors anonymous. Today, the Christian Democrats also are the recipients of funds from unknown industrialists who consider Christian Democracy a valuable antidote to the radical left. A lawyer serves as the intermediary between the contributors and the labor groups. ASICH's overseas sources are located primarily in Europe, especially among trade unionists in France and Belgium, who pay solidarity dues to African, Asian, and Latin American labor. Inasmuch as Latin America offered the best hope in the 1960's for Christian Democratic expansion, more than 60 per cent of the total amount funded reached the Western Hemisphere and a large portion of that stopped in Chile.[90]

When one comes right down to it, there are two basic weaknesses in Chilean labor's ability to develop a stronger financial foundation. First, most workers simply earn too low a salary to be able to contribute even the most modest amounts to dues. For the second reason, one only has to return to that perennial inhibitor of labor development, the Labor Code. The code discriminates against craft unions by forbidding them to form a union shop even when more than a majority wishes it. Nor can craft unions obtain the right to a checkoff of dues, which would ensure a larger and more regularized flow of revenues. No unions may build up "resistance" funds for strikes. However, this is so important if a union is to be able to call upon its principal bargaining weapon that many unions do it anyway.[91] Except for the equivalent of about 15¢ U.S., unions may not keep any cash on hand. Instead, all money must be deposited in the National Savings

[90] Interviews with José Goldsack and with Beatriz Marescotte, secretary of finances of the Confederación Latinoamericana de Sindicalistas Cristianos, in Santiago, February 12, 1964.

[91] Alexander, *Labor Relations in Argentina, Brazil, and Chile*, p. 294.

Bank and, other than in small amounts, it may not be withdrawn without the approval of the local labor inspector. The reasoning behind this rule theoretically holds great merit—to avoid as much defalcation as possible of union funds by disreputable leadership; but in practice it serves to delimit union activities unnecessarily and places one more dimension of trade unionism under governmental supervision. Union officers frequently side-step this requirement by "pocket banking," a necessary process that simply transfers cash from one person's pocket to another in order to facilitate carrying on daily business.

Leadership. In a sense, the financial restrictions heaped upon labor expose a third major shortcoming in Chilean trade unionism—the effectiveness of labor leadership. The code flatly states that the "functions of directors of Unions shall be gratuitous."[92] This means that union leaders must be gainfully employed in a regular job and then provide direction to their trade union on a part-time basis, subject to whatever energy and time might remain. The president of CUT in 1963–1964, Oscar Núñez, worked the long days of a schoolteacher and then provided direction of Chile's biggest central during his off hours and holidays. This is repeated hundreds of times among the local unions, federations, and confederations of Chile. Fortunately, most labor leaders are extraordinarily dedicated to trade unionism and display a high sense of responsibility to their organizations. There are very few instances of criminal procedures being instituted among labor leaders for improper associational actions. Nonetheless, Chilean trade unionism suffers greatly from leaders who labor full-time on their regular jobs and then must put the union's organizational needs in order, deal with pervasive government regulations and controls, and bargain with employers for gains for their fellow workers.

Of course, as happens so often with Chilean labor law, not everyone is subject to the same restrictions, nor do all groups enjoy the same benefits. For example, the copper workers, who carved out a highly preferred status for themselves in the code, need not adhere to the same prohibitions as the rest of labor. The executives of the Confederación de Trabajadores de Cobre, under a special statute of 1955, are

[92] Article 377, Díaz S., *Legislación social*, p. 136.

permitted to work on union business for two months as salaried officers, then return to their regular position with the copper company the third month.[93] Furthermore, in some cases where legal recognition is not a question, the law is skirted. It is generally accepted that Communists underwrite many of their labor leaders so they can act in a full-time capacity with their unions. Undoubtedly this is one of the most important of several factors contributing to the Communists' strong position in the labor movement. A few democratic union heads also receive outside financial aid, but their number is very small. One of these is the highly capable secretary general of the private employees' main federation (CEPCH), who was dismissed for attending an international labor convention abroad and then "blacklisted" by management.[94] Other financial sources, mostly from international labor organizations, came to his aid to keep his talents in organized labor. Such an example among moderate trade unionists is, however, rare.

In spite of the difficulties inherent in this legal insistence upon unions not paying salaries to their directors, considerable attention has been directed to upgrading the labor consciousness of workers, spotting potential leaders, and strengthening the qualifications of existing officers. Known by the term *capitación*, these efforts toward leadership training are vital in an atmosphere where there is such a high turnover in executive officers, largely due to the great demands placed upon them when they must, in essence, work at two jobs.

Undoubtedly, this is one of the most rewarding functions of national and international labor bodies. Most federations and centrals devote a major share of their time to *capitación* and perhaps see some of their best efforts allocated to this function.

CLASC, the Christian Democrats' regional organization, centers its training institute for South America in Santiago (and one in Caracas for Middle America) and provides more than 40 per cent of its entire budget for improving all levels of union leadership. Besides the principal headquarters in Santiago, three other *capitación* schools are located in Concepción, Valdivia, and Antofagasta. Altogether they

[93] Interview with Antonio Esperidión, technical secretary of the Confederación de Trabajadores del Cobre, in Santiago, February 4, 1964.

[94] Interview with Enrique Sánchez.

train 3,500 unionists a year. CNT offers training programs to labor groups that are not affiliated but in fraternal contact with its organization as well as to its own members. During 1963, 350 individuals passed through labor courses sponsored by CNT's provincial councils in Valdivia, Concepción, Talca, and Iquique.[95]

An interesting and highly fruitful seminar was held in April, 1964, under the auspices of the Cultural Affairs Section of the United States Information Service, the British Embassy, and the International Labor Office. Headed by Benjamin Martin and Hernán Troncoso, both highly knowledgeable in labor matters in the United States and Chile, respectively, and strengthened by the addition of competent experts from the United Kingdom, Argentina, and Mexico, seminars were held for three days at a mountain resort some twenty minutes from Santiago. Beginning with panel discussions on various aspects of collective bargaining in Chile, the United States, Great Britain, Argentina, and Mexico, the meetings then were thrown open to an interchange of ideas among all participants.[96]

One of the most intensive leadership-training programs in all of Chile is the maritime workers' highly successful Seminar on Labor Education held in cooperation with the hemispheric groups, Inter-American Regional Organization (ORIT) and the Institute for the Development of Free Trade Unionism (IDSL),[97] and under the directorship of COMACH's secretary general, Wenceslao Moreno. A typical program got under way in Valparaíso in October, 1963, when eight instructors and fifty-five participants assembled for almost a week of lectures and discussions about some of the challenges and obligations of labor leadership. One of the questions confronted was "Why are leaders not followed by their bases?" In the most candid fashion, problems of personal empire building, rivalry between lead-

[95] Interview with Alfredo di Pacce.

[96] The seminar's deliberations were summarized in a pamphlet issued by the Cultural Affairs Section of the U.S. Embassy, entitled "La negociación colectiva en sociedades democráticas."

[97] IDSL is a curious organization dominated by U.S. labor and management elements. If its intentions appear to some to be laudable, it has come in for considerable criticism from many Latin Americans for its failure to truly represent Latin American interests.

ers, ill-prepared leaders, and related matters were treated openly by the instructors and their groups. Other topics dealt with the purposes of a union, how to go about resolving a union problem, how to draw out the apathetic or timid in a union gathering, techniques for running a good conference, the use of propaganda and information sources, the accessibility and utility of correspondence courses and other educational programs, the union relative to its place of work and to the community, functions of the union, and countless other themes significant in the daily operation of a union. Upon the seminar's conclusion, the contents of the various lectures and discussions were brought together in a book for widest possible dissemination throughout COMACH and for use by the graduates of the seminar when they returned to lead their own locals.[98]

Capitación programs reach only a small minority of organized labor and, unless they are dynamic in mood and highly informative in content, they will have a very limited impact on the participants. Still, they do present one significant avenue for labor itself to try to overcome some of the grave handicaps to effective leadership development imposed by the Labor Code.[99]

Goals. In addition to problems related to cohesion, finances, and leadership, Chilean trade unionism also endures a certain disorientation and disagreement over its proper goals. Tied to the lack of cohesion, this problem also has wider origins and ramifications that give it separate definition.

The Chilean working classes manifest a deep unsettlement that periodically erupts into anomic actions. Such actions stem from the fact that most workers are discontented about their working and living conditions; in addition, most union officials express dissatisfaction with the economic and political systems in which they endeavor to grab some portion of the scarce resources. One sample of local union presi-

[98] Interviews with Wenceslao Moreno and Juan Lubiano. Also, see COMACH, *Conclusiones seminario.*

[99] One study for local union leaders indicated that only 15 per cent of those sampled had attended such a seminar and only 6 per cent believed that *capitación* had helped them more considerably than other learning techniques (Landsberger, Barrera, and Toro, *El pensamiento del dirigente sindical chileno*, p. 23).

dents in Santiago, Valparaíso, and Concepción revealed that all agreed that the best approach to achieving needed economic and social progress would be to change existing institutions. They only differed in the rate of change—34 per cent favoring immediate systemic restructuring; 44 per cent wanting the same to occur, though at a slightly slower pace; and the remaining 22 per cent opting for a gradual evolution of existing institutions.[100]

However, there is a distinct lack of certitude as to how to bring change and what to try to accomplish. Every labor leader interviewed by this author expressed deep unhappiness with the Labor Code, though the copper workers were not as militant as most; but there was no unanimity as to what should be changed beyond a few obviously irritating articles. Wenceslao Moreno perhaps expressed the situation most pointedly when he observed that "the labor code is very antiquated and should be rewritten in general," but "labor is at fault here, too, because they must get together as to what they want to accomplish."[101] He felt that his maritime workers, the copper miners, and a few other groups had gone ahead and pushed through alterations in the code to favor themselves. Still, most laborers were hurt by labor legislation presently on the books and they needed to find some bases of agreement to bring desired improvements.

A far more grievous division among trade unionists regarding goals is a direct outgrowth of the presence of political ideologies in most, though not all, of the federations and confederations. Thus, one schism splits organized labor between those groups which are heavily politicized and envisage a primary major political role for the centrals and those which out of disenchantment with political struggles seek only economic reforms and "bread and butter" goals. CUT clearly falls into the first category; the Maritime Confederation and the Confederation of Private Employees of Industry and Commerce lean toward basically apolitical ends.

A second attitudinal disagreement over goal orientations is to be found within the politicized sectors of the labor movement where

[100] *Ibid.*, p. 25.
[101] Interview with Wenceslao Moreno.

countless currents flow. In CUT's formative years, for example, the Radicals were committed to democratic precepts and progressive labor legislation, but ambiguous and ambivalent about general needs; the Christian Democrats also held to democratic forms while calling for a major overhaul of the economic system; Communists and Socialists labored to reconstitute society along Marxist lines, though differed over details; and the Anarcho-Syndicalists advocated a militantly revolutionary approach, but one that had to be purely unionist and that would avoid compromises with political parties.

These doctrinal divergences were mirrored in CUT's struggles to adopt a platform upon which all labor could stand. However, Marxist domination of the founding congress in 1953, brought forth a strong socialist statement with overtones of Anarcho-Syndicalist militancy: "[CUT's objective is] the organization of all the workers of the city and of the country without distinction of political or religious creeds, of nationality, color, sex or age, for the struggle against the exploitation of man by man until achieving integral socialism."[102] By 1962, the split-off of the Anarcho-Syndicalists and the rising tide of Christian Democracy forced CUT's leadership to search out a more representative expression of its organizational purpose. The result was the replacement of the goal to achieve "integral socialism" with a watered-down aspiration to bring about "the total emancipation of the workers and the political transformation of the society, so as to definitively secure social justice, freedom and the welfare of salaried workers."[103]

Even this catchall did not expunge disagreement over specific goals. For example, the question of whether to affiliate with an international organization saw CNT and COMACH associating with the ORIT; CUT found it expedient to keep itself formally aloof from international affiliations, although the various political groupings kept friendly relations with their counterparts at the regional and international levels. Moreover, Socialist and Communist efforts to present a united delegation of CUT's major political components at the Congress of Labor Unity of the Workers of Latin America, held in Brazil in Jan-

[102] Barría, *Trayectoria y estructura del movimiento sindical chileno*, p. 144.
[103] CUT, *Chile necesita cambios de fondo*, p. 10.

uary, 1964, fell stillborn when the Christian Democratic representatives rejected the invitation.

Opinions also differ regarding the role of government in the economy, relations with management, and the proper line for Chile to take vis-à-vis other nations. Such labor sections as the Christian Democrats boost the slowly emerging Latin American Common Market (ALALC) as of immense importance to the future growth of Chile's economy, while the far left describes it as merely facilitating the expansion of United States economic imperialism throughout South America. Attitudes toward the Alliance for Progress and sundry other programs follow a similar pattern.

In short, organized labor in Chile is handicapped as a bargaining agent because of a certain amount of internal dissidence—mostly impinging upon politicization—as well as resulting from other organizational, financial, and leadership encumbrances. This in turn sheds light upon the styles and tactics that labor employs to issue its claims into the political system in its contention with the inordinately influential management structures.

Management and Labor: Influence and Methods

Management

Both political influence and control of political resources are unevenly distributed in all of the world's societies. The nature of this distribution in Latin America generally can be classified as a "cumulative inequality, where greater control over one resource, such as wealth, is closely related to greater control over most other resources."[104] Until the 1960's, this depicted Chile's situation rather closely as well. Throughout most of its history, Chile was dominated by a small economic elite that controlled the political resources of the nation. The first important exception to this pattern occurred in the 1920's when the new middle sectors broke onto the political scene behind Arturo Alessandri. The landed oligarchy adjusted to the gradual appearance of industrial-commercial elitist forces and the resulting accommodation perpetuated oligarchical sway over the decision-making process.

[104] Robert A. Dahl, *Modern Political Analysis*, pp. 32–33.

For the most part, the oligarchy was a benevolent one and it succumbed periodically to persuasion from its more progressive members to liberalize political processes. Thus, major control of political (as well as economic and social) resources remained in the hands of a few who ensured a relatively stable political environment in which competing elements and ideas were channeled through orderly electoral and political processes. Often described as a "democracy of the oligarchy," Chile's political system held fascination for many foreigners who considered it quite remarkable in the sea of violence and instability dominating most of the continent. That perspicacious interpreter of the Americas, James Bryce, described an election he observed in Chile when a chief executive was to be selected by Congress—then in the majority hands of Liberals:

> The discussions and the votings in their gatherings went on for several weeks, but force was never threatened; and the Chileans told their visitors with justifiable pride that, although twelve thousand soldiers were in or near the capital, no party feared that any other would endeavor to call in the help of the army. Chile is also the only South American state which takes so enlightened an interest in its electoral machinery as to have devised and applied a good while ago a system of proportional representation which seems to give satisfaction. . . . The result was foreknown, because there had been an arrangement between Liberal sections which ensured the victory of the candidates they had agreed upon, so there was little excitement. Everything seemed to work smoothly.[105]

At the heart of oligarchical power were great banking interests that gradually fused and spread their influence into industrial, agricultural, mining, and commercial enterprises. By the end of the nineteenth century, such financial houses as the Banco de Chile, Banco Edwards, Banco Español, and Banco Sud-Americano intervened so successfully in the political process that a Liberal congressman thundered: "It is the banks in Chile which have command of politics."[106] Later, enormous industrial groupings created banks to further their own expansion; but interestingly enough these new banks (e.g., Banco Pan-

[105] James Bryce, *South America*, pp. 222–223.

[106] Quoted in Ricardo Donoso, *Alessandri, agitador y demoledor*, p. 72.

americano, Banco Nacional del Trabajo, Banco Continental, and Banco de Crédito e Inversiones) continued to function economically and politically in the same fashion as their nineteenth-century predecessors.

Ricardo Lagos has drawn a fascinating picture of the nature and extent of economic concentration in contemporary Chile along with the political implications emanating from such concentration.[107] He concludes that eleven groups are overwhelmingly dominant in his country's economy. Eight of these groups are banking establishments (Banco Sud-Americano, Banco de Chile, Banco Edwards, Banco Nacional del Trabajo, Banco Español, Banco Continental, Banco de Crédito e Inversiones, and Banco Panamericano). Of the remaining three, one is identified by the region where the bulk of its holdings reside (Punta Arenas Group) and two by the major enterprises within them (Grace-Copec Group and Cosatán Group). Their total assets are remarkably extensive. Together, the eleven groups control 22.4 per cent of Chile's corporations; even more incredible, their holdings constitute 70.6 per cent of all the capital invested in the nation's firms. The diversity of these holdings is prodigious: "The great concentration which the Chilean economy presents reaches to all economic sectors and activities: copper, textiles, glass manufacturing, construction, tobacco, breweries, income buildings, transportation (of all kinds), newspapers and radios, distribution of products, insurance, banks, mines, etc. There does not exist any sector in our economy, however small it may be, that cannot be found tied in one form or another to the groups which in fact integrally control national economic activity."[108] In brief, these eleven groups—of which three (the Banco de Chile, Banco Sud-Americano, and Banco Edwards) can be classified as super groups because of their enormous economic power—heavily influence or control outright through regional and national organizations a huge proportion of domestic and foreign enterprises by means of interlocking directorates.

The political implications of this spreading economic power were

[107] The following discussion draws heavily upon Ricardo Lagos, *La concentración del poder económico, su teoría, realidad chilena*, pp. 93–177.

[108] *Ibid.*, p. 165.

further unveiled by the Communist periodical, *Vistazo*.[109] Often sensationalist and certainly reflecting an anticapitalist political orientation, *Vistazo* does build many of its feature stories upon exceedingly accurate reporting. Whereas Ricardo Lagos generally avoided naming specific individuals, *Vistazo* delineated the oligarchical families in terms of their interlocking corporate positions as well as of their political relationships. The powerful Edwards family, for example, not only exercises preponderant influence in the bank that carries its name, but also exercises sway in the councils of innumerable enterprises from Compañía Agrícola Chilena and Compañía Industrial to the sprawling press empire of *El Mercurio*. Other great family names—Aldunate, Serrano, Alessandri, Vial, Letelier, Subercaseaux, Claro, Ibáñez, Correa, Braun, Barros, Opaso, Yarur, and Amunátegui, to mention a few—claim similar economic power and hold persuasive pivotal positions in the political system that range from congressmen to directors of government agencies, from cabinet posts to presidents of the republic. As a specific example, Gabriel González Videla, major Radical party leader, who served as President of Chile from 1946 to 1952 and subsequently held numerous political posts—including running the Democratic Front electoral coalition in 1963–1964, was cited by *Vistazo* as exercising control over or strongly influencing 6 banks and 116 companies.

Unfortunately, the lines of such control are not always precise and evaluations of the economic power of a person or group may be greatly exaggerated to make a point. Still, the basic premise seems to be irrefutable that a few powerful nuclei—whether families or groups—comprise a highly cohesive force strongly influencing economic enterprises and political decision making.

Not only did the oligarchy customarily endeavor to mesh their economic and political power bases, but they also institutionalized their representation on major policy-effectuation agencies of government, thus ensuring them a voice on many of the most important public and

[109] See *Vistazo* (Santiago) for March 20, 27, 1962, March 30, August 6, 13, 20, and 27, 1963.

semipublic councils. These agencies perform in a broad span of functions that include investment and development (e.g., Corporación de Fomento de la Producción, Banco Central, Banco del Estado, and Empresa Nacional de Minería); labor and social welfare (e.g., Servicio de Seguro Social, Caja de Accidentes de Trabajo, Junta de Conciliación y Arbitraje, Servicio Nacional de Salud, and Caja de Empleados Particulares); education (e.g., Consejo de la Universidad Técnica del Estado and Comité Asesor del Consejo de Rectores Universitarios); and general administration (e.g., Junta General de Aduanas).

The nature of their dominance on these agencies and the method by which their representation is determined can be illustrated by the make-up of the governing board of the tremendously influential Banco Central, which largely determines national monetary policies for the Chilean nation. For a long time, the Banco Central's directorate was made up of fourteen officers: three selected by the President of Chile, four appointed by Congress, four being representative of stockholding groups, one jointly serving the Sociedad de Fomento Fabril and the Sociedad Nacional de Minería, one representing both the Cámara Central de Comercio and the Corporación de Ventas de Salitre y Yodo, and finally a trade unionist.[110] Actually, the trade unionist almost always came from a company union rather than from the mainstream of organized labor. By the early 1960's, two changes occurred relative to the representational make-up of the Central Bank's directorate. For one, the congressional representation was removed and, second, CUT uncovered a long-hidden technicality that enabled it to finally elect one of its own delegates to the directorate. Still, the representational nature of the Banco Central and other public agencies clearly favored employers' groups and disadvantaged organized labor; this was also true even on agencies, such as the Social Security Service and the Work Accidents Bank, that obviously are of inestimable value to workers and that directly bear on working-class matters.

Accordingly, employers' groups by and large enjoyed direct penetration of the decision-making process, by means of representation in both elective and appointive offices, and they have been able to buttress

[110] Carlos Fredes, *Curso de economía: Elementos de economía chilena*, pp. 58–60.

this influential vantage ground by their notable leadership, financial, and organizational resources. Above all, their combined influence permitted methods that continuously, directly, and specifically reached into the political system in a steady flow of demands upon the policy-making and policy-effectuation process—a process of which they themselves formed a predominant part.

Labor

For its part, labor can claim few commensurate advantages in the pressure field. Trade unions were late to appear, having to await major industrial expansion and, even more important, urbanization, which would amalgamate a sizable number of workers in a limited area. Ideological rifts within the labor movement and opposition from management and government inhibited the establishment of strong structural solidity and cohesion. Also, as has been noted, labor legislation has tended to encroach upon almost every aspect and action of trade unions. But because of the open political system and the absence of any excessive dedication to "going by the book," some statutory features are very much modified in practice. Sometimes this accrues to the advantage of labor, as when the governing regime tacitly recognizes "free" unions and deals with them as though they had obtained legal status (e.g., the railroad workers' federation); on other occasions it can work a hardship as occurs when minimum wages are not enforced (e.g., in 1964, the minimum wage in the nitrate mines was over 1,800 pesos per hour, but the actual hourly amount paid was closer to 1,000 pesos).[111]

Of course, labor has friends in Congress, especially in the Communist, Socialist, and Christian Democratic camps and, to a lesser degree, among Radical senators and deputies. Some labor groups have constructed a fairly effective procedure for dealing with Congress when they seek to alter existing legislation or to propose new laws. The railroad workers utilize a two-pronged attack. Officers of the federation search out all congressmen, whatever their political colors, who will talk with them in order to explain labor's needs and endeavor to per-

[111] Interview with Bernabé Valenzuela B., secretary-treasurer of the Federación Industrial Nacional Minera, in Santiago, February 10, 1964.

suade the legislators to give sympathetic attention to a particular bill. Meanwhile, union members who are militants of particular political parties go to their own partisans in Congress to enlist their aid.[112]

Other labor groups, probably the vast majority of them, find it a unique experience to see their requests carried out. Until the congressional elections of March, 1965, trade unionism generally considered the legislative branch to be controlled by anything but a prolabor majority. Typically, according to many labor leaders, congressmen "talk but do not act" (*hablan, pero no actuan*).

Insofar as the executive branch of government is concerned, labor's fortunes are even more closely tied to the rise and fall of sympathetic regimes. For, even more crucial in many ways than legislative enactments is the way law is interpreted and administered. President Pedro Aguirre Cerda (1939–1941) and his Popular Front government launched progressive reforms that captured the imagination of organized workers and clearly redounded to their benefit. But this was a short-lived era and exceptional in its understanding of labor's wants. As a matter of routine, labor must open channels to administrators if it is to prosper. Some, like the copper, maritime, and railroad workers' federations, enjoy relatively easy ingress into the highest offices of government. When the railroad workers' federation (FIF) anticipates the desirability of policy changes, its member organizations engage in a series of conferences in which they specify exactly what they hope to accomplish and then, at a final meeting at the summit, they set out their requests in point-by-point form. If they fail to convince managerial ranks of the feasibility of their claims, they next go directly to the President of Chile. FIF has profited from good rapport with all Chile's presidents since its founding and, even when they have disagreed on policy questions, both have dealt toward each other with mutual respect.[113]

Nonetheless, as with labor's relations with the legislature, this is an exceptional case. There are many functions of government that touch upon organized workers where labor would like to acquire better representational rights. Democratic methods of selecting labor representa-

[112] Interview with Edmundo Polanco.
[113] *Ibid.*

tives to local boards usually prevail in local situations. For example, unions submit lists of candidates to departmental governors in order to fill positions on the Conciliation Councils; the councilors' names are then drawn by lot.[114] Nevertheless, except for CUT's one spokesman on the Banco Central, the central labor structures complain that they do not exercise the same privilege on the national level. Instead, history has always seen such "trade unionist" delegates coming from unaffiliated or company unions.

To sum up, then, most of labor feels itself cheated out of its representative rights on government boards, since the President of Chile hand-picks labor delegates and, except for the Bank of Chile where a CUT-chosen man was one of fourteen on the directorate, these are not truly representative of organized labor. This is quite a serious matter, for trade unionists find it difficult to be heard in many board meetings that, like the National Health Service, Social Security Service, Labor Accident Fund, Council of Conciliation and Arbitration, and Private Employees Fund, are of tremendous significance to them.

If labor considers itself disadvantaged by underrepresentation in government, what techniques can it employ to press for wanted policy decisions? As has been mentioned at several points, some groups are unique in being able to open executive and legislative doors with relative ease. The maritime workers' generally harmonious working arrangements with management and their tremendous importance to the economy have ensured better accessibility to government than the bulk of labor can muster. The same holds true for the copper workers, primarily because of their enormous contribution to national revenue. The style of their approach is personal and direct, relying upon face-to-face persuasion for selling their programs to policy makers. Also, at times labor generally has found channels to the executive quite open, as during the Aguirre Cerda administration. In such periods one of the most important conditions for the peaceful resolution of conflict prevails: "The likelihood of peaceful adjustment to a conflict is increased if there exist institutional arrangements that encourage consultation,

114 Alexander, *Labor Relations in Argentina, Brazil, and Chile*, p. 314.

negotiation, the exploration of alternatives, and the search for mutually beneficial solutions. Conversely, the prospects of dead-lock and coercion are increased if institutional arrangements severely inhibit such activities."[115]

Unfortunately, by the 1950's favorable institutional arrangements diminished in number or could only be intermittently pursued as the Chilean society became more complex and the regimes of Carlos Ibáñez (1952–1958) and Jorge Alessandri (1958–1964) too often refused to welcome labor into their councils. Alessandri particularly rejected partisan politics and thus found it difficult to relate to the highly politicized CUT. Since the bulk of labor failed to open many doors to government, it increasingly turned to wider pressure tactics hoping to attract sympathetic attention among the populace and force the government to recognize working-class needs. (Moreover, the government's pervasive involvement in the economy as a major employer, regulator, and purveyor of services placed it in the position of being a bargaining agent with whom labor was forced to negotiate—thus additionally stressing labor's political role.)

Oftentimes labor has encountered difficulties in its efforts to present a favorable image to the public. In part, this stemmed from its very limited access to radio and from its treatment by an antagonistic conservative press, which more often than not ignored labor's side in a specific controversy and which largely mirrored the antipathy of managerial elites to trade unionism generally. The existence of a few equally one-sided prolabor periodicals never quite offset the initial disadvantage of a much greater circulation of those publications that were antagonistic to labor. Furthermore, labor is disadvantaged by schisms within its own house that periodically break out in open bitterness. Obviously, attacks hurtling back and forth between labor groupings only detract from trade-union solidarity.

Along with these negative features, Chilean trade unions by and large have developed only the most primitive public relations facilities for projecting a more positive image of themselves to the general

[115] Dahl, *Modern Political Analysis*, p. 77.

public. One of the best of these is maintained by the maritime workers' confederation. Its Publicity Department regularly prepares materials for general release and keeps a professional reporter on its payroll who is in constant contact with the newspapers.[116] But this typifies only a small handful of labor associations, the great bulk of them being handicapped by a shortage of funds and an inability to penetrate the barriers set up by the conservative press.

For its part, CUT relies heavily on the Marxist newspapers and upon technical help from the left-wing political parties to formulate its publicity efforts. Several weapons stand out in CUT's arsenal of devices to be employed against recalcitrant policy makers, but all of them emphasize quantity. That is, sheer numbers of data or people are at the center of most of its campaigns.

One level of such action is what the head of the miners' federation refers to as "protesting with statistics."[117] In this regard, CUT can call upon the aid of a number of economists and statisticians in and out of its organization to draw up presentations for use in bargaining procedures and before the general public. They deal with such current problems as low salaries, rises in the cost of living, inadequate housing, educational inequities, and the Labor Code. Thus, a steady stream of data is thrown out in formal statements to the government and through the friendly press; less technical presentations are circulated as leaflets in the streets and as posters pasted on the sides of buildings.

A second level of CUT's quantitative approach relies upon the promotion of mass meetings and street demonstrations. Once a campaign of statistical and propagandistic protest has been launched, it commonly will be reinforced by great public gatherings.[118] Typically, these begin

[116] Interview with Wenceslao Moreno.

[117] Interview with Roberto Lara.

[118] Such a protest meeting is exemplified by CUT's decision to protest a rise in the cost of wheat, flour, and bread in January, 1964. *El Siglo* reported the decision to assemble as follows: "CUT resolved to call, in the nature of an emergency, a meeting of federations, unions, neighborhood councils, slum dwellers, labor organizations, housewives, students and popular political parties, for tomorrow, at 19 hours in Compañía 1477 [the headquarters of CUT], with the object of adopting practical and immediate measures in order to in-

with announcements that unionists and their friends are called to assemble in union headquarters, at a park, in a theater, or (with increasing frequency) in front of the Congress building. A speech or two later, the congregation moves out into the streets carrying signs, perhaps singing militant songs or chanting slogans. The original nucleus of workers and politicians now swells with new adherents to the cause—especially students and transients. Many of the latter are unemployed drifters who possess only a slight notion of what the issues are, but who are glad for some excitement, the opportunity to release frustrations, and even for the possibility of some gain either from the demonstration's organizers or from looting if that unlikely eventuality should actually arise. Of course, this is rather standard procedure for similar anomic manifestations around the world. One important characteristic of such activity in Chile, though, is that customarily it is quite orderly and does not become perverted to expressions of a violent sort.

A final form of labor protest is the strike. In Chile, strikes are almost always of short duration because the law forbids unions the right to form strike funds and because workers are unable to accumulate personal savings from their meager salaries that would sustain their families through a lengthy work stoppage. A notable exception to the rule of brief strikes took place in 1960 in the coal mines of Lota and lasted three months. The strike's unusual duration was generally attributed to management's desire to keep the mines closed down because of overproduction and to the timidity of the government about intervening in the situation.[119]

Actually, a very large percentage, perhaps 80 per cent, of strikes are illegal.[120] Some of this can be laid at the door of inconsistencies between the Labor Code and actual practice—for example, the code forbids unions of government workers, though these are organized and do strike. On the other hand, many illegal strikes stem from a failure to follow the established formal practices of conciliation, usually requiring several weeks of negotiations.

---

tercept this and all the rises, in general, with which the present Government is regaling the people" (*El Siglo* [Santiago], January 8, 1964).

[119] Florencio Durán Bernales, *La política y los sindicatos*, p. 114.

[120] *Ibid.*, pp. 118–119.

Moreover, many strikes are marked by extremely political overtones, leading one author to define the strike simply as "a means of coercion with political ends."[121] This can be explained by the deep political commitments of most labor leaders and, consequently, by the close relationships between them and the political parties. Trade unionists with leftist tendencies in particular, being devoted to revolutionary changes in the social system, lace their demands for economic reforms with an insistence on the necessity of political reconstruction if their "bread and butter" wants are ever to be fulfilled.

Then, too, not all unionists agree as to what the preferred duration of a work stoppage should be and in this difference of opinion rests one more bone of contention frequently splitting Chilean trade unionism. The confusion grows out of the divergencies in political and ideological beliefs held by labor leaders.

On the one side, most Socialists, as well as the few Trotskyites and Anarcho-Syndicalists, prefer the unlimited strike—that is, one that lasts as long as it can be sustained. Their intent is to employ the maximum pressure to break the power of management and their partners in government and, at the same, to bring about a climate of opinion more receptive to labor's demands.

In contrast, the Communists, though laboring to achieve a full revolution, and those Christian Democrats and Radicals of an evolutionary but strongly reformist bent, prefer a limited strike hoping in the process to strengthen labor organization and tactics and thus build up an over-all working-class solidarity and consciousness before running head on into the power of the oligarchy. Also, they fear that an unlimited general strike runs the danger of provoking the government into taking repressive measures against labor, the outcome of which could well find labor possessing even fewer freedoms of action than prevailed prior to the strike.

Those favoring the limited strike point with horror at several precedents that seem to underscore their contention that the unlimited strike holds only calamity for organized labor. One of the most tragic of such experiences involved the abortive general strike of January, 1956.[122]

[121] *Ibid.*, p. 114.
[122] Oscar Núñez, *Diez años de los trabajadores chilenos*, pp. 13–15.

Its prelude saw a rash of work stoppages breaking out in 1955 in defiance of anti-inflationary measures, which had been recommended by the Klein-Saks Commission to Chile and which President Ibáñez was determined to effectuate to the fullest extent possible.[123] Rightly or wrongly, labor concluded that it would be taking the brunt of the effect of such measures because of a provision for holding the line on workers' salaries while, it was believed by the trade unions, inflation would continue to escalate. Harsh feelings on both sides of the controversy raised antagonistic feelings to a fever pitch. At the same time that some radical trade unionists issued inflammatory revolutionary manifestoes, on May 1, 1955, President Ibáñez in a radio broadcast to the nation denounced CUT as an illegal organization, controlled by foreign influences, which disrupted economic production and destroyed public order. The chief executive further threatened to call upon his coercive powers under the Laws for the Defense of Democracy and then requested Congress to grant him powers to impose a state of siege when he deemed it necessary. Labor's answer was to strike.

In the next few months CUT initiated two general strikes, and at various times transportation, communications, health service, social security, and Treasury Department workers stayed away from work. Finally, CUT requested its adherents to begin an unlimited general strike on January 9, 1956. The result was disastrous for labor. President Ibáñez, falling back upon both his ordinary and emergency powers, prorogued the legislative session, declared a state of siege, and moved to decimate the organized labor movement. Many trade unionists, especially from CUT's locals, were seized and transported to various points of the nation. Scores of top labor leaders found themselves under house arrest or incarcerated; CUT's president, Clotario Blest, and its treasurer, Juan Vargas Puebla, were sentenced to jail for 110 days. This set of circumstances seriously threatened the entire national labor movement. In particular, CUT suffered an organizational weakening, reduced assets, and a demoralization of its membership—all of

[123] For the Klein-Saks proposals, see *El programa de estabilización de la economía chilena y el trabajo de la Misión Klein y Saks.*

which combined to lessen its ability to perform as a bargaining agent.[124]

In the next half-dozen years, CUT slowly recovered from this low ebb; but Chilean labor still remained factionalized and lacking in the necessary combative qualities and resources to effectively contend with its managerial opponents. Above all, trade unionism in Chile continued to be so highly politicized that, with its deep ideological cleavages, it usually was next to impossible to find common agreement on fundamental tactics and goals. Such limitations perpetuated a shortage of regularized channels into the decision-making agencies of government that inhibited the conversion of claims into long-desired economic and social reforms.

Some two decades of trade unionism's frustrations under governmental regimes that, at least to labor, seemed far more sympathetic to management, finally boiled over in the presidential and congressional elections of 1964 and 1965. By then, labor's lot appeared more strongly than ever tied to the fortunes of political parties, and countless thousands of unorganized urban and rural workers—in most instances for the first time—responded to the political appeals of reformist and radical party groupings. Indeed, probably at no previous moment in Chilean history had such a diversity and quantity of societal sectors sought economic salvation by means of political action.

124 Barría, *Trayectoria y estructura del movimiento sindical chileno*, pp. 85–106.

CHAPTER FIVE

Political Parties

THE EARLY DEVELOPMENT of political parties in Chile duplicated a pattern of political activity observable in most of the Latin American nations. Its origins can be traced to struggles that began shortly after independence between largely aristocratic factions and gradually evolved into rivalry between two main political parties, the Conservatives and the Liberals. Throughout most of the nineteenth century these parties remained rather closed corporations, though slight differences in their bases of membership and somewhat more discernible variations in their issue orientations marked each with certain distinguishing characteristics of its own.

However, the basically two-party nature of Chilean politics failed to live out the century. Ultimately, new societal elements and new ideologies broke out on the national scene and inevitably disrupted the tidy traditional arrangement. Indeed, by the 1960's six major parties vied for control of the government and offered the Chilean voters numerous doctrinal alternatives. But if the contemporary party system now provided an openness and dynamism unparalleled in the history of the the republic, the very plethora of partisan camps—and the societal cleavages they mirrored—also introduced immobilist features into the decision-making process that created uncertainty about the viability of government in its existing form and about the social and economic directions the nation would pursue. Consequently, the developmental aspects of Chilean parties together with an explanation of their contemporary organization and doctrine as well as of their relations with each other offer important clues to reasons for the systemic difficulties in Chilean national life and possible avenues to their resolution.

PARTY ORIGINS

Conservatives, Liberals, and Radicals

The earliest glimmerings of party activity began in partisan disputes that sprang up in the 1820's. At that time, those Chileans who were actively engaged in the affairs of state tended to cluster either as *pelucones* or *pipiolos*.[1] Both names were coined by their adversaries as derisive epithets. The term *pelucones*, or bigwigs, derived from the ceremonial powdered wigs worn by colonial aristocrats and was meant to suggest an anachronistic bent of the well to do who populated these ranks; the *pipiolos*, or greenhorns, obtained their label because of the lower social rank of some members. (In time, both elements provided their own appellations, Conservatives and Liberals respectively, and the names carried on down into the twentieth century.)

In 1823, the dictatorship of Bernardo O'Higgins, Chile's principal

[1] Among the hundreds of studies on nineteenth-century Chile a few useful references are Isaac J. Cox, "Chile," in *Argentina, Brazil and Chile since Independence*, ed. A. Curtis Wilgus, pp. 279–369; Ricardo Donoso, *Las ideas políticas en Chile;* Alberto Edwards Vives, *La fronda aristocrática*, and *La organización política de Chile*; Francisco A. Encina, *Resumen de la historia de Chile*, Vols. II and III; Francisco Frías Valenzuela, *Manual de historia de Chile*; Luis Galdames, *A History of Chile*, trans. and ed. Isaac J. Cox; Federico G. Gil, *The Political System of Chile*, Chap. II; and Fredrick B. Pike, *Chile and the United States, 1880–1962*, Chaps. I–IV.

independence leader, was ended and the nation subsequently suffered a period of political adventurism, governmental experimentation, and general chaos that typified the growing pains of many of the hemisphere's new nations. This epoch, lasting for seven years, saw the *pipiolos* politically dominant. Then in 1830, the *pelucones*, victors of a civil war, seized power and ushered in a new period under the strong-willed conservative, Diego Portales. Although assassinated in 1837, Portales lived long enough to stabilize Chile and set a pattern of autocratic governing to persist for decades.[2]

In these formative years of Chilean politics issues were obscure and the choice between political groups did not always seem too attractive. One Chilean politician complained that the "banner of one of these parties carried the inscription: 'Liberty even if in anarchy' while that of the other read: 'Order even if in despotism.' And in both cases the motto was sometimes inscribed in bloody characters."[3] Be that as it may, several programmatic tendencies eventually served to sharpen distinctions between the two main political currents. The root cause of most dissension probably erupted over the Church-State issue. Actually, it was a manifestation of a certain amount of popular anticlericalism, rather than (at least in the early years) of governmental policies. Alberto Edwards Vives described such anticlericalism as "a spontaneous movement, common to all Christian peoples, independent of active politics."[4]

This attitudinal environment served as a foundation for political disagreement when an appropriate issue would trigger it. For example, the installation in 1845 of an intensely antisecular archbishop of Santiago, Rafael Valentín Valdivieso y Zañartu, provided the rallying point for conservative elements and a focal point of liberal opposition.[5] On another occasion, in 1856, the climate of disagreement was fired by a minor issue when President Manuel Montt, an implacably independent-acting chief executive, supported the Supreme Court's ruling

[2] Pike, *Chile and the United States*, pp. 10–13.

[3] René León Echaíz, *Evolución histórica de los partidos políticos chilenos*, pp. 26–27.

[4] Edwards, *La fronda aristocrática*, p. 93.

[5] Pike, *Chile and the United States*, pp. 15–16.

that the high clergy could not oust the sacristan of the Cathedral from his post and inferred that the archbishop might be exiled if he did not abide by the Court's decision. Although a compromise was reached, the die was cast for an authentic issue to separate political groups. In the 1856 instance, proclericals heretofore participating in the Montt government withdrew their support and officially formed themselves into the Conservative party.[6] Liberals and later partisan groupings took up the antithetic role in a dialogue that saw the Church's powers slowly but inexorably curtailed over the next few decades.

Other differences split the political activists besides the Church issue. Some issues were rather well defined and specific (e.g., whether to establish a federal or unitary governmental form and whether to install a presidential or parliamentary system); other argumentation assumed a more philosophical tone.

Intellectual ferment in the 1840's, referred to as the "literary renaissance" and coinciding with the establishment of the University of Chile, fostered a reawakening of liberalism.[7] Several literary journals were founded that thrust some exciting new figures onto the Chilean intellectual scene. José Victorino Lastarria, Francisco Bilbao, and several other youths attacked the vestiges of colonialism still prevalent in Chilean society and spoke on behalf of a more open political society. In 1850, they created Chile's first workers' organization, La Sociedad de la Igualdad. Although attacked by conservatives and, in some cases, even banished from Chilean soil for a time, their voices were heard by an ever-enlarging circle. By mid-century a Liberal party appeared, headed by Lastarria and representing a loose assemblage of older liberals and the more progressive youth, many of whom had been inspired by the radicalism of the French Revolution of 1848. Lastarria defined the party's goals in his *Bases de la reforma* as seeking to create an environment "in which all citizens aspire to the progress and aggrandizement of the nation and to the enlargement of their freedoms."[8]

[6] John R. Stevenson, *The Chilean Popular Front*, pp. 13–15.
[7] Sergio Guilisasti Tagle, ed., *Partidos políticos chilenos*, pp. 74–75.
[8] *Ibid.*, p. 75.

Although the main historical foundations for the Conservative and Liberal parties had been laid by the middle of the nineteenth century, in no sense could their unfolding be considered regularized or disciplined. In fact, oftentimes they were hopelessly fragmented; on occasions elements moved back and forth between the two party groupings; and more than once substantial numbers of Conservatives and Liberals joined together in governmental coalitions. Periodically, party names changed and issues became obscured by the exigencies of practical politics.

Meanwhile, the economy underwent recurring changes that readjusted old coalitions and propelled new ideas and new societal elements onto the political scene. Beginning in the 1840's agricultural production was augmented by road-building projects, the opening of new land, and the appearance of farm machinery. Chile's great mineral resources, especially in the north, brought important new sources of revenue to the national treasury, as did an expansion of foreign trade.

Gradually, a dissident political element emerged who felt contempt for oligarchical control of the political process and who were intent on doing something about it. Comprising southern landowners, many anticlericals, and the modest-sized but growing middle sector (i.e., mostly teachers, bureaucrats, and merchants), for some time they had constituted the more progressive wing of the Liberal party and thus were imbued with the same radical roots. However, they believed that these principles had been unfulfilled and so moved to the left of the political spectrum. Calling themselves Rojos, or Reds, the disaffected Liberals enunciated their radicalism through the leadership efforts of Pedro León Gallo and of the journalist-brothers Manuel Antonio and Guillermo Matta. Their vigorous opposition to the Montt government in its last years and the extremism of their doctrine for that time led to a direct confrontation with the ruling oligarchy. Thus, when the Rojos held meetings to arouse public opinion to their cause, they ran afoul of the governing regime. In short order, the government declared a state of seige in the central provinces, accused the Rojos of sedition, and jailed scores of their socially prominent members. The Rojos responded in early 1859 with insurrectionary outbreaks in numerous towns to the south and north. Within a few months government troops had smashed the rebellion; but the experience forged an intense esprit de corps among the Rojos, who moved to formalize their separate political identity by converting themselves into the Radical party. In March, 1862, the Matta brothers' publication, *La Voz de Chile*, set out the main postulates of the new party to be constitutional reform, public education, administrative decentralization, and electoral freedom.[9]

As has been indicated, then, the Conservative, Liberal, and Radical parties all owe their principal origins to the thirty years following 1830 when three presidents governed Chile—General Joaquín Prieto (1831 to 1841), Manuel Bulnes (1841 to 1851), and Manuel Montt (1851 to 1861). Their era often referred to as the Age of Autocracy, its form tempered by the iron will of Portales, the chief executives tended to rule with little regard for the political parties. However, the passage of Montt from power introduced political innovations whereby presidents sought the support of political parties and to some measure reflected party wishes. During this time, lasting until 1891, the Liberals, though almost constantly torn by factionalism, dominated the government. Chile fought a small war with Spain in 1864 and emerged the victor over Peru and Bolivia as a result of the War of the Pacific in 1879 to 1883. These episodes served to strengthen Chilean national consciousness and the War of the Pacific garnered impressive new sources of wealth for the country. A wave of prosperity permeated most of Chile and even filtered lightly down into the working classes.

Then in 1891, Chile suffered a serious setback when the nation fell into an eight-month civil war. It seems likely that the dissension erupted primarily because the one umbrella that could shelter most Liberals, the clerical issue, disappeared during the 1880's when the Church question was largely ameliorated. Since there was nothing else to cement the contentious factions together, the Liberals fell to squabbling among themselves and dragged other political cliques along with them. The controversy revolved around the age-old question of just how much power the President should possess. Hence, when

[9] *Ibid.*, pp. 132–134; Galdames, *History of Chile*, pp. 298–304.

President José Manuel Balmaceda (1886–1891) endeavored to initiate economic reforms with currency manipulation and land-reform measures, he provoked the ire of the large landowners, the wealthy exporters, and the powerful foreign nitrate holdings. These economic interests and others opposed to presidential omnipotence combined in Congress to oppose Balmaceda down the line. Violence between the President and the Congress concluded with Balmaceda's loss and the virtual destruction of executive preeminence.[10]

Now Chile had come half circle—from the Age of Autocracy and presidential paramountcy to the Age of Parliament and congressional supremacy. The relatively orderly nature of the earlier period gave way to virtual chaos during the next three decades and, according to one Chilean historian, the Parliamentary Age could only be defined as "systematic disorder."[11] The administration of government became irresponsible and corrupt and the electoral process was rampant with vote buying. Politics moved along erratically above the heads of the bulk of the citizenry, who remained largely apathetic to national events.

Nevertheless, occasional glimpses of changes to come surfaced from time to time as the bases of an expanded multiparty system built upon profound ideological diversity—though fraught with deep cleavages—were being implanted in this historical span. Coalitions were necessitated by the failure of any single partisan structure to secure a congressional majority, and legislative voting blocs rose and fell in tireless repetition. A host of partisan units, mostly speaking for moneyed and aristocratic interests, contended for political resources: The Conservatives continued to be a confessional party, drawing their major backing both from the farm population and from urban proclericals in the central provinces. The Liberal party still constituted the largest single grouping, though it remained badly fragmented. The National party merged splinter elements from the Liberal as well as the Conservative parties and consisted of little more than a personalist coterie of wealthy bankers and merchants. The residue of Balmaceda's following underwrote the Liberal Democratic party and, while persisting in their preference for a powerful presidential system, they did not

[10] Frías, *Manual de historia de Chile*, pp. 548–562.
[11] *Ibid.*, p. 561.

seem unhappy about taking their slice of the spoils available under a strong congressional arrangement. More than any other party, the Radicals catered to the growing middle sector and to the youth—bases of strength that would lift the Radicals to unprecedented political importance after the First World War. Finally, the Democratic party represented a faction that had split away from the Radicals in protest against the parent group's failure to consider the plight of the working classes.[12]

The splits and fusions that characterized these parties during the Parliamentary Age defy efforts at clarification. Two presidents, Jorge Montt (1891 to 1896) and Ramón Barros Luco (1910 to 1915), received the general support of all voting parties in uncontested elections. Germán Riesco (1901 to 1906) achieved the presidency with the aid of the Liberal Alliance, a combination of Radicals, Democrats, and the more progressive Liberals. Another group, known simply as the Coalition and formed of Conservatives, moderate Liberals, and the National party, succeeded in placing two men in the presidency —Federico Errázuriz Echaurren (1896 to 1901) and Juan Luis Sanfuentes (1915 to 1920). Still another arrangement, the National Union—this time National and Radical parties and factions of the Liberal and Conservative parties—placed Pedro Montt (1906 to 1910) in the presidential chair. Throughout, the small but influential Liberal Democratic party moved its money from coalition to coalition.[13]

Although presidents served out their full terms, they scarcely were able to govern. Simply to present the barest outlines of an administration required chronic juggling of the cabinet. The acuteness of this problem can be observed in the fact that between 1891 and 1920, 348 ministers wandered through eighty-five cabinets. This compared unfavorably with the 30 ministers and fourteen cabinets in the three decades of the Autocracy and with the 118 ministers and thirty-six cabinets during the thirty years of the Liberal Republic.[14] Moreover,

12 Guillermo Feliú Cruz, "Durante la república. Perfiles de la evolución política, social, y constitucional," in *La Constitución de 1925 y la Facultad de Ciencias Jurídicas y Sociales*, pp. 59–305.

13 Frías, *Manual de historia de Chile*, pp. 566–567; Edwards, *La fronda aristocrática*, pp. 157–205.

14 Feliú, "Durante la república," pp. 282–291.

electoral practices reached the apex of corruption. The dead voted and vote buying was ubiquitous. A senatorial post went for from 100,000 to 250,000 pesos and a deputy's seat for roughly 50,000 pesos.[15]

But despite the prodigious excesses of the Parliamentary Age, the seeds were being sown for fundamental alterations in the Chilean political system. In fact, it was an era of relative political quietude in which the freedoms of speech and assembly were respected. This permitted the middle- and working-class sectors, now growing at a measurable pace in a period of general prosperity, to accustom themselves to political role playing. Literacy increased from about 30 per cent to more than 50 per cent of the population, thanks largely to the expansion of a public educational system that enabled many poorer families to enter their children in schools.[16] General educational and economic improvements especially benefited the enlarging middle class, which railed against the oligarchically controlled Congress and determined to enhance its own position in the policy-making councils.

Initially, and most importantly, happenings in northern Chile rallied vigorous opposition to the status quo. There the burgeoning nitrate and copper industries agglomerated thousands of workers exposed to the most lamentable living and working conditions. Desperate conditions in Valparaíso, Santiago, and Concepción similarly activated workers in those areas. Numerous protest organizations sprang up and middle-class leaders commonly stood at their helm. However, if the middle class provided the bulk of the leadership for fomenting change, it could not anticipate the fulfillment of its goals without the actual involvement of the industrial workers who "supplied the necessary violence and strong-arm methods which the order-loving middle class could not have been expected to provide."[17]

Strikes by maritime workers in Valparaíso (1903), laborers protesting high living costs in Santiago (1905), and railroad workers in Antofagasta and nitrate workers in Iquique (1907) experienced the full repressive force of the aristocratic government, which slaughtered

[15] *Ibid.*, p. 297.
[16] Eduardo Hamuy *et al.*, *El problema educacional del pueblo de Chile*, p. 10.
[17] Stevenson, *Chilean Popular Front*, pp. 26–27.

thousands of strikers.[18] One author estimates that between 1911 and 1920 (excepting 1915), more than 155,000 workers participated in 293 strikes. Although their record of success was very limited, the workers did score partial satisfaction of their wants in 93 cases and major victories in 51 instances.[19] But even this percentage of successful actions whetted labor's appetite for increased militancy and swelled the rolls of newly formed trade unions.

By 1920, many brooms were ready to sweep out the political home of aristocracy. Federico Gil notes that this change "had come swiftly —an industrial revolution and social upheaval hand-in-hand—the machine, the proletariat, the metropolis and the intellectual middle class appearing almost simultaneously on the scene."[20] Out of the presidential election of 1920 arose the implementor of that change—the charismatic, impulsive, and dynamic Arturo Alessandri Palma. Although frustrated by residual oligarchical control of the Senate until congressional elections four years later, the supreme shock to his reform efforts occurred in 1924 when his own majority in Congress fell into wrangling among themselves—thus leaving the impatient President deprived of legislative action he so desperately sought.

In rapid succession, the military entered the political scene after a century on the sidelines and supported demands to force through the proposed reforms. Alessandri brought army General Luis Altamirano in as cabinet chief, who in turn ordered a congressional action with the implied threat of military intervention if Congress did not respond properly. Years of legislative inaction were immediately replaced by the adoption of all of Alessandri's requests in one hour's time. But the President, sensing his own loss of position to the army, fled to the U.S. Embassy where he resigned his office and then left the country. An oligarchy-oriented military junta governed briefly only to be overturned by more reformist-minded officers of the middle sector who were backed by a soldiery from the working classes. Alessandri was

[18] Moisés Poblete Troncoso and Ben G. Burnett, *The Rise of the Latin American Labor Movement*, pp. 58–59.
[19] Alberto Cabero, *Chile y los chilenos*, p. 339.
[20] Gil, *Political System of Chile*, p. 56.

recalled to the presidency in March, 1925, after less than six months in exile and moved to establish a consitutional assembly for the purpose of refurbishing Chile's governmental system. Under the new constitution, approved by popular plebiscite in August, 1925, the parliamentary system was scrapped for a presidential arrangement in which the chief executive reassumed a greatly strengthened role in the decision-making process. Also, the guarantee of impartially administered elections and universal voting rights to males of majority age ensured that the old oligarchy could no longer monopolize policy formulation.[21]

Socialists and Communists

The economic and social ferment of the parliamentary epoch and the political guarantees enlarged and protected by the Constitution of 1925 augured well for the growth of mass-based political parties. The older party structures now were challenged by more radical groupings, which appealed not only to some of the middle sectors but to the urban poor as well. (In time, they also would seek to extend their influence into the impoverished rural regions.) Thus, a reconstitution of the Chilean party system began to occur: the Conservatives and Liberals coalesced on the right; the Radicals, heterogeneous and thus often ambivalent, moved across a wide area in the center; and the more recently formed Marxist parties held down the left.

At the turn of the century, the fledgling trade-union movement spawned the earliest Marxist political associations. In effect, socialist elements established a viable base among organized workers and then picked up labor and moved it into the political system. Thus in 1897, elements from Iquique, Valparaíso, Talcahuano, Lota, and Punta Arenas assembled in Santiago and created the Unión Socialista. A year later, the Partido Obrero was formed and in 1901 the Partido Socialista appeared. These were ephemeral groupings, but they articu-

[21] Among the countless analyses and memoirs of this era, see Carlos Andrade Geywitz, *Elementos de derecho constitucional chileno*; Samuel Gajardo, *Alessandri y su destino*; Augusto Iglesias, *Alessandri, una etapa de la democracia en América*; Emilio Rodríguez Mendoza, *El golpe de estado de 1924*; Arturo Olavarría Bravo, *Chile entre dos Alessandri.*

lated their doctrines to an ever-widening audience through countless labor-socialist publications—including *El Trabajo*, *El Obrero*, *El Proletario*, *La Voz del Pueblo*, *El Rebelde*, *La Tromba*, *El Socialista*, and *Germinal*.[22] By 1902, the Socialist party claimed thirty sections distributed throughout the nation. From the beginning, the Socialists drew their lines of battle clearly when they declared their complete opposition to the established order and announced their intent to replace it with a "just and more equalitarian one" of but one class, the workers, in which production and its benefits would be enjoyed by all. Achieving this goal necessitated converting private property into collective or common ownership.[23]

Luis Emilio Recabarren, socialism's prime catalyst in its formative years, helped to congeal socialist thought in 1912 with the creation of the Partido Obrero Socialista.[24] His preeminence in this party and in the recently launched labor central, the Federación Obrera de Chile, placed him at the forefront of Chilean radicalism. In 1921 at the party's convention in Rancagua, on the high tide of the Bolshevik Revolution, Recabarren rather easily transformed the Socialist party into the Communist party, the Chilean section of the Third International.[25] This proved to be the only instance in all of Latin America when a Socialist party was delivered intact into Communist hands.[26] (For its part, FOCH affiliated with the Red International of Labor Unions, or Profintern.)

During much of the 1920's the Communists were buffeted about by unfriendly regimes and ran into especial difficulties when the government sought to bring trade unionism under its official control. Still, the Communists demonstrated a certain amount of staying power

22 Guilisasti, *Partidos políticos chilenos*, pp. 255–256.

23 Julio César Jobet, "Acción e historia del socialismo chileno," *Combate* 2, no. 12 (September–October 1960): 33.

24 An important study of Recabarren and the early socialist movement is Julio C. Jobet, *Recabarren: Los orígenes del movimiento obrero y del socialismo chilenos*.

25 A year earlier, Recabarren attempted to make the same move; but he was vigorously opposed by Manuel Hidalgo, who wanted to maintain national autonomy (Pike, *Chile and the United States*, pp. 202–203).

26 Rollie E. Poppino, *International Communism in Latin America*, pp. 67–68.

when, in the presidential elections of 1927 in the face of severe persecution, they placed on the ballot the name of Secretary General Elías Lafertte—then jailed on a remote island—as the only opponent to Dictator-President Carlos Ibáñez. Subsequently, the Communist party took such a battering from the Ibáñez regime that it appeared moribund for a time. This condition was further exacerbated by internal power struggles between Lafertte's Stalinist wing and a Trotskyite faction led by Manuel Hidalgo. Finally, the Lafertte group emerged in 1937 as the official Communist party.[27]

Meanwhile, Chile's modern-day Socialist party evolved out of circumstances that colored it with a profound uniqueness and that effectively differentiated it from its apparent counterparts in other Western democracies. This is pointed up by Ernst Halperin, who notes that just because the Chilean Socialist party "calls itself Socialist and proclaims its ideology to be Marxism naturally leads the foreign observer to assume that this is a social democratic party of the familiar European type. The Chilean Socialists were for a long time victims to a similar but opposite illusion in believing that the European socialists had some affinity with them. However, both sides finally found out that they had nothing in common, and the Chilean Socialists' relations with the Socialist International were broken off."[28]

An explanation of this peculiar situation finds its roots late in the Ibáñez dictatorship when the temporary bankruptcy of Communist leadership on the left impelled the formation of a number of small Marxist groups seeking to fill that void. However, like other leftist elements, these minor political factions and university groups (including El Partido Socialista Marxista, Nueva Acción Pública, and Orden Socialista) all felt the heavy boot of the Ibáñez dictatorship until its demise in 1931.[29]

In the next months the office of the presidency was passed from hand to hand like the baton in a relay race. After only one day as chief executive, Pedro Opazo Letelier appointed Minister of the Interior

[27] *Ibid.*, pp. 69–70; Elías Lafertte, *Vida de un Comunista*, Part IV.
[28] Ernst Halperin, *Nationalism and Communism in Chile*, pp. 121–122.
[29] Jobet, "Acción e historia del socialismo chileno," p. 36.

Juan Esteban Montero to serve as acting President; less than a month later, Montero moved his own minister of the interior up to acting President in order to qualify himself as a candidate in the presidential elections scheduled for October 4, 1931. Montero won the election, but his conservative and lackluster approach to the disastrous domestic effects of the world-wide depression produced political alienation that spilled over into street protestations. Six months to the day after taking the oath of presidential office Montero was dumped by a coup d'état directed by Colonel Marmaduke Grove, the commander of the air force.

A junta composed of General Arturo Puga, Carlos Dávila, and Eugenio Matte shared executive power in the new government; Colonel Grove took the post of minister of defense. Matte and Grove, who actually dominated the government, held Socialist leanings. In short order they declared Chile a Socialist Republic, prorogued Congress, and issued several decrees easing the banking situation, which won them some popularity. Their initial success proved short-lived, however, and in less than two weeks the junta fell apart.

Once again, the presidency assumed the appearance of a kaleidoscope with six different regimes heading the government in 101 days. The chronic instability characterizing these months pushed Chilean politics to the right as the nation expressed an overwhelming preference for order and, in 1932, returned a now very conservative Arturo Alessandri to the helm of the republic. The temper of the times was observable in the fact that Alessandri and two other conservative presidential candidates received a convincing 80 per cent of the total votes cast, the Socialist Grove and the Communist Lafertte obtaining the tiny remainder.[30]

Throughout Alessandri's second administration (1932–1938) social and economic reforms were shunted aside in preference for order and adherence to the Constitution of 1925. On leaving office, Alessandri expressed his content over the success of this dedication when he said:

[30] The actual vote distribution to the conservatives was Alessandri (183,744), Rodríguez (45,267), and Zañartu (42,273); and to the leftists, Grove (60,261) and Lafertte (4,621).

"I governed six years with the Constitution always in my hand, making a supreme effort to defend constitutional government."[31] In point of fact, President Alessandri underwrote some repressive procedures in his pursuit of that goal, which further alienated the Marxists. Above all, they feared the presence of a fifty-thousand-man paramilitary group, the Republican Militia, formed of well-to-do youths who were determined to underscore Alessandri's concepts of order and constitutionalism.[32]

The government's conservatism and periodic resort to coercion induced the fragments of Chilean socialism to reassess their situation. In 1933, they pulled themselves together as the Socialist party of Chile and, moving into the leftist leadership vacuum occasioned by the Communists' weakened status, they soon exercised major sway among trade-union centrals. This momentary dominance of the left, however, was soon shattered as the Communists eventually rallied under Lafertte (while Hidalgo's Trotskyites merged with Socialists and produced additional heterogeneity in the Socialist party) and entered a Popular Front that carried Pedro Aguirre Cerda to the presidency in 1938.[33]

The Popular Front with the Radicals undoubtedly benefited the Communists far more than it did the Socialists. For the Communists, it gave them a certain air of respectability and reduced some of the taint of being considered a party directed by a foreign (i.e., Moscow) power. Since the Socialists suffered from no such opprobrium, there was no similar advantage to be gained from tying their fortunes to the Radicals. Clearly, the Socialists were pulled into the Popular Front "under the hypnotic effect of European political slogans that had no relevance to the Chilean political situation, and thus from the beginning they felt cheated and dissatisfied."[34]

The upshot of the Popular Front arrangement insofar as the Marxist parties were concerned was to cause chronic dissension among the

[31] Stevenson, *Chilean Popular Front*, p. 58.

[32] Galdames, *History of Chile*, p. 395.

[33] Stevenson, *Chilean Popular Front*, Chaps. V–VII. Also see Alberto Baltra Cortés, *Pedro Aguirre Cerda*, and Alberto Cabero, *Recuerdos de don Pedro Aguirre Cerda*.

[34] Halperin, *Nationalism and Communism in Chile*, p. 126.

Socialists that enervated them through the war years while the Communists acquired internal strength and an improved public image. Indeed, as their reward for helping the Radical presidential nominee, Gabriel González Videla, to become elected Chile's chief executive in 1946, the Communists gained three cabinet posts and the overt support of the new President in their efforts to seize hegemony over organized labor. This era of good feeling between González Videla and the Communists was symbolized in the conventions of the Socialist and Communist wings of the big labor central, the Confederación de Trabajadores de Chile, which assembled in December, 1946. The President and several of his cabinet members appeared before a Communist gathering of more than fifteen thousand people in the National Stadium, while the Socialists could only garner a few thousand delegates in a small Santiago auditorium.[35]

Flush with so much success, the Communists now demonstrated a disquieting aggressiveness not only from their official positions in government but also in direct street confrontations with the Socialists. In the ensuing violence numerous deaths occurred on both sides. The Communists chalked up gains among workers at the expense of the Radicals, but tended to slip in the aggregate as many laborers returned to the Socialist fold.[36] Meanwhile, Liberals and then Radicals pulled out of the cabinet and González Videla was left with a minority government based on the untrustworthy Communists. Moving quickly, the President ousted the Communists and reconstituted his administration with Radical party participation and with congressional support from the Liberals. After a few weeks the disestablished Communists moved to counter the new regime with a series of short but highly disruptive strikes.

By October, 1947, González Videla had assumed such a militantly anti-Communist posture that he severed diplomatic relations with the Communist nations and ordered the arrest of hundreds of Chilean Communists. Less than a year later, he pushed through Congress the repressive Laws for the Defense of Democracy. This was to be his harsh-

[35] Robert Alexander, *Communism in Latin America*, pp. 200–201.
[36] *Ibid.*, p. 202.

est weapon in his battle against opposing political and trade unionist leaders.

Earlier, the President had opened the door to the Socialists to enter his cabinet, but they were again mired in the throes of factionalism. Youthful radicals, led by Raúl Ampuero, rejected the Old Guard's willingness to seek a conciliation with the traditional parties in order to coalesce against the Communists. Instead, Ampuero advocated combating communism by seizing a doctrinal position on the farthest left of ideological politics.[37] This led to a split in the Socialist camp with Ampuero reorganizing his fraction into the Popular Socialist party.

In 1952, in one of the many twists and turns that characterize the history of Chilean political parties, the older Socialist group reversed its former antipathy to the Communists and wooed Communist endorsement of its presidential nominee, Dr. Salvador Allende. In 1957, a rapprochement between the dissident Socialists and the Old Guard brought them back together as the Chilean Socialist party. A year later, the Socialists found common ground with the Communists and created an electoral alliance, the Frente de Acción Popular (FRAP), which fell only 33,000 votes short of winning the 1958 presidential election.

Much has been written about the Socialists' repeated shifts in emphasis and tone during the last three decades. To some observers they inevitably resulted from doctrinal schisms in a movement that combined, as it did, several brands of Marxism, anti-Marxian anarcho-syndicalism, and moderate social democracy.[38] Others stress Socialism's "extreme susceptibility to political fashions imported either from other continents or from other Latin American countries."[39] Whatever the case, the Socialists have passed through a number of phases in their history that sometimes pitted them against the Communists and allied them together in other periods; at various times they entered a Popular Front, flirted with Peronism, raised the flag of Titoism, lauded Castro-

[37] The Socialists' ideological position on the left is interestingly discussed in Halperin, *Nationalism and Communism in Chile*, pp. 121–144.

[38] Gil, *Political System of Chile*, p. 285.

[39] Halperin, *Nationalism and Communism in Chile*, p. 135.

ism, and have contained a pro-Peking element in their midst. At the very least, the shifting Socialist stands revealed a flexibility—if not an ambiguity—that the Moscow-oriented Communist party generally lacked.

Christian Democrats

While the several political parties mentioned were splitting and regrouping to adjust to changing conditions in Chilean life, a new political movement appeared that was destined to achieve almost unprecedented electoral successes in the middle 1960's. This movement, in time known as the Christian Democrats, traces its origins back to a cluster of youths within the Conservative party who had been inspired by the liberal encyclicals of Pope Leo XIII and who were stimulated to political activism by the liberal social programs of two Jesuit priests, Fernando Vives del Solar and Jorge Fernández Pradel.

In the main, the Conservative party itself had voiced approval of the *Rerum Novarum* and *Quadragesimo Anno* encyclicals simply because they constituted official pronouncements by the Church, and the Conservatives, as members of a confessional party, felt obliged at least to render lip service to them. In fact, however, the Conservative hierarchy deplored such liberalism and never really intended to implement the encyclicals. As a consequence, the disaffected youths emerged in 1935 as a recognizable faction of the Conservative Youth espousing Christian social views and determined to give substance to the economic and social reform called for by the encyclicals. It soon became completely intolerable for them to continue to work within the Conservative party and so, in 1938, they broke out of Conservative ranks under the banner of the Falange Nacional or National Falange, led by a number of intelligent and dynamic men—including Bernardo Leighton, Eduardo Frei, Rafael Gumucio, Sergio Fernández Larraín, Radomiro Tomic, Alejandro Silva Bascuñán, and Manuel Garretón.[40] For a time relations with the Conservative party remained rather cordial; then, due to the impact of the Spanish Civil War and the Falange's

[40] Luis Vitale, *Esencia y apariencia de la Democracia Cristiana*, pp. 108–109.

increasing ideological absorption of the philosophy of Jacques Maritain, the two became estranged.[41]

During the 1940's the Falange's following remained quite small—never reaching as high as 5 per cent of the total votes cast in any of the municipal and congressional elections of that decade. In part, its inability to expand membership stemmed from the existence of a rival Christian social party, the Partido Conservador Social Cristiano, which tended to dilute the Falange's area of appeal. That challenge was removed in 1957 when the Falange absorbed the bulk of the Partido Conservador Social Cristiano and reconstituted itself as the Christian Democratic party (Partido Demócrata Cristiano, or PDC).[42] From then on, Christian Democracy swelled rapidly. Hundreds of thousands of voters swung over to the Christian Democratic party and several small political parties (e.g., the Partido Agrario Laborista, mostly comprising southern farmers, and the Nueva Izquierda Democrática, a split-away from the National Democratic party) merged with the Christian Democrats. Electoral statistics clearly indicate the remarkable extension of Christian Democracy throughout the nation: In 1953, the Christian Democrats could garner only 2.9 per cent of the total votes for congressional candidates; in municipal elections ten years later, they had leaped to 23 per cent of the vote and stood as Chile's largest single political party.

Doctrine

Conservatives and Liberals

(In 1965, the Conservatives and Liberals recognized that little actually separated them and that they could represent their constitutents and programs more effectively by joining in common cause. As a consequence, they reconstituted themselves into one structure, the National party. However, for purposes of analysis and to build that analysis toward the 1964 and 1965 elections, the Conservatives and Liberals will be treated separately until the concluding chapter.)

Although the heyday of Chile's traditional parties of the right, the

[41] Guilisasti, *Partidos políticos chilenos*, pp. 199–202.

[42] Most of the remaining members of the PCSC returned to the Conservative party.

Conservatives and the Liberals, has long since passed, these century-old structures both show a political acumen and agility that periodically reinstates them in the highest political councils—as occurred between 1958 and 1964 when they served the presidency of Jorge Alessandri. The raging issues that heretofore made them enemies have long ago disappeared and their continuing electoral decline in the face of advancing centrist and leftist political groups has forced them to collaborate in order to aggregate the claims of the small, but still immensely powerful conservative oligarchy.[43] The last important issue to separate them was the Conservatives' confessional stance; this anachronistic position found the Conservatives trying to hold on to their ancient relationships with the Catholic church even while the high clergy moved to a far more progressive position. Typical of the old ways was the presentation of Monsignor Luis Arturo Pérez at the Conservative party's national convention in 1947 when he quoted another prelate who said that "the Church recognizes in the Conservative Party its better children, those who sacrifice themselves for the defense of its rights, those who confess in public their Christian faith without being ashamed of it, those who stand courageously before attacks of its adversaries, those who foot by foot defend the cause of God in the government of peoples. For this Party the Church has its affections of gratitude and its better blessings."[44] More recently, the head of the Conservative party, Senator Francisco Bulnes Sanfuentes, affirmed this proclerical posture when he acknowledged that the "philosophical foundation of the Conservative Party is Catholicism" and it has "as its supreme aspiration the *social Christian order*."[45] Moreover, natural law governs the universe; private property "has its foundation in natural rights and its inviolability is the principal basis of the welfare of the [whole society.]"[46]

[43] For a useful source on Conservative doctrine, see Marcial Sanfuentes Carrión, *El Partido Conservador*; and on Liberal doctrine, Raúl Marín Balmaceda, *Derechas o izquierdas*.

[44] Ignacio Arteaga Undurraga, comp., *Partido Conservador XIV—Convención Nacional—1947*, p. 129.

[45] Guilisasti T., *Partidos políticos chilenos*, p. 32.

[46] Arteaga U., *Partido Conservado XIV—Convención Nacional—1947*, p. 147 (errata).

The Conservative party also proclaims its dedication to democratic ideals, but it favors a strong infusion of authority in government. In the economic sphere, Conservatives admit that some governmental intervention in the economy may be necessary to give it direction and growth, but such actions must not intrude upon or in any way weaken free enterprise. Finally, the Conservative party ostensibly favors equity between management and workers, though its tactics generally seem to belie this stand.[47]

In fact, Conservative doctrine contains almost nothing that would keep the Liberals from joining in common cause. The Church issue no longer impels them to a serious separation, since the Conservatives oppose the clergy's entrance into politics and the one possible basis for dissension—conservatism's preference for religious teaching in the public schools—is not pushed strongly enough by the Conservatives to offend the Liberals. Like the Conservatives, the Liberals are completely devoted to the preservation and expansion of private property and they believe that capitalism "constitutes the only system which secures democracy, liberty and dignity for man."[48] Similarly, the Liberal party recognizes that occasional state direction of the economy may be desirable. Nevertheless, the Liberals point out that state intervention may be medicinal or it may prove toxic. It is their contention that by the 1960's the latter was the case and that an excessive dosage hindered economic recovery.[49]

Of the two rightist groups, the Liberals are somewhat more adaptive to political exigencies of the moment and from time to time search out coalitions with centrist movements. But when all is said and done, there appears to be a lack of dynamism in the Conservative-Liberal side of the political spectrum. Their doctrinal posture is a rather rigid

[47] See Francisco Bulnes S., "Principios de orden político," and Bernardo Larraín, "Principios de orden económico-social," in Guilisasti, *Partidos políticos chilenos*, pp. 32–70.

[48] Guilisasti, *Partidos políticos chilenos*, p. 110.

[49] Interviews with Ivan Urzua Ahumada, secretary general of the Liberal party, in Santiago, May 8, 1964, and Oscar Fuenzalida E., secretary of the Liberal party, in Santiago, April 13, 1964. Also, see Eduardo Moore, "Principios de orden político," and Pablo Aldunate, "Principios de orden económico-social" in Guilisasti, *Partidos políticos chilenos*, pp. 87–127.

one, ordinarily unyielding to contemporary political currents,[50] though their tactics have led them to make strategic arrangements with centrist groups in order to survive. It probably is symptomatic of the Right that, in a brief official history of the Liberal party published in 1963, great attention was given to the rise of the party and to the unfolding of its doctrine up to the Constitution of 1925, whereas the years since are passed off with the simple statement that many "events have occurred since 1925."[51]

Radicals

The Radical party is the third major political structure to evolve out of the political struggle of the last century. However, its membership clings to a far broader range of beliefs than do the Conservatives and Liberals and largely fall into a more progressive, centrist position.[52]

The main tenets attributed to Chilean radicalism are secularism, defense of liberties, government based upon political parties, concern for public education, a civil and juridic sense, equality of woman with man, defense of the parliamentary regime, concern for the working classes and the desire for an eventual classless society, evolutionary methodology, rationalism, and tolerance.[53] Unfortunately for the Radicals, the "constants" of their doctrine proved difficult to spell out and the more progressive features deteriorated during the fourteen years (from 1938 to 1952) when they held the presidency. Then they seemed more devoted to securing government jobs for themselves—at the time being widely referred to as an "employment agency"—than to implementing the reforms they earlier had promised.[54]

[50] However, both parties have made some gestures to change. Thus in the late 1950's, the Conservatives came out in favor of a small amount of agrarian reform and the Liberals showed some sympathy for labor reform (Gil, *Political System of Chile*, pp. 247, 254).

[51] José Miguel Prado Valdés, *Reseña histórica del Partido Liberal*, p. 29.

[52] A summary of left-wing Radical views can be found in *El Siglo* (Santiago), January 26, 1964.

[53] Interview with Sergio Cifuentes, pro-secretary general of the Radical party, in Santiago, May 11, 1964. Also, see Marcial Mora, "Principios de orden político," and Humberto Enríquez, "Principios de orden económico-social," in Guilisasti, *Partidos políticos chilenos*, pp. 147–196.

[54] Donald W. Bray, "Chile: The Dark Side of Stability," *Studies on the Left* 4, no. 4 (Fall 1964): 85–96.

As Chile's single pragmatic, bargaining party, the Radicals have been more peculiarly prone to a mixture of strengths and shortcomings than any of the other major parties have known. For example, the fluidity and even ambiguity of their programs furnished the Radicals with a doctrinal umbrella large enough to shelter an amazingly heterogeneous following. They ran the gamut from the provincial well to do, who originally founded the party in order to combat the Santiago-dominated Liberal party, to the urban middle sectors, who increased rapidly in numbers as a result of urbanization and industrialization and practically grew up with the Radical party, to the later addition of laborers attracted by the reformist features of radicalism in those years. On the other hand, the very success the party enjoyed in admitting such a variety of societal elements frustrated its efforts to locate itself doctrinally. As a consequence, it frequently gave the impression of excessive opportunism and ambivalence. This image was reinforced by what seemed to be chronic irresponsibility; repeatedly it agreed to enter a coalition government, only to withdraw just prior to the next election in order to enjoy freedom to campaign and to attack the incumbent regime.

By the same token, its wide membership base and programmatic vagueness enabled the Radicals to move left in a Popular Front coalition with the Marxist parties or to the right in a Democratic Front with the conservative parties when special conditions warranted such associations. The efficacy of these maneuvers was obvious in an era when the voting population was rather limited and large segments of the lower economic strata remained politically quiescent; but the situation started to change suddenly in the late 1950's as an ineffectual government and the activist efforts of revolutionary and more highly committed reformist parties aroused previously nonpolitical urban and rural poor to demand genuine structural alterations of the political, social, and economic order. And not only did these newly politically activated elements gravitate toward more liberal parties, but countless university students, trade unionists, and others long affiliated with the Radicals now slipped from their grasp. Certainly the Radicals could not be counted out as a political force in Chile, though undoubtedly the coherent and extensive programs of the more ideologically inclined parties on the left attracted far greater attention among the lower economic strata in the mid-1960's.

Christian Democrats

In addition to a strong organizational sense, a dynamic leadership, and their appearance on the Chilean political scene at a propitious time, the Christian Democrats owe much of their success to the enunciation of a broad and reformist ideology, the main tenets of which have been set out by Eduardo Frei in a host of books and articles.[55] Throughout his writings, Frei has stressed six primary concepts of Christian Democracy; they are Christianity, democracy, humanism, revolution, nationalism, and communitarianism.[56]

The Christian ingredient led some of the PDC's enemies to impute that it was both a clerical and a confessional party. Frei countered that "Christian Democracy is neither a Catholic or confessional party which demands that its militants be believers and which by act and right pretends to assume the representation of the Church or of Catholicism. . . . It is possible that the name Christian Democracy induces quibbling. It is not a question of an exclusive democracy, only for Christians; not even of a democracy under the control of Christians."[57] Instead, the PDC welcomes to its ranks Protestants as well as Catholics, Jews as well as nonbelievers. This admission policy has been built upon the views of the party's early leaders, the path followed by counterpart groups in Europe, as well as upon the very practical consideration that there are many non-Catholic minorities in Chile and that, even among the so-called Catholic majority, perhaps as high as two-thirds are uninterested in the Church, only nominally Catholic, or even athe-

[55] Among his book titles are *Chile desconocido*, *La política y el espíritu*, *Pensamiento y acción*, *Sentido y forma de una política*, *La verdad tiene su hora*. Also, see Eduardo Frei, "Principios de orden político" and Juan de Dios Carmona, "Principios de orden económico-social" in Guilisasti, *Partidos políticos chilenos*, pp. 213–251.

[56] Much of the following material is based upon interviews with Eduardo Frei, in Santiago, May 18, 1964, and with José de Gregorio, secretary general of the Christian Democratic party, in Santiago, May 12, 1964. Also, for an interesting explanation of the stages through which Christian Democratic ideology developed, see Gil, *Political System of Chile*, pp. 267–268.

[57] In Guilisasti, *Partidos políticos chilenos*, p. 219.

istic.[58] Thus, just as the Frapistas quiet down their anticlericalism in order not to ruffle the feathers of the believers, the Christian Democrats have had to fight a clerical tag or run the danger of scaring off people who are suspicious or resentful of church-oriented groups in politics.

Besides extolling a Christian value system, the PDC believes that democratic goals must finally be fulfilled rather than just vaguely pursued as has been the case to date. For too long a paternalistic type of democracy has been the norm in all of Latin America; it is time that Lincoln's definition of democracy as "government of the people, by the people, for the people" take hold: "Government must no longer be imposed on the people. It is now a matter of helping a new state to be born from innermost reaches through a human process in which the people will feel that they are generating power and creating wealth, and sharing in their creation and distribution. Only then can restrictive and paternalistic democracy be replaced by a democracy that is truly respectful of human values."[59] Furthermore, authentic democracy will not come about simply by writing a new constitution or by instituting an alternative democratic governmental form; real democracy is only possible when certain specific types of statutes are enacted and a selective bank of laws currently on the books are enforced with an end to democratizing power and making certain that government represents the authentic will of the people. At one level this necessitates widening the electoral base, for democracy "not only must formally guarantee rights, but it has to structure them in a form so as to permit all the citizens the plain exercise of them."[60] This and other strengthenings of the law will conduce to a true sociopolitical pluralism, the key to democracy, which is "based upon the principle of equality of rights for all citizens and social groups."[61]

Democracy also connotes humanism, which recognizes and emphasizes the basic dignity and worth of man himself. Accordingly, the

[58] Based on a study carried out by the Institute of Sociology of the University of Chile (Halperin, *Nationalism and Communism in Chile*, p. 202).

[59] Eduardo Frei, "Paternalism, Pluralism, and Christian Democratic Reform Movements in Latin America," in *Religion, Revolution, and Reform*, ed. William V. D'Antonio and Fredrick B. Pike, pp. 38–39.

[60] In Guilisasti, *Partidos políticos chilenos*, p. 224.

[61] *Ibid.*

educational system must be infused with humanistic teaching, not just technical teaching, in order for Chile to achieve and "maintain a level and a conscience as a nation."[62]

In searching out the correct path to a humanistic and pluralistic democracy, Frei experienced a minor semantic dilemma. Early in his efforts to define a conceptual framework for Christian Democracy, he observed that there existed two obvious approaches to combating the traditional paternalism found throughout Latin America. They were revolution and reform. Revolution sought to destroy the old regime in a sudden, violent, and total manner. In the Marxist scheme this would simply substitute state capitalism for private capitalism, bureaucrats for private holders of capital, supermonopolies of the state for private capitalist monopolies. Frei rejected both economic systems and implicitly opted for a reformist methodology that would peacefully restructure society.[63] By the 1960's, the exigencies of campaign politics demanded a more dynamic terminological response to the Marxists' nomenclature that made no bones about offering "revolution" as their alternative to the existing system. Consequently, the Christian Democrats came up with the more attractive definition of their aims to be "revolution in freedom," thus offering everything FRAP suggested in changing economic and social processes and relationships, while preserving democracy. Eduardo Frei explained the PDC's stand persuasively:

> In Latin America there is need for a true revolution. Indeed, it is already in ferment, but the revolution must take place in freedom and under the control of a democratic movement. Old and inefficient social organizations that paralyze the economic system must be replaced, but only through institutional and administrative reforms that will permit authentic participation of the people in civic life. Only through reforms in land tenure, tax, educational, and other systems can all obstacles be removed. Only through development of the people's responsibility in municipal government, unions, and cooperatives, and through a policy for the protection and promotion of the family will the ground be laid for true democracy. Only

[62] *Ibid.*, p. 221.

[63] See Frei's lecture, "Hacia una economía humana," in *Pensamiento y acción*, pp. 27–49.

through accelerated economic development can the standards of living be increased rapidly. All of these reforms simultaneously require a social policy for a more equitable distribution of income.

To such ends, democratic planning will be necessary. We have come to a point where it is absolutely necessary to make organized use of all the resources of the nation, and most especially of the human factor. The effort is of such scope and urgency that goals and means must be established; dispersion is no longer tolerable. This requires the cooperation of management, organized labor, the entire educational apparatus, the people in general. And it requires that outside and domestic resources be made adequate.[64]

The tactical efficacy of promising revolutionary solutions to Chile's problems, though within the context of political democracy, proved overwhelming in the 1964 and 1965 elections. But another doctrinal plank that aided in those victories involved a dialogue with the Frapistas over nationalism. Much of FRAP's ideological strength hinged on its insistence that the nation's great natural resources, largely "looted" by foreigners, be nationalized and thus entirely accrue to the benefit of the Chilean people. The Christian Democrats preferred a more moderate position—to "Chileanize" the country's resources. This meant that the Chilean government should purchase controlling interests in several major enterprises held by foreigners, rather than pushing all foreign capital from the nation because of expropriation.

In the aggregate, the foreign-owned enterprises under contention were the holdings of United States firms. Frei had recognized this fact in a speech he presented to the Chilean Senate in 1954 when he observed that three strains of nationalism seemed to predominate in the nation's politics.[65] One of these he called the nationalism of surrender (*entreguismo*), which views everything the United States does as good and which values all U.S. investments as a great favor to Chile. He classified a second variety as the nationalism of strategic hatred (*odio estratégico*) against the United States; Frei believed that this attitude only "paralyzes the possibilities of economic develop-

[64] In D'Antonio and Pike, eds., *Religion, Revolution, and Reform*, p. 38.
[65] Frei, "Política americana," in *Pensamiento y acción*, pp. 226–231.

ment."[66] Rejecting both of these nationalist forms, Christian Democracy considered a third approach preferable, what he labeled the nationalism of constructive cooperation (*cooperación constructiva*). This brand of nationalism recognizes the United States as a wealthy and highly democratic society; but it is "a democracy made, in part, at the expense of a world-wide economic imbalance."[67] Then he issued a suggestion as to the role the United States could play within the context of constructive cooperation:

> If the United States would understand that it cannot have a continent at its back, where mistrust and hatred are increasing; that it is not enough for it to gain votes in conferences and formal agreements with governments, agreements which many times are imposed on people and which are not the result of their consent; if the United States would understand that the better friends of American cooperation are those who defend the legitimate interests of those nations; if the United States would understand that those who speak a language of frankness are much more capable tomorrow of constructing a policy of solidarity, then it would be taking an effective step toward the solidarity of America.[68]

In short, the nationalism of constructive cooperation rejects the nationalism of submissiveness and hatred toward other international powers; rather it seeks the development and dignity of the Chilean nation by means of cooperative endeavors on a plane of equality with other states.

What, though, will be the eventual nature of Chilean society in the Christian Democratic order? It is to be a communitarian one and a new phase in the development of civilization.[69] All men who work in the same enterprise will be organized together so that instead of capital and labor being separated as they now are, they will be gathered as

[66] *Ibid.*, p. 228.

[67] *Ibid.*

[68] *Ibid.*, pp. 228–229.

[69] Some observers of Christian Democracy claim that there is a shadow of fascism in communitarianism. This contention is based mostly upon Frei's early work, *Chile desconocido*, especially his summary on pp. 162–164. Frei vigorously denied any fascist meaning in conversation with this author. Also, the fascist implication is rejected by Halperin in *Nationalism and Communism in Chile*, pp. 182–189.

one "in the same hands."[70] Old-fashioned individualism is not the answer, for paradoxically it destroys the individual's worth and the "free play of individual appetites has never succeeded in producing the common good."[71] Contained in the concept of communitarianism is belief in the inevitability of its eventual attainment, though man will enjoy it sooner by working to bring it about. Tactically, this pursuit of the communitarian ideal includes fostering trade unionism among agricultural workers and expanding and strengthening urban labor groups. Necessarily, this will lead to some conflict at first with managerial groups. However, once the organized workers have forced the upper classes to adjust to working-class needs, all will live in a more just and equitable society:

> In Latin America we must today shoulder the responsibility of entering a new phase. The people wish to break with the old paternalism and ancient privileges, but do not wish to be led into dictatorships of any kind. They wish to progress and create new forms of social life. Latin Americans will not copy formulas that may have been suited to others but that are of no avail to them. I dream of a synthesis of justice and freedom in an economy that is based entirely on man's ability, not on inherited factors of money, class, or race. In Latin America it is man that must be made great.[72]

Communists and Socialists

The Christian Democrats' most serious contenders for political power in the electoral contests of 1964 and 1965 campaigned together as the Popular Action Front (or FRAP), a coalition of Communists and Socialists plus an almost moribund group of hangers-on, the Partido Democrático Nacional (or PADENA). The two large partners in the coalition, while built on a number of similar ideological pillars, basically disagree on several doctrinal points.

Although avowedly Marxist,[73] the Socialists reject any utopian label,

[70] In Guilisasti, *Partidos políticos chilenos*, p. 214.

[71] *Ibid.*, p. 218.

[72] In D'Antonio and Pike, *Religion, Revolution, and Reform*, pp. 39–40.

[73] Much of this section is based upon an interview with Salvador Allende, in Santiago, May 12, 1964. Also, see Salvador Allende, "Principios de orden

claiming instead to provide a well-defined "answer to the vital need for collective progress."[74] Socialism is anticapitalistic, anti-imperialist, and antifascist. It considers Marxism to be in constant change and growth rather than static and does not accept the dogmas of Marxism in their entirety—"for Socialism, Marxist theory has value only as a method for foreseeing collective development, or as an auxiliary set of tools for advancing its objectives."[75] Nevertheless, the Socialists adhere rather closely to the broad outline of Marxist thought, contending that the existing capitalist system divides society into two antagonistic classes, the powerful exploiters and the much larger element of the exploited who toil at subsistence wage levels. Once the upper class is destroyed and a classless society is achieved, the state will lose its oppressive qualities and instead will act to direct, harmonize, and protect society. This necessitates the alteration of private property into collective ownership for the benefit of all. Only in this way can real individual freedom be assured. The restructuring of society, with its destruction of the dominant and unprogressive bourgeois class, requires a revolution based upon working-class elements—industrial laborers, miners, peasants, artisans, white-collar groups, and intellectuals. Reform is "useless for combatting the deep contradictions, injustices, and privileges" that the capitalists have wrought in "an undeveloped, semifeudal and semicolonial country."[76] Ultimately, the Chilean Socialists seek the formation of a continental Federation of Socialist Republics, which will serve as the first step on the road to a world-wide Confederation of Socialist Republics.

For their part, the Communists closely follow the Marxist-Leninist line and generally sound much like their Socialist counterparts in Chile.[77] They accept dialectical materialism with its class struggle and

político," and Raúl Ampuero, "Principios de orden económico-social," in Guilisasti, *Partidos políticos chilenos*, pp. 271–306. The Socialists' monthly publication, *Arauco*, is a rich source of ideological discussion.

[74] In Guilisasti, *Partidos políticos chilenos*, p. 298.

[75] Julio C. Jobet, "Teoría y programa del Partido Socialista de Chile," *Arauco* 3, no. 27 (April 1962): 15–16.

[76] *Ibid.*, p. 17.

[77] See Luis Corvalán, "Principios de orden político," and José Cademartori, "Principios de orden económico-social," in Guilisasti, *Partidos políticos chi-*

the inevitable workers' revolution; they are anti-imperialist, antifeudal, and antimonopolist. As such, they champion liquidating the holdings of foreign imperialists, along with those of the domestic monopolists and latifundists; they also wish to bring under state ownership the nation's basic resources (e.g., copper, iron, and nitrates), electrical energy, the metallurgy industry, banking, the major part of distributive commerce, and the large landholdings. Contrary to what their enemies say of them, the Communists claim to favor a pluralistic society, with a government of several parties that represent the vast majority of the population:

Consequently, we do not conceive of one-party government, but of the widest and most united popular bloc. Moreover, we want the people to be represented in all organs of power and the workers to have real access to the public institutions, to the administration of the State and of its enterprises. Not only do we fight for a government *for* the people. We make our formula as Abraham Lincoln defined his concept of democracy: *that of a government* OF THE *people,* BY *the people and* FOR *the people.*

We are partisans of universal, direct and secret suffrage for literate and illiterate, civilian and military men and women over 18 years of age.

We announce ourselves for a State of Law with Executive, Legislative, and Judicial Powers.

We prefer a unicameral Parliament, which would count among its powers and essential features that of selecting the President of the Republic, Ministers of State and members of the higher organisms in charge of administering justice.

We are for freedom of conscience, of religion, of speech, of press, of assembly and association, for inviolability of person and domicile; for the right of the voters to revoke the mandate of the elected; for the right to work, to rest, to education and culture; for the social, economic and juridic equality of women.

All of this requires the dictation of a new Political Constitution, new Codes, new laws, new institutions or a profound transformation of those that exist. Basically, these regulations serve the ruling and minority classes. On the people's achieving power, they will create or transform institutional

lenos, pp. 323–356. The monthly, *Nuestra Epoca*, and the bimonthly, *Principios*, are very useful Communist publications for ideological matters.

functions so that all the apparatus of the State will be at the service of the majority and of the revolutionary objectives.[78]

These comments bring into focus one of the Communists' paramount tactics, to offer a democratic image to the Chilean voter and, consequently, to verify their right to contend for power in the Chilean democratic context.

Furthermore, the Communist party repeatedly stresses its dedication to the *vía pacífica*, or peaceful road, to the Socialist revolution. In 1872, Marx specified that revolution could be achieved in certain countries by peaceful methods; Lenin repeated this point following the overthrow of the Czar in February, 1917; and the peaceful way was resurrected at the Twentieth Congress of the Communist Party of the Soviet Union. The head of the Chilean Communist party, Luis Corvalán, writing in the party's ideological journal, *Nuestra Epoca*, observed that Chile is one of those nations of the world most apt to achieve a socialist revolution peacefully because of the confluence of a number of special conditions: the presence of a strong coalition of anti-imperialist and antifeudal political parties in FRAP, a political-electoral system that for all its limitations will permit a sufficiently well-organized and active popular majority to come to power, a preference among the vast majority of the population for nonviolent methods, and a ground swell of popular reaction and activism against the antidemocratic reactionaries.[79]

Finally, the Communists portray themselves as the most nationalist of Chilean political parties because the Communist party "defends with patriotism the riches of the country and national sovereignty" as well as "the interests of the working classes."[80] In brief, Chilean communism appeals to the voter on the basis of a democratic, humanistic, and nationalistic doctrine that utilizes a nonviolent methodology.

The Frapist coalition functioned well in the early 1960's. Both of the Marxist parties were of approximately equal strength and each

[78] In Guilisasti, *Partidos políticos chilenos*, pp. 331–332.

[79] "La vía pacífica es una forma de la revolución," *Nuestra Epoca* 3, no. 12 (December 1963): 3–4.

[80] José González, *Curso elemental sobre el partido*, p. 15.

party was fairly safe from membership raids or invasions by the other. Nonetheless, no love was lost between leaders of the two parties and in nonparty structures, especially the trade unions, they often engaged in power squabbles. Periodically, their differences erupted into public notice; then the pattern of their disagreements became especially manifest. By and large, the Socialists railed against the parliamentary system as merely an instrumentality of the oligarchy, whereas the Communists found they could operate quite comfortably within the parliamentary process. Also, the Socialists claimed to be more nationalistic than the Communists, since, in contrast to Communist ties with Moscow, they remained independent of outside dictation. (This helped to explain the presence on the Socialists' left of an influential pro-Peking element as well as the Socialists' tendency to sympathetically attach themselves to various non-Soviet Communist movements, while the Communists stood shoulder to shoulder with the Soviet Union.)

Early in 1962, an ideological debate broke out between prominent officials of the two parties.[81] What started as an open discussion between Orlando Millas, a Communist deputy and member of the Politburo, and Raúl Ampuero, senator and secretary general of the Socialist party, before long was a controversy in which others became embroiled. Some of the wrangling dealt with practical programs (e.g., the Socialists' repudiation of Communist urban reform programs, which in part aimed at converting renters into owners of their domiciles); more serious, however, were their differences of opinion as to the role of international Marxism. Raúl Ampuero summed up his party's preference for national solutions for national problems:

I would say in synthesis that the Socialist Party does not believe in a single world-wide direction of the revolutionary movement. We believe that each country and each people must choose their own roads, suitable to their own conditions, in order to build socialism. Consequently, we refuse to accept either a single ideological and political command or a determined national hegemony over the rest of the planet. In that regard, we have always applauded with enthusiasm the attitude of the Yugoslav Govern-

[81] The debate was reported extensively in the Marxist press. The bulk of the argument appeared in Central Committee of the Partido Socialista, eds., *La polémica socialista-comunista.*

ment and people when they defended their right to build socialism in the Yugoslav manner. Because of this we believe today that the repetition of a similar attitude of the USSR regarding Albania, although we are not in absolute agreement with the Albanians, implies a rupture of the meaning of the principle of self-determination of peoples.[82]

Orlando Millas responded that this accusation of "Russian hegemony" was an old imperialist propaganda trick to cloud the laws of social processes and he deemed it incredible for a Socialist senator to echo that view. After all, Yugoslavian revisionism was based upon its own anti-Soviet attitudes and certainly no one could blame the Soviet Union for violating self-determination as far as Albania was concerned.

At another point, Senator Ampuero repudiated military blocs, such as that which the Soviet Union had imposed upon its partners in the Warsaw Pact, and the explosion of atomic bombs as warlike acts. He contended that such actions created a military conflict in the world at a time when each nation had the seeds within itself for its own economic transformation. Ampuero admitted that the military orientation of the Soviet bloc was obviously being influenced by the similar position of the United States and its allies; but if that situation could be neutralized, it would permit a long period of world peace in which popular movements could achieve their goals.[83]

Orlando Millas objected to this line of thought with the observation that once again Ampuero was simply mouthing imperialist propaganda emanating from the press services of UPI and AP and he expressed his incredulity at Ampuero's apparent indignation over the Socialist nations' endeavors to defend themselves. Speaking for the Politburo of the Chilean Communist party, Luis Corvalán made this point abundantly clear when he pointed out that the Defense Treaty of the Warsaw Pact nations did not come about until 1955 after "North American imperialism had created a whole series of pacts and bases around the socialist countries, after its aggression against the Socialist State of North Korea, [and] after it had cleared the way for the remilitarization of Western Germany."[84]

[82] *Ibid.*, pp. 6–7.
[83] *Ibid.*, pp. 7–8.
[84] *Ibid.*, pp. 22–23.

Finally, Ampuero cited disagreement over the function of Marxist theory itself as a major ideological stumbling block dividing the Socialists from the Communists:

And, finally, I would say that there also is a problem of interpretation in the ideological order. For us Marxism, to which we feel ourselves intellectually tied, is above all a method of interpretation of reality. It does not constitute a dogma; we do not construct a liturgy around it. We consider it to be a scientific method for better recognizing what is happening in the heart of our society and for choosing the roads which will permit us to transform it. Facing that, the Communists traditionally have had an attitude that we consider quite dogmatic and sectarian in the sense that they suppose that Marxism and the same historical conclusions that its ideologues have brought forth in other epochs are irrefutable, definitive and more or less eternal. It is because of that that we also have in our workings a freedom of criticism and a play of ideas much livelier and more dynamic than that which occurs in the Communist Party.[85]

Deputy Millas objected strenuously to this whole line of thought:

Does not Senator Ampuero suspect that sectarianism, dogmatism and prejudice rather belong to those who cannot or do not want to be convinced of the vigor of creative Marxism and of scientific Communism? Regarding his reprimands of the internal life of the Communist Party, they proved, to say the least, inopportune, when the nation has been able to observe its expression of revolutionary and proletarian democracy in the internal discussion process which culminated in the XIIth National Congress.

The Socialist Senator outlines a definition of his and of his party as not Marxists-Leninists in that they only feel "intellectually tied to Marxism," though they consider that their conclusions are not "irrefutable, definitive and more or less eternal." For those who are acquainted with Marxism and therefore understand the dialectic connection between the relative and the absolute, especially regarding theory of knowledge and scientific truth, they must be surprised at the invocations of "liturgy" and "dogma" in a tone that would seem to compare them to some type of eclecticism. Finally, it is certain that no people in the world has advanced toward socialism with such ideological standards. A few days ago a Latin American Marxist-Leninist, Fidel Castro, wisely and profoundly condemned these attitudes.

[85] *Ibid.*, pp. 8–9.

We Communists feel fine in his company. We understand perfectly that many of our allies have other thoughts and we respect them. We are not accustomed to presenting these matters in such an intransigent tone as Senator Ampuero, but with the calm firmness of those who understand that history each time proves us more right.[86]

These doctrinal thrusts and parries between the two Marxist parties assumed graver proportions following the 1965 congressional elections, when the direction and even the survival of FRAP came into question. Although it remains a moot issue as to whether the Socialists' or the Communists' methodology holds more applicability for Chile, the Socialists' claim to greater flexibility in the operative sphere may be somewhat specious. At least that has been the impression of Lautaro Ojeda Herrera, secretary general of PADENA, the small non-Marxian socialist group that is a minor partner in FRAP. Basing his evaluation upon working relationships with Marxists that go back to 1920, Ojeda had come to the conclusion that the Communists are "flexible, practical people who know their own limitations; they live a kind of religion or mysticism of their own and possess great discipline. Their greatest shortcoming is their international connections and obligations which frequently contain them too much and at times make them act or be too conservative."[87] Admitting that the Socialists are not handicapped by the kind of international obligations for which they criticize the Communists, Ojeda nevertheless asserted that the Socialists in fact "are much more inflexible and rigid" than the Communists.[88]

Membership and Organization

The several political parties' organizational arrangements possess certain resemblances to each other in that they all center their national organization in Santiago, they all have a pervasive territorial dispersement (while concentrating their structural bases in the larger urban areas), and they all claim widespread involvement in party decisions from local through regional to national machinery. In fact, of course,

[86] *Ibid.*, p. 9.
[87] Interviews with Lautaro Ojeda Herrera, secretary general of PADENA, in Santiago, April 29, May 4, and May 5, 1964.
[88] *Ibid.*

the party structures do differ substantially in spirit and procedure if not so considerably in form. Nevertheless, the apparent deep commitment of the great majority of Chileans to democratic processes demands that all the parties at least give considerable attention to maintaining the appearance of internal democracy.

Although much has been written in Chile about the weakness of local governments—some cities even going so far as to brand them meaningless—the parties find the boundaries of some of these local and regional administrative divisions convenient for defining organizational strata. The major political division of regional government is the province, of which there are twenty-five.[89] Within the provinces are eighty-seven departments, which in turn contain subdelegations; below the subdelegations are even smaller units, the districts. None of the officials heading up these local governmental units is elected to his post; instead there is a chain of command that runs directly down from the President of the republic. Administratively, however, Chile's provinces are also subdivided into communes; the governance of one commune or of several communes grouped together is within the province of a municipality—made up of a mayor and a number of councilmen. These municipal officials are the only officers below the national government who are selected in popular elections. All the political parties utilize the communal area and, in some cases party subdivisions thereof, as the principal base level of organization. The regional stratum follows departmental or provincial boundaries.

Conservatives and Liberals

In large measure, the Conservative and Liberal parties can be equated to the nation's economic elite. The Conservatives predominately draw from the rural aristocracy, while including some well-to-do elements in the cities; Liberals mostly recruit membership from among urban businessmen and industrialists, though they also attract a small number of the rural upper class. Of the two, liberalism tends to spill over somewhat more measurably into middle-class and even into a few working-class homes. And although both parties occasionally co-opt particularly

[89] A brief description of local government can be found in Guillermo Gandarillas M., *Curso de educación cívica*, pp. 135–147.

promising middle-sector adherents into the highest party councils, it is the economic oligarchy that overwhelmingly officers and operates party organization.

Besides their slight differences in membership bases, the Conservatives and Liberals also differ somewhat in their internal operation. That is to say that the Conservatives place great store in the party office and they grant great respect and homage to the one who holds high party position. Undoubtedly, this coincides with their penchant for authority. Somewhat in contrast, the Liberal hierarchy is composed of several influential family groupings and partisan factions who occasionally act as divisive influences. Intraparty struggles, consequently, typify Liberal decision-making processes far more than is the case with the Conservatives and personal influence and position count for more than party position.[90]

The two conservative parties' structures reflect their oligarchical nature in that they are the only political groupings lacking subcommunal organization.[91] This derives from political forms in the past when suffrage restrictions and electoral coercion negated the need for smaller units; party membership was small and local party control resided with a few leaders. (In contrast, with the democratizing of the electoral process during the twentieth century, other political parties sought to attract popular bases and required smaller units that would be closer to their clientele.)

Consequently, both the Conservatives and Liberals still recruit members into their communal assemblies. New members must file requests for admission with the assembly directorate, a small governing body of between five and eleven officials in the Conservative party and numbering a half-dozen in the Liberal party; the directorate in turn forwards membership lists to national headquarters. Applicants must swear their acceptance of party program and bylaws and, in the case of Conservatives, adherence to the Roman Catholic faith.

Out of a total of 263,000 votes, which the Liberals gained in the 1963 municipal elections, perhaps 10 per cent constituted party mili-

[90] Gil, *Political System of Chile*, pp. 254–256.

[91] See Partido Conservador, *Estatutos del Partido Conservador*, and Partido Liberal, *Estatuto orgánico del Partido Liberal.*

tants. Of these, a large proportion were small merchants. The percentage of members in the Conservative party relative to its 227,000 votes in 1963 probably fell well below 10 per cent of the total because many Conservatives were landowners while a great bulk of their votes traditionally came from farm workers who voted according to the dictates of their employers but who were not enrolled on party membership lists.[92]

In addition to recruiting, the local organs carry out such other customary functions as fund raising, propagandizing, and preparing for elections. With respect to elections, the local party units perform a participatory role in selecting candidates. The assemblies directly nominate councilmanic candidates; they indirectly participate in nominating deputies and senators to the national Congress by means of delegates to regional deliberative bodies—at the departmental level for deputies and at the provincial level for senators. For these purposes, the Conservatives maintain departmental *directorios* and provincial *consejos*; the Liberals rely upon *consejos agrupacionales* at the departmental and provincial levels.

Both parties function nationally through their conventions, directorates, and executive councils as well as through several specialized ancillary organs.[93] The conventions are large assemblages of party militants drawn from national, regional, and local organizations; they also agglomerate certain governmental officials and others tied to the party. The Conservatives are supposed to assemble every four years and the Liberals every five years. According to the bylaws, the principal business of the convention is to enunciate general policy and to revise rules and regulations. Actually, beyond issuing pronouncements, mostly on general issues, and serving as fraternal get-togethers, conventions rarely act as truly deliberative bodies. As will be seen, decisions regarding such major matters as who will lead the party and whom the party will support as its presidential candidate in the national elections are in the domain of other party agencies.

[92] Interviews with Ivan Urzua A. and Oscar Fuenzalida E.

[93] These include youth, labor, feminine, municipal, electoral, and other departments.

In fact, the hierarchical nature of the two rightist parties allocates increasing decision-making authority the higher one goes up the organizational ladder. At the top is the small and powerful Governing Board (Mesa Directiva) of the Executive Council (Junta Ejecutiva). The Liberals' *mesa* is made up of the party president, two vice-presidents, the secretary general, and a treasurer; the Conservatives include nine members on their *mesa* in addition to the president and two vice-presidents. In each case, the president holds immense power as the main voice and guiding force of the party.

Periodically, in order to secure a more representative party mandate for its policies or in a critical situation when it no longer commands a clear control over party structures, the Mesa Directiva will turn to the larger Junta Ejecutiva for support or direction. The Conservative *junta*, totaling twenty-three members, is composed of the *mesa*, five congressmen, the president of the youth movement, the head of the women's section, three members who represent occupational groups, and the treasurer. The Liberal *junta* is even more sizable; basically it is constituted like its Conservative counterpart, but it pulls in more congressmen, two councilmanic representatives, and a large, but varying, number of other regional and national leaders. Since most members of the *junta* reside in Santiago, it is a relatively easy matter to convoke a meeting of this body. Moreover, because it reflects a wide cross section of national and regional views, most issues can be settled at this point.

The Directorate (Directorio General) is scheduled to meet annually. However, if party matters dictate it, it may be called into special session. The party's maximum authority for selecting party officers and for establishing on-going policy directives, the Directorio General brings together national, regional, and local leaders. The Conservative directorate numbers five hundred and the Liberals' more than twice as many.

Discliplinary questions customarily originate with an assembly or other party organ that brings charges against an individual. These in turn are announced by the Junta Ejecutiva, which then refers the question to a special agency, the Supreme Tribunal (Tribunal Supremo).

The Supreme Tribunal is an ad hoc body of five former high-ranking party leaders whose names have been selected by lot; its deliberations are secret. In point of fact, expulsion occurs very rarely. For example, in the ten years prior to 1964, the Liberals expelled only four members.[94] Invariably, expulsions result from a member's unwillingness to go along with electoral arrangements the party has agreed to or from his refusal to support the party's presidential nominee. But despite the rarity of expulsions, they often are of a sensational nature, since they almost always come during a campaign and manifest cleavages in party leadership.

A better picture of the role of each of these party structures can be obtained by tracing several critical events the two parties faced during the hectic campaign for the presidency in 1963-1964. At that time the Conservatives and the Liberals were participating in an electoral coalition with the Radicals known as the Democratic Front (Frente Democrático). The front's standard-bearer, Senator Julio Durán, had been one of the six whose names the Radicals' National Assembly had proposed to their Conservative and Liberal partners for consideration. Discussions among the Conservative and Liberal leaders concluded with a preference for Durán; in May and June, 1963, the Conservative and Liberal directorates formally approved the selection. Nevertheless, aggressive elements in the hierarchies of both parties considered the choice unacceptable. In October, 1963, a prominent Liberal congressman, Enrique Edwards, canceled his party membership in the misguided belief that he would be able to muster support for changing the Chilean Constitution to permit incumbent President Jorge Alessandri to seek immediate reelection. Hugo Gálvez, ex-minister of labor, lauded Edwards' views, but disagreed with his resignation from the party. Gálvez' statement constituted a serious breach in the professed unanimity of Liberal support for Durán and he was peremptorily expelled from the Liberal camp by the Junta Ejecutiva on the request of the Mesa Directiva. Gálvez objected vigorously that the *junta* could only propose expulsion under the bylaws and that the definitive

94 Interview with Ivan Urzua A.

act necessitated a full hearing before the party's Supreme Tribunal.[95] Legally, Gálvez was quite right.[96] The only action the *junta* was permitted to take by itself was "to admonish or to suspend" a member, not to expel him. Liberal party President Sergio Sepúlveda countered that the Directorio General's agreement to support the Durán candidacy was amplified by an order from the Junta Ejecutiva for all militants to fall in line, and let it go at that.

The high-handed manner in which the Sepúlveda cabal dealt with dissidence evoked charges of dictatorial methods, which gave Conservative leaders second thoughts about utilizing the same techniques to resolve a similar annoyance. Senator Francisco Bulnes, the Conservatives' president, chose instead to demonstrate the widest possible backing for his stand by turning to the same Directorio General that had originally opted for Durán. Bulnes and the rest of the Mesa Directiva resigned their posts requesting an overwhelming and unqualified endorsement from the Directorate or the replacement of the entire Mesa Directiva. As it turned out, most of those favoring Alessandri's reelection were in Conservative Youth and held few seats on the Directorio General. As a consequence, the Mesa Directiva received a solid 85 per cent majority approval. Immediately thereafter, Bulnes ordered the reorganization of Conservative Youth and, thus, a threat to the entrenched leadership was headed off.[97]

Another leadership crisis broke out in March, 1964. Then, a great deal was riding for Durán and the other two front-running presidential candidates (i.e., the Christian Democrats' Eduardo Frei and FRAP's Salvador Allende) on the outcome of a by-election in Curicó to fill a vacancy from that district in the Chamber of Deputies. In many ways it gave the appearance of a trial run for the presidential election. All of the political parties poured tremendous quantities of money and effort into ensuring a good showing and Durán even went

[95] The press gave considerable attention to these events. See especially *El Mercurio* (Santiago), October 17, 19, and 27, 1963.

[96] Partido Liberal, *Programa y estatuto orgánico del Partido Liberal*, Articles 164, 165.

[97] See *South Pacific Mail* (Santiago), November, 1963.

so far as to declare his intention to withdraw from the race if the Democratic Front's candidate for deputy failed to win. The outcome was disastrous for the Duranistas and Durán did, in fact, pull out of the campaign (though later the Radicals forced him back in). At this juncture, the Democratic Front fell apart and the Conservative and Liberal *mesas* resigned under a cloud of opprobrium because of the defeat.

Now, renewed jockeying for control of the parties and a search for unity between the Liberals and Conservatives developed. The latter met first in mid-April and its Directorio General installed a new governing board headed by Deputy Luis Valdés Larraín. Unofficially, a strong preference for joining the Frei campaign as a last resort became obvious during the deliberations; but the Directorio General preferred to grant the final decision to the smaller Junta Ejecutiva in order to facilitate rejoining the Liberals. On April twenty-third, the Liberal Directorio General selected Hugo Zepeda Barrios, president of the National Senate, to preside over the new *mesa* and by a vote of more than three-fourths of the members present decided to side with Frei.[98] A few days later the presidents of the two parties met privately to confer on the situation and to make final arrangements for bringing the Conservatives to the same decision. This was not easy for the Conservative party, whose relations with the Christian Democrats had been characterized by a marked coolness for several years. (In the 1958 presidential election, Frei had sent a note to the Liberals requesting their help in his campaign, but he had ignored the Conservatives.)[99] Still, the Conservatives were left with little choice in the matter if FRAP were going to be defeated. Consequently, an enlarged version of the *junta* met in secret session on April thirtieth and cast forty-one votes for lining up the party with Frei; only one opposed the new arrangement and two members abstained. In open session an hour later, the Junta Ejecutiva proclaimed its unanimous approval of Eduardo

[98] The actual vote was 301 for following Frei; 119 requested a meeting of the Junta Ejecutiva to select a new candidate; and 19 wanted to permit party members to vote their own conscience (*El Mercurio* [Santiago], April 24, 1964).

[99] *Ercilla* (Santiago), April 8, 1964.

Frei "because he represents the maintenance of the democratic regime and he has the best possibility of defeating the Marxist candidate."[100]

In short, the highest national party organs usually can bulldoze the rest of the party into accepting, or at least not openly opposing, their stands. Indeed, except in moments involving virtually cataclysmic happenings, as transpired in the Curicó by-election, the Mesa Directiva enjoys great leeway in determining who will be the party's presidential nominee, in entering into electoral pacts, and in becoming involved in various other bargaining situations. The command process from top to bottom only rarely allows for local autonomy in regular party functions. Usually, the bases enjoy freedom in selecting candidates for municipal posts and to some degree they are free to nominate congressional candidates.[101] Although the national hierarchy may exercise its influence in the final determinance of congressional nominees, changes in electoral laws have conduced to more local say in such matters. One example of this was related by a Liberal deputy regarding his first attempt to become a candidate from the province of O'Higgins:

> There were five of us who wanted to be considered for the deputyship —two attorneys, a farmer, a white-collar employee, and a merchant. The farmer was the one picked by the local party organization in O'Higgins. Unfortunately, he had very poor stage presence, used to read speeches badly and myopically. So, several leaders of the party in the district asked national officers to ease out the farmer and get a more dynamic candidate. The national organization flatly refused saying that the man was liked by his colleagues, who selected him to be their candidate. The important thing now was to get him elected so that the Liberals would have one more vote in the Chamber.[102]

In fact, local and regional groups are obligated to search out most of their own financial sources. And whatever the problems this may offer

[100] *El Mercurio* (Santiago), May 1, 1964.

[101] Federico Gil believes that the local units enjoy even less autonomy (*Political System of Chile*, pp. 252, 256).

[102] In earlier times this was not the case. Under previous electoral procedures, the national party organization would draw up a list of candidates totaling, say, the number of deputies to be elected from a district and rank them in preferential order. Local units had next to nothing to say about who went on the list or about their ranking (interview with Ivan Urzua A.).

to marginal party bases, the system does allow primary party units to perform day-to-day activities of a nonpolicy-making sort.

Radicals

The Radical party differs quite markedly from the two rightist parties.[103] First of all, it encompasses a far more heterogeneous membership agglomeration than the Conservatives and Liberals, or for that matter any political party in Chile. Undoubtedly at its core is the urban *empleado*, or white-collar worker, though it is probably literally true that party membership is representative of all regions, occupations, socioeconomic strata, religious views, and ethnic groups.[104]

As Chile's one great secular, pragmatic, bargaining party, it has long prided itself on its open admission policy and internal vertical mobility irrespective of a person's social or economic standing. During the first years after its formation, the Radical party especially comprised southern landowners and northern miners who objected to the dominance of Santiago elements in the Liberal party as well as middle sectors scattered throughout the cities who were attracted to its program. Beginning around the turn of the century, a sizable number of workers gravitated to the party as well. Then, their years of governing located Radicals overwhelmingly among public employees and additionally involved them with the business community when they fostered governmental entrance into the economy. At various points in time, Arabs, Jews, Protestants, and other ethnic and religious segments of the population further swelled party membership. Thus, the extremely varied, and oftentimes contentious, nature of Radical membership underscores the already-mentioned doctrinal problems the party has experienced and the strategic difficulties of coalescing right or left or going it alone in the center.

Another Radical feature that contrasts with the conservative grouping is its organizational proximity to workers by means of small structural units, known as *grupos gremiales* in the bylaws, but commonly

[103] A sympathetic history and analysis of the Radical party is Florencio Durán Bernales, *El Partido Radical.*

[104] See Gil, *Political System of Chile*, pp. 260–263, and Kalman H. Silvert, *Chile: Yesterday and Today*, pp. 100–102.

referred to as *grupos funcionales*—both terms stressing their occupational basis.[105] At their twenty-first national convention, held in 1961, the Radicals approved the fostering of another basic unit, *núcleo* (or nucleus), to agglomerate five to fifteen members. However, the *núcleo* did not catch on in the next four years and the few that did appear, such as the *núcleo femenino* of the Caja de Previsión de Empleados Particulares, were far less numerous than the long-established *grupos*.

The most important local deliberative body is the *asamblea*, at least one and as many as seven being located in every commune in the nation. The form and spirit of the communal assemblies, as well as of those at regional and national levels, is one of open debate in full public view and with press coverage. The truly public, deliberative nature of their assemblies' work is one of the most outstanding characteristics of the Radical party, and one that causes them to be unique among Chilean political parties. To a large degree, this feature derived from the Chilean Radicals' emulation of the free-thinking, libertarian nature of their French namesakes. At the same time, the Radicals experienced certain difficulties in maintaining these open and purposeful deliberations. During the middle 1960's the number of party militants stood at more than seventy thousand and, while a communal assembly is only required to inscribe a minimum of twenty members on its rolls, the tendency is for the *asambleas* to be much larger. One of them lists eighteen hundred members.[106] Consequently, one of the major efforts at reorganization of the party bases has been to split up assemblies, especially in communes covering a large territorial extension. Until that can be accomplished, it is problematic to find a meeting place large enough to hold a conference of all the membership and to ensure an atmosphere facilitating the give and take so dear to Radical procedures.

Another problem emanating from so many over-sized assemblies showed itself in April and May, 1964, when the Radicals were searching for the preferred line to follow after the Curicó debacle. Then, argument centered on whether to give support to their own candidate for the presidency, to the Frapistas' Salvador Allende, or to the Chris-

[105] Partido Radical, *Estatutos*.
[106] Interview with Sergio Cifuentes.

tian Democrats' Eduardo Frei, or to permit each individual to vote his own conscience. It was alleged by many high-ranking party leaders that the Communists took advantage of the open, large assemblies to penetrate meetings and shout on behalf of opting for Allende. The situation deteriorated so severely in Santiago's Eighth Commune that the National Executive Committee, by a narrow vote, appointed a committee to investigate further and reorganize the assembly in that commune.[107]

This action was quite exceptional, since local party organs, as well as regional groups (*consejos provinciales*), enjoy considerable autonomy. Horizontal links are especially strong, as communal assemblies share information and suggested lines of action with each other, and provincial councils do the same. National organs customarily confine themselves to national matters and leave subordinate structures to select candidates for municipal and congressional offices, to initiate disciplinary actions against members, and generally to work out their own problems. Communal assemblies and provincial councils select their own executive boards (*mesas directivas*), election committees (*comisiones electorales*), and disciplinary committees (*comisiones de disciplina*) to facilitate this process.

The supreme authority of the party is the National Convention (Convención Nacional), which has the sole jurisdiction to affirm or alter the Declaration of Principles, the Bylaws, and the Party Program. Its membership—ranging from five hundred to eight hundred in attendance—draws from a wide assortment of officials representing all levels and departments of the party as well as current and former governmental officers. Regular conventions are supposed to convene every four years in order to define "the political position of the Party."[108]

Interim adjustments in the party's political position may be handled by the National Assembly (Asamblea Nacional), a significant consultative body meeting regularly in May and October each year and in extraordinary sessions on the call of the party's president or by petition from two-thirds of the Assembly's membership. Slightly more than two hundred delegates will be present when there is full attendance.

107 *El Mercurio* (Santiago), May 1, 1964.
108 Partido Radical, *Estatutos*, Article 48.

Approximately sixty of these constitute national officers and the rest are elected for two-year terms from congressional electoral districts—one for each three thousand votes received by the party in the last balloting for deputies. Besides considering the party's political line, the assembly enjoys wide latitude in other fundamental areas of action: setting norms for congressional strategy, criticizing acts of the National Executive Committee, removing (by absolute majority) members of the National Executive Committee and filling vacancies on the committee, supervising and censuring activities of the various departments and national component groups, deciding upon proposed electoral pacts, readmitting expelled members, determining the process for picking a presidential candidate, and convoking extraordinary meetings of the National Convention.[109]

Executive business falls in the domain of the National Executive Committee (Comité Ejecutivo Nacional), simply referred to as CEN, and to its Mesa Directiva. CEN's nineteen officers include eleven chosen by the National Convention (who are not congressmen); two representing the party's senators and two the deputies; the national president of Radical Youth; the secretary general of the National Labor Organization; the president of the National Organization of Municipal Councilmen (*regidores*); and the president of the National Women's Organization. For its part, CEN picks a president, two vice-presidents, and a secretary general to serve as the Mesa Directiva.

The functions of CEN range widely—including carrying out orders from the National Convention or the National Assembly, making organizational changes (excepting any involving the National Assembly and the Supreme Tribunal), granting permission to members to serve in high governmental offices (as well as demanding their resignation from government), setting internal elections, approving the budget, fixing lines of action for its congressmen, arranging electoral pacts (though these must be ratified by the National Assembly), and handling numerous other matters confronting the party. In most cases, CEN holds sufficient power to deal with issues quickly. This was demonstrated in late September, 1963, when CEN determined that the

[109] *Ibid.*, Article 46.

policies of Chilean President Jorge Alessandri were running contrary to Radical interests and voted to withdraw from participating in the cabinet. The following March, CEN approved a motion to split entirely with the Alessandri regime and ordered all Radicals in appointed posts to resign their positions. More than a dozen top-ranking officials (e.g., Chile's ambassadors to the United Nations and to the Organization of American States) were affected. The finality of the decision was indicated in the terse cablegrams, without any explanation, sent out by the party president, which simply stated: "Party order of the present immediately resign your post."[110] Failure to have complied with the order could have led to automatic expulsion from the party.

The interplay of the several Radical sectors and the functioning of party structures can be illustrated in the outgrowth of events following Durán's resignation as the presidential candidate of the Democratic Front in March, 1964. As has been mentioned, Durán had indicated before the Curicó by-election that he would withdraw his name from the presidential race if the Democratic Front's candidate for deputy failed to win an impressive victory. True to his word, on the candidate's loss, Durán resigned. CEN's meeting on March twentieth recognized this fact and proclaimed the end of the Radicals' year-and-a-half-old electoral pact with the Conservatives and Liberals. Now, as the party sought to find a solution to the dilemma, local assemblies all over the country convened to debate the possible directions open to the Radical party. Deputies, senators, and national component organs followed suit. By the time CEN met again on March twenty-third, it had received myriad communications from member groups suggesting possible solutions to the crisis. Consequently, it recognized the necessity for calling a special consultative gathering of the National Assembly in order to air party differences. In the interim, open debate raged through meeting after meeting of structures at all levels of the party hierarchy. Four currents of thought dominated the discussions: reinstate Durán; join the Allende camp; put up another candidate with an end to supporting Frei; declare for no candidate and thus free individual Radicals to vote as they wished. The first two views appeared

[110] *Diario Ilustrado* (Santiago), March 22, 1964.

to party regulars to be the most persuasive. As noted, Duranistas accused Radicals who favored Allende of having enlarged their voice through Communist penetration of local assembly meetings. But the tip-off to majority sentiment came on April third, the first day of of the National Assembly's special session, when members voted 115 to 57 to install a panel of pro-Duranist presiding officers. The next day, this partisanship was confirmed when 139 delegates chose to stay with Durán (in the belief that the presidential election very likely would have to be decided by Congress and the Radicals would then constitute the decisive voting bloc); only 29 stood in opposition and 11 abstained. However, deep rifts within the party remained and dissidents demanded the opportunity for additional debate and still another vote on the question at the Assembly's regular session in May. By then, a fourth presidential candidate, Jorge Prat running as an independent, had withdrawn and the Liberals and Conservatives had swung over to Frei. Extensive discussion culminated in a reaffirmation of the April meeting, though a number of members left the assembly hall when the balloting began. CEN was granted full powers to enforce discipline in the party and, a few days after the Assembly adjourned, it did in fact initiate measures to expel two Radicals who continued to favor Allende and one who still battled in Frei's behalf.[111]

All in all, there was much to commend the Radicals in their maintenance of long-standing democratic procedures during an especially critical time in their history. Whereas the Conservatives and the Liberals tended to come to major conclusions behind closed doors, then bring their decisions into the open, and to enforce discipline early and from the top, the Radicals fostered open, public debate at the bases and in higher levels of party organization. Moreover, sanctions against dissidents and the reorganization of units were not introduced until after two assemblies had established the Radicals' political direction. The one additional measure that could have been taken and regarding which Radical leadership balked was to call a special National Convention. Vice-President Bucher spoke for his colleagues on the Mesa Di-

[111] These events were closely watched by all the press. For example, see *El Mercurio* (Santiago), March 21–23, 25, 29, 31, April 1–6, 16, 21, 30, May 7, 11, 14, 1964.

rectiva when he noted that only a few local assemblies had called for such a convention and that it would serve no purpose. In fact, he observed, the party lacked the funds for such a large undertaking at that time.

Christian Democrats

While the Democratic Front was breaking up and its erstwhile political party members deliberated over their future tactics, the Christian Democrats maintained an image of exceptional confidence and security. In no small measure, this resulted from the probable shift of several blocs of votes from the defunct Frente Democrática to Frei's cause. Beyond this advantage, though, the Christian Democrats enjoyed an esprit de corps and organizational solidarity at this time to pay dividends in the next months. Basically, Christian Democratic leadership had accumulated a reservoir of confidence from its rank and file, which permitted it to act quickly and efficiently in the face of various political-electoral crises without having to worry about internal dissension during the campaign. By the same token, the leadership kept party bases involved in policy making by means of numerous conferences that considered specific reform proposals destined to be incorporated into Frei's "Plan of Government" should he become President. This kind of involvement imbued party members with a feeling of excitement and a sense of purpose and it served to cement together militants of long-standing fealty to Christian Democracy with the countless new elements who daily knocked at the party's doors for admission.[112]

Christian Democracy's ballooning size in the early 1960's was achieved by making sharp incursions into the middle classes, who for decades had owed their major loyalty to the Radicals, and by attracting followers among the politically awakening urban and rural working classes. The principal nucleus of professionals who came to lead the party belong to the generation of the 1920's—an element that came into prominence with the rising middle sector at a time when the government rather haphazardly expanded its economic and social func-

[112] This author was greatly impressed with the level of involvement and morale among the Christian Democrats throughout practically all of Chile during 1963–1964.

tions. The generation of the 1920's especially deplored the often inefficient and occasionally corrupt nature of government and called for reforms that would "technify" administration as well as enlarge the realm of social and economic progress.[113] Such political and socioeconomic programs, together with the high level of capability and the personal standards of Christian Democratic leaders—both in Santiago and in the provinces—proved to be an unbeatable combination for many middle- and working-class Chileans. These attributes also won the allegiance of an exceptionally large percentage of Chilean women who were fully enfranchised by 1952 and who subsequently registered in ever-greater numbers.

Chilean Christian Democracy's emulation of its European counterparts (Eduardo Frei personally greatly admires former German Chancellor Konrad Adenauer and an enormous picture of Adenauer stands in party headquarters) has led it to assume something of the stance of a "movement" and to incorporate varied religious and nonreligious, ethnic, and economic clusters of society under its aegis. Thus, the relatively broad spectrum of the party's adherents, though not quite so broad as that characterizing the Radicals, has engendered some of the same kinds of factional difficulties that have beset the Radical party. During the electoral campaigns in 1964 and 1965, party officers adjusted their differences well and no important divisions broke the surface. Nonetheless, both ideological and tactical disagreements between the moderates and leftists remained to threaten party unity once Frei assumed the presidency.

Christian Democratic organization is rather similar to Radical party arrangements, but internal procedures and links between local and national organs mark it with a flavor of its own.[114] Reflecting one of their most frequently voiced ideological tenets, communitarianism, is the lowest level of party groupings—the neighborhood communitarian groups (*grupos comunitarios vecinales*) and communitarian workers' groups (*grupos comunitarios de trabajadores*), each with an executive

[113] See Silvert, *Chile*, pp. 103–104.

[114] Interview with José de Gregorio. Also, see Partido Demócrata Cristiano, *Estatutos del Partido Demócrata Cristiano*, and Edward J. Williams, *Latin American Christian Democratic Parties*, Chap. IV.

board (*mesa directiva*). Communal councils (*juntas comunales*) stand on the next higher rung of the hierarchical ladder and in turn work through smaller directive organs, *consejos comunales*, with their *mesas directivas*. These units deal with the various organizational, membership, financial, and electoral matters for the territory within their jurisdiction.

Members are inscribed at the communal level, a would-be adherent going through a thirty-day waiting period during which time his qualifications for membership may be challenged. The president or another leader of the communal council conducts the swearing-in ceremony as follows:

Official: "Do you wish to belong to the Christian Democratic Party?"
Militant: "Yes, I do."
Official: "Do you accept its principles, its Program and Bylaws?"
Militant: "Yes, I accept them."
Official: "I invite you, then, to swear or promise, repeating with me the following words:
Both: "I swear (or I promise) loyalty to the Christian Democratic Party."
Official: "Therefore I declare you in solemn and public manner, a militant of the Christian Democratic Party."[115]

Upon taking the oath, the new member signs the rolls, fills out an information sheet, which is forwarded to the Department of Organization and Control, and in due time receives a card affirming his membership. In mid-1964, the number who had completed this process and became militants was estimated to be approximately 120,000, a very high percentage relative to the 453,000 votes the party received in the 1963 municipal elections.[116]

The large deliberative body at the provincial level is the *junta provincial*, which selects a smaller *consejo provincial*, a *mesa directiva*, and a disciplinary court, the *tribunal provincial de disciplina*. The *junta* derives its membership from the communal *juntas*, party *regidores* and congressmen of the province, provincial leaders of the party

115 Partido Demócrata Cristiano, *Estatutos*, p. 6.
116 Interview with José de Gregorio.

and of its affiliates, and representatives from the province who sit on the national *junta*. The *consejo* may be enlarged into a *consejo plenario provincial* with the addition of presidents of the communal *mesas*. The provincial party organization reviews and scrutinizes communal activities, reporting these to national leaders, selects candidates for *regidores*, and proposes candidates for the national Chamber of Deputies and the Senate.

National party organization follows a pattern much like the provincial set-up, except that it is more elaborate. Supreme authority resides with the National Congress (Congreso Nacional), a body of 1,200–1,500 representatives from communal, provincial, and national organs as well as incorporating current and former legislators, former cabinet members, and delegates from labor and student groups and from the media of communication. Scheduled to meet every three years, it primarily concerns itself with the party bylaws and program. Between its assemblages, the congress grants full power to the Junta Nacional. Comprising 350 members from all party levels, it convenes annually and, in addition to acting on any question ordinarily within the domain of the National Congress, the Junta Nacional also assumes the responsibility for choosing the party's candidate for the Chilean presidency. In the campaign for 1964, this decision was little more than perfunctory because of Eduardo Frei's preeminent position.

Most of the remaining national structures assemble more frequently and are operative on a more continuing basis. The powerful Consejo Nacional is composed of the five officers from its executive board (Mesa Directiva), twelve councilors appointed by the Junta Nacional (of whom two are labor leaders, one is a youth director, one is a women's leader, one speaks for agricultural workers, and several are drawn from miscellaneous sources), and a deputy and a senator selected from their own blocs. The Consejo Nacional's duties are extensive. It makes the final determinance as to who will stand for congressional seats and whether party members may assume cabinet posts in the national government. It directs deputies and senators in their official capacities, initiates disciplinary action, may reorganize any party organ (except the Junta Nacional and the National Tribunal of Discipline), and, in short, treats virtually any subject demanding attention. This body, then, along with its *mesa* (i.e., the party president, two vice-presidents, the secretary, and treasurer) constitutes the locus of party power in day-to-day matters. Semiannually or exceptionally the Consejo Nacional expands into a plenary session (Consejo Plenario Nacional) with the addition of provincial presidents and national departmental directors (i.e., sixty members plus the party's deputies and senators) in order to review interim party activities and to consider such unusual items as entering into electoral pacts. The Mesa Directiva is charged with over-seeing the large secretariat (Secretaría Nacional) with its many departments.

Fortunately for the Christian Democrats, they have not been obliged to call upon the Tribunal Nacional de Disciplina very often to consider requests for expelling particular members. An exception occurred in 1963 when a Christian Democratic mayor publicly threw his weight behind the campaign of several Democratic Front candidates for city councilmanic posts; a year later disciplinary charges were invoked against a Christian Democrat who was found to be involved in a contraband scheme. Both men were dropped from the party rolls.

Links between national and provincial and communal party structures generally have been strong, hence facilitating a good flow of information and directives from headquarters to the bases.[117] In 1963, for example, national leaders requested that subordinate units confer on local needs that would be brought together into regional planning conferences and ultimately incorporated into an over-all program of social and economic reform for the nation. The response was immediate and enthusiastic as local groups throughout Chile set out proposals in the form of "green reports," which then were taken by provincial representatives to regional congresses and hammered into final proposals.

One such regional congress met in Concepción in November, 1963, following earlier provincial deliberations, and compiled final recommendations for the provinces of Nuble, Concepción, Arauco, Bío-Bío, and Malleco regarding bases for regional development, administrative

117 However, the party expanded so rapidly in such a short time that weaknesses began to crop up in links between communal and lesser units soon after the 1964 election.

reforms, education, health, housing and urbanization, industry, energy and combustibles, transportation and communications, agriculture and forestry, and the role of municipalities in regional growth.[118] The Christian Democrats' high quality of provincial leadership and the pervasive territorial coverage of the problems and programs considered funneled an impressive array of suggestions for societal reform to the party's top decision-making centers. Moreover, this deliberative process helped to keep morale high and, along with Frei's stature and the party's ideological attractiveness, it undoubtedly aided in party recruitment and in converting many passive members into activists. The local study sessions, in particular, encouraged party volunteers to work diligently for the campaign with the belief not only that they were contributing to winning the presidential election, but also that their proposals would actually reach fruition in Frei's reforms when he became President. All this counteracted a tendency in all Chilean political parties (far less so among the Radicals) to be highly centralized and, consequently, often to stultify local endeavors.

FRAP Parties

The last of the political groups to be considered here are those parties coalescing in the Popular Action Front—the Socialists, the Communists, and the small PADENA element. Little needs to be said about the fading National Democratic party (Partido Democrático Nacional or PADENA), a residue of Carlos Ibáñez' followers who fused together in 1960. Hierarchically, it follows the usual three levels of structures.[119] Locally, there exist subcommunal organisms (*organismos subcomunales*) and base committees (*comités de base*); above them are the communal assemblies with their *mesas directivas*. In 1964, the party claimed 300 of these local organs spread over the nation. In fact, the number of these was declining rapidly and many could hardly be said to maintain their minimum of 5 to 15 members. Provincial

[118] Interview with Emilio McNamara, dierctor of the Christian Democratic Provincial Command, in Concepción, March 5, 1964. Also, see Congreso de Planificación Regional, "Informe Final," mimeographed.

[119] Interviews with Lautaro Ojeda H. Also, see Partido Democrático Nacional, *Declaración de principios, programa fundamental, y estatutos.*

councils, with *mesas* and disciplinary courts (*tribunales provinciales*) are located at the intermediate level. And at the top of the pyramid stand the National Congress, supposedly gathering 750 to 1,000 members; the National Executive Council (Junta Ejecutiva Nacional), a 30-member body that can be expanded into the 150-delegate Pleno Nacional; the Mesa Directiva, with 5 officers; the Supreme Tribunal; and various departments and committees. The Mesa Directiva and Junta Nacional provide day-to-day direction and generally handle any matter affecting the party.

PADENA has suffered from a steady loss of rank-and-file members and of voters; but, even more damaging, it experienced a wholesale abandonment of the party by officeholders, which depleted its reservoir of leadership disastrously and further diminished its ability to recruit new militants. At one point, in 1963, when a crisis developed over whether to remain in FRAP, five of PADENA's twelve deputies and three *regidores* broke ranks to join the Christian Democrats. There remained little doubt but that PADENA would follow the path of so many of Chile's minor parties and disappear.

In contrast, the Communists and Socialists remain vigorous parties with fairly strong membership ties and active recruitment procedures. Both draw primarily from the urban working class—overwhelmingly from organized labor—and from professional and intellectual elements in the middle class. However, the Communists have been more successful in holding on to trade unions and in capturing the allegiance of new unions than the Socialists; on the other hand, the Socialist party has agglomerated more of the middle groups. Each has staked out regions of electoral predominance (e.g., the Communists in the north and the Socialists in the far south); but in some provinces, as in the coal-mining district near Concepción, they compete for followers. Since the 1950's, the Marxist parties have devoted considerable organizational effort on behalf of agricultural workers.

The two Marxist parties are practically identical in organization.[120]

[120] Poppino, *International Communism in Latin America*, Chap. VI; Partido Comunista, *Estatutos*; and Partido Socialista, *Estatuto del Partido Socialista*. Additional information was obtained at each of the party's national headquarters.

Occupational and residential groupings—called cells (*células*) by the Communists and nuclei (*núcleos*) by the Socialists—constitute the basic units; it is here where recruitment into the party occurs. A new Socialist adherent, after having been endorsed by a party militant and receiving the approval of all the nucleus members, takes an oath in which he promises "loyalty to the Party, to the working class, and to the common people";[121] for his part, a newly accepted Communist declares: "I promise the firmest loyalty to the principles of Marxism-Leninism and to the Program of the Communist Party of Chile, strengthening its unity and discipline, seeing to the fulfillment of its Bylaws and fighting tirelessly for the application of its political line in defense of the supreme interests of the working class and the common people, and for the arrival of socialism and communism in Chile."[122] The smallness of the base units helps to reinforce ideological loyalty, though factional disputes do erupt periodically. The Socialists as well as the Communists proclaim their internal governance to be by the principle of "democratic centralism," which refers to:

a) The elective character of all the leadership organisms of the Party, from bottom up to the top.
b) The obligation of the leadership organisms of the Party periodically to give an account of its action before the respective organizations of the Party.
c) The obligation to observe Party discipline and the subordination of the minority to the majority, and
d) The obligation for the inferior organisms to rigorously carry out the agreements of the superior organisms.[123]

The next higher level of organization is located in the communes and subdelegations where the Socialists maintain *comités seccionales* with congresses and the Communists establish their *comités locales* (or *comités de empresa*), each with a conference and a congress. The parties are administered in the provinces by regional committees and congresses; the Communists also provide for regional conferences.

121 Partido Socialista, *Estatuto del Partido Socialista*, Article 3.
122 Partido Comunista, *Estatutos*, Article 3.
123 *Ibid.*, Title VIII; Partido Socialista, *Estatuto del Partido Socialista*, Article 2.

Regarding the subnational structure of Communist parties in Latin America generally, Rollie Poppino suggests that their vertical nature is rarely altered. However, "the number of units in each echelon below the national level is highly flexible, subject to bellows-like expansion or contraction with changing party fortunes. This horizontal flexibility, which enables the party to absorb thousands of new recruits at one time and to withstand a sudden dramatic loss of members at another, is the great organizational strength of the Communist movement in Latin America."[124] The necessity for this format has not always been as obvious in Chile as in other countries in the hemisphere. Still, the sudden reaction of the González Videla regime against the Marxists, beginning in the late 1940's, saw the Communist party drop measurably from 50,000 members in 1947, to 35,000 in 1952, and to a low point of 25,000 in 1957. By 1963, it had climbed back to 30,000 and it continued to expand through the middle of the decade.[125]

At the top of the party pyramid stand the National Congress, except in times of internecine struggles a rubber-stamp assemblage; the Central Committee, which can be expanded into a larger advisory body, El Pleno Nacional; and the Secretariat, a powerful inner group dominating the various departments and their bureaucracy. In both the Socialist and Communist camps, the single most powerful repository of party authority and the guiding force in policy formation is the Political Commission, headed by the highly influential secretary general. (See Chart 2.)

To reach the highest echelons in the Communist party requires at least ten years of active dedication and repeated testing of one's qualifications of leadership. On the other hand, the Socialist party, while usually demanding long service to the party in order to advance to high-ranking positions, is more flexible in occasionally pushing outstanding leadership prospects to the forefront quickly despite a relatively short tenure in the party.

Actually, both secretaries general in the mid-1960's—the Communists' Luis Corvalán Lépez and the Socialists' Raúl Ampuero Díaz—boasted long records of leadership in their political movements. Cor-

[124] Poppino, *International Communism in Latin America*, pp. 118–119.
[125] *Ibid.*, p. 231.

CHART 2

The Secretary General and the National Administration of the Chilean Socialist Party

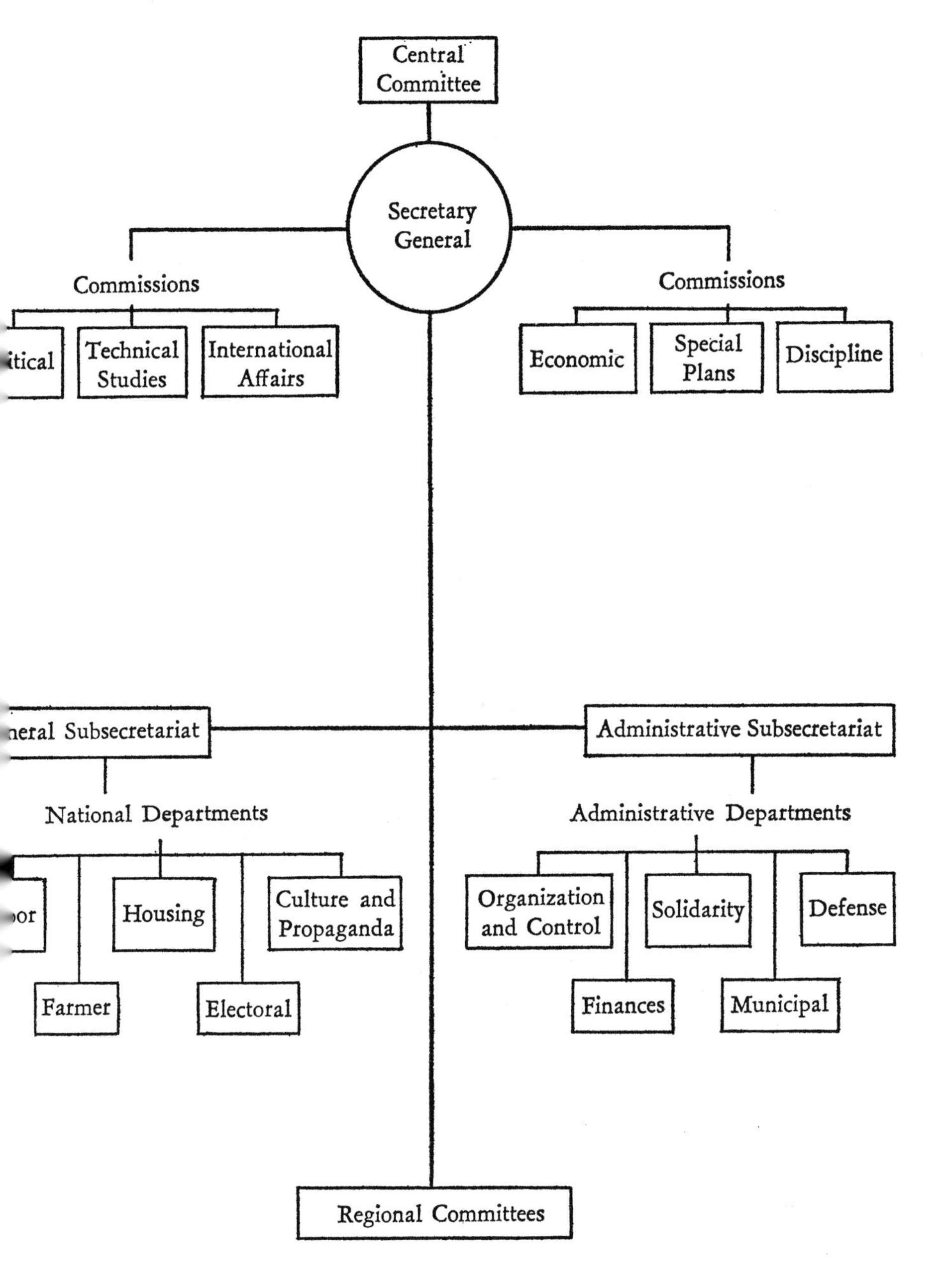

valán, who entered official ranks in 1932, taught school briefly and later acquired a name as an important Marxian journalist. In 1957, he succeeded Galo González as secretary general and, in 1961, entered the Senate from the electoral district comprising the provinces of Concepción, Nuble, and Arauco. Ampuero, an attorney by profession, entered the Socialist camp in 1934 as a founder of Juventud Socialista; in 1946 he was elevated to the post of secretary general in his party and, after 1953, represented Antofagasta and Tarapacá in the Senate. Despite the enormous personal power held by both Corvalán and Ampuero in their party structures, periodically each had to contend with internal factionalism. For the most part, party squabbles have related to ideological and other developments in international communism and the relevance of such happenings to Chile.[126]

Very early in his career as party leader, Corvalán was confronted with the Cuban Revolution and the need to determine a line for the Chilean Communists to follow insofar as Castroism was concerned. For a time, Corvalanistas wavered between a preference for the peaceful road to power (*vía pacífica*) and a desire to combine peaceful with violent tactics as their strategy. Then in August, 1961, they clashed with Clotario Blest, the head of CUT and a militant Castroite, who advocated immediate and violent revolution. At that time, Corvalán attacked "adventurers and provocateurs" who demeaned his group's efforts to bring about a revolution by peaceful means. After all, Corvalán said, "We need not play at revolution and Sierra Maestra in order to be revolutionaries."[127] He further admonished his adversaries by reminding them that the "Chilean people will not be hauled along by adventurism, nor eradicate their disputes by any force."[128]

Still, inside of two months Corvalán felt obliged to modify his statement because of Castro's apparent decision to install a Communist state in place of his personal dictatorship—a move that enhanced Castro's standing among Marxists. Accordingly, Corvalán explained

[126] For a discussion of factionalism in the Marxist parties, see Halperin, *Nationalism and Communism in Chile.*

[127] Partido Comunista, *El Partido Comunista de Chile y el Movimiento Comunista Internacional,* p. 153.

[128] *Ibid.*

that what he really had meant in his earlier presentation was that a violent road might be necessary if the conservative oligarchy were to institute armed force against the people. In addition, he expressed fraternal sympathy to all those choosing violence so long as they were not mere adventurers—directing this jab at Clotario Blest and his coterie.[129] In fact, Corvalán's dedication to the *vía pacífica* for Chile was repeatedly reasserted in the following years.

A more serious intrusion in party harmony, the Soviet-Chinese rift, found the Corvalán element firmly in Moscow's corner. Nonetheless, a few Communist leftists (as well as a number of Socialists) articulated strong pro-Chinese views. In large measure, these pro-Peking expressions were channeled through a publishing house known as Espártaco Editores, which appeared early in 1963. The Communist intellectuals in the firm came to be referred to simply as the Spartacus Group. In the next months a barrage of Pekinista propaganda emanated from their presses. One of their most sensational attacks was built around an open letter from the Albanian Central Committee to the Chilean Central Committee, which the Spartacus Group circulated in party circles and also leaked to Santiago's far-right daily, *Diario Ilustrado*. In particular, the Albanian letter bitingly condemned Corvalán, his cohorts, and *El Siglo* as divisionists "blindly obedient to the baton of Moscow."[130] Something of a showdown occurred in September, 1964, when the long months of verbal exchanges moved toward demonstrations of organizational strength. The confrontation revolved about the fourteenth anniversary of the Communist Chinese Revolution. By means of ubiquitous announcements posted on walls and buildings throughout Santiago, the Pekinistas called for a celebration of that event—at ten in the morning on Sunday, September twenty-ninth. The Vanguardia Revolucionaria Marxista (VRM), mostly comprising Communists tossed out of the party back in 1950, sponsored a reunion in the Teatro Esmeralda; another faction, the Movimiento de Apoyo a la Revolución Antiimperialista (MARA), which included a number of former low-echelon Communists whom the party also had expelled,

[129] *Ibid.*, pp. 171–180.

[130] All this was lengthily reported in *Diario Ilustrado* (Santiago), February 11–15, 1964.

called for another commemorative assembly in the Teatro Baquedano. Now the orthodox Communist organization moved into action. A number of its members, including several prominent names, had agreed to participate in the MARA meeting. The Political Commission publicly warned them through *El Siglo* against doing so and contacted Socialist higher-ups requesting a similar action—a request with which the Socialist hierarchy complied.

Subsequently, most of the more known Communists and Socialists refused to attend, several even alleging that they had been listed as sponsors without their permission. Communists who failed to heed their party's directives arrived at the Teatro Baquedano only to find fellow-Communists picketing the assemblage and taking note of party recalcitrants entering the theater. Meanwhile, Corvalán's group not only actively discouraged party militants from attending the Pekinista gatherings, but by the same token sought to counter whatever propaganda value those meetings might have by scheduling a mass meeting of its own at ten o'clock on that same Sunday morning. Consequently, some three blocks from the Baquedano movie house, in the open Parque Bustamante, the official Communist leadership rallied its own supporters. Several thousands heard speeches by Chile's most famed poet, Pablo Neruda, and by Luis Corvalán and others—all interspersed with musical entertainment.[131] Somewhat paradoxically, the leader of the capitalist world, John F. Kennedy, was lauded (for recently having signed the nuclear test ban treaty), whereas Chinese Communists came under blistering attack on "Homage to the Chinese Revolution" day. Neruda told of his visit to China where he saw thousands of Soviet technicians aiding in all kinds of public works and of how much the Chinese owed to the Soviet Union for its advances. Regrettably, Neruda pointed out, the Chinese now suffered from "a personality cult" and were "reactionary."[132]

[131] Halperin indicates that "a rather meager crowd of perhaps fifteen hundred Communists" assembled at the Parque Bustamante (*Nationalism and Communism in Chile*, p. 110). This writer estimated the gathering to be at least four thousand and a friend, Professor Myron Glazer of Smith College, estimated the total to be closer to five thousand.

[132] From notes taken by the author. Also, see *El Mercurio* (Santiago), September 29, 1963, and *El Siglo* (Santiago), September 30, 1963.

Shortly afterward, however, factional differences quieted down in order for the Chilean left to unite behind Allende's candidacy. Actually, Corvalán's position was never seriously threatened by the disagreements, though FRAP's failure in the 1964 presidential election would reopen holes in the façade of Communist harmony.

Whereas Corvalán's opposition emanated mostly from purged Communists who voiced their antagonism to the *vía pacífica* outside party circles, Ampuero was forced to contend with enmity from within the Socialist party. Dissension mounted in the months prior to the Socialists' ordinary National Congress, scheduled to meet in Concepción during February, 1964. On the one side stood the domineering Ampuero, whose "soft line" favored sticking with the present Communist leadership. In vigorous disagreement, the scholarly Socialist Deputy Clodomiro Almeyda demanded a "hard line," meaning immediate, all-out social war.[133]

The Ampuero-Almeyda split at first lurked in the background as the two adversaries cooperated in fostering Allende's candidacy; but by early 1964, they even came to differ over Allende's campaign tactics, Almeyda insisting upon the necessity for more militancy. Their first big clash occurred in January, 1964, when the Regional Committee of Santiago, headed by Almeyda, assembled to elect delegates to the Socialists' forthcoming National Congress. At that time, Almeyda's *antioficialistas* secured all twelve seats. Ampuero then ordered the Organizing Committee of the National Congress to review the Santiago proceedings. An *antioficialista* chairmaned this committee, but the remaining three committeemen were *oficialistas* and voted according to Ampuero's wishes. First, they annulled the elections for delegates held by a congress of Santiago's Regional Committee; then they rejected the Santiago congress itself with the allegation that its leaders had run a "machine" that made free expression of the bases impossible.[134]

A week after the first Santiago Regional Congress, Ampuero con-

[133] Halperin, *Nationalism and Communism in Chile*, pp. 144–177.

[134] These and subsequent events were described in *Ercilla* (Santiago), February 19, 1964; *Diario Ilustrado* (Santiago), February 10 and 16, 1964; *El Mercurio* (Santiago), February 17 and 18, 1964; and *El Siglo* (Santiago), February 16, 1964.

vened Santiago Regional Congress No. 2—this time in the national headquarters of the Socialist party, which Ampuero controlled, rather than in the offices of Almeyda's Regional Committee. Not surprisingly, the rump congress chose twelve *oficialista* delegates.

By the time the Twentieth National Congress opened in Concepción, bitterness in the Almeyda sector ran rampant. Nevertheless, despite the fact that Concepción was Almeyda territory, the outcome of the Ampuero-Almeyda clash never was in serious question. First, Ampuero placed a paid statement in *El Sur*, one of Concepción's daily newspapers, in which he delineated his side of the events leading up to the moment. Next, the Ampuero-controlled party administration went to work. The Commission on Powers and Discipline refused to admit some twenty Almeydistas from various districts into the congress, whereas it did certify the delegation from Santiago's Regional Congress No. 2. Almeyda's request to be admitted as a delegate from Santiago was denied, though the commission pointed out that as a deputy in the Chilean congress he enjoyed automatic membership in the Concepción gathering.

Ensuing developments followed a similar pattern. By voice vote, Ampuero was reelected to the secretary generalship and the Central Committee, now enlarged from thirteen to seventeen members, fell even more heavily to the Ampueristas. Seeing his delegation reduced to a thin minority, Almeyda departed from the congress on the pretext of illness in the family, while his followers clamored in the streets outside the congress against the Ampuero "dictatorship." The Regional Committee of Socialist Youth of Concepción went so far as to publicly repudiate party leadership and to threaten to form themselves into a new leftist movement.

In the wake of the Concepción discord, a number of Socialists resigned from the party. One of these, Baudilio Casanova Valenzuela, former secretary general of CUT, spoke for them when he said: "Internal democracy has not existed since the moment in which Mr. Raúl Ampuero lost influence in the bases and he and his intimates ran the danger of losing control of the Party. The process was evident during the preparation of the last congress at Concepción, where the majority of the delegates planned the total renovation of its leadership. It was necessary for Mr. Ampuero, using his power and that of his intimates and of the Party's bureaucracy, to eliminate legitimately elected delegates, in order to designate others of his own determination."[135] For the time being, Ampuero had successfully thrown off this threat to his monopoly of power; but the specter of discontent in the bases was to reappear to haunt him in the following year.

SUMMARY

Thus, in the mid-1960's, six major political parties endeavored to aggregate claims on the political system by Chile's diverse societal elements. As the campaigns for the 1964 presidential election and for the 1965 congressional election bore on, several characteristics regarding the Chilean political parties stood out.

Ideologically, the allocation of Chile's political parties into Right, Center, and Left compartments—a situation that often has been likened to Western European multiparty systems—offers a doctrinal choice that can accommodate virtually all the Chilean electorate. In 1964, only the extreme right and left fringe elements (e.g., the Fascists and the more violence-oriented Marxists) found difficulty in obtaining official recognition from the major parties. However, the doctrinaire fascists, after a flurry of importance in the 1930's, probably no longer constituted a very measurable viewpoint in Chile; the militant Marxists who advocated immediate and violent revolution, did find some expression of their views in a few leaders of the major Marxist parties as well as through minor political organizations of their own.

Such an assortment of ideological stands, while offering choice to the voters, also points up a political fragmentation that almost always has necessitated coalition governments—leading to immobilist features in policy formation not unlike the French Fourth Republic. Nevertheless, the at-least-surface instability that this might imply is mitigated by the fact that Chile possesses a presidential rather than a parliamentary system and by the presence on the Chilean political spectrum of several political parties (especially, of course, in the Center) the diversified make-up of which permits relatively easy movement to the

[135] *El Mercurio* (Santiago), April 1, 1964.

left and right in governmental coalitions, electoral pacts, and congressional bargaining groups.

Closely related to this feature is the comparatively pragmatic nature of most of the parties' leaders, who on occasions sacrifice doctrinal tenets for tactical expediency. Hence, Radicals coalesced with the Marxists in Aguirre Cerda's Popular Front government and co-governed with the Liberals and Conservatives in Jorge Alessandri's regime; they also participated in an electoral front with the two conservative parties for a time in the early 1960's and voted in Congress with the Communists in the mid-1960's. Christian Democrats welcomed the support of the Liberals and the Conservatives in the 1964 presidential election; yet earlier they had voted with the Communists on several important congressional items and joined with FRAP in a tactical maneuver against the Democratic Front in the Curicó by-election.[136]

In the last years, the fulcrum of the party system has decidedly moved to the left. This was due in part to the resurrection of the Communist party after 1958 when it was no longer outlawed. But it also was evidenced by the meteoric rise of the reform-minded Christian Democrats and the general success of certain leftists, especially among the Radicals. Several reasons can be offered for this leftward trend. Above all, frustrations have built up among the bulk of Chileans about the inability or unwillingness of moderate-conservative and conservative regimes to resolve endemic socioeconomic problems. Antioligarchical attitudes are directed against community as well as national leadership. (An example of disenchantment with local moderate-conservative leadership is Valdivia where the disastrous earthquake and tidal wave of 1960 destroyed many domestic industries, bridges, and roads. Most of these were not rebuilt; unemployed and underemployed workers placed the blame for job shortages on the owners of the industries, whom they associated with the Democratic Front.)

Furthermore, the reformist and radical political parties have evinced a far greater dynamism and their solutions to long-time problems have

[136] It was alleged that the Democratic Front had deposited a large amount of money in a Curicó bank to be used for buying votes. Frapistas and Christian Democrats physically prevented the Democratic Front from withdrawing the money for that purpose.

proved more convincing to the impoverished strata of society at a time when the traditional parties offered the same old palliatives and sought political support in many areas by buying rather than winning votes. By the same token, the leftist groups exercised a greater hegemony in organized labor and were largely responsible for politically activating countless unorganized urban and rural elements; once politicized, this latter stratum overwhelmingly gravitated to the left.

In addition to these ideological attributes, the Chilean political parties are interesting in their organizational set-ups. As noted, they are structurally similar in being territorially dispersed at local, regional, and national levels—though the Liberals and Conservatives have not endeavored to implant the small primary bases typifying the other major parties. Moreover, in contrast to political parties in the United States, they are all subject to considerable centralized control (the Radicals, of course, being less so than the others). Local involvement in some aspects of party decision making seems to be best in the Radical party, varied in the Christian Democratic party, and very limited in the parties of the far right and left.

In general, the quality of Chilean party leadership is probably as good or better than anywhere else in Latin America. A principal reason for this is the presence of a number of viable economic interest groups, the officers of which are generally very politicized and who thus form a ready reservoir of leaders for the political parties. Most cut their teeth politically as early as high school and, of those who went on to the university, many gained public stature and partisan training as student-body leaders. Also very important, the general absence of dictatorial regimes and of chronic military intrusion into the political system has helped Chile to avoid the stultifying effects on leadership recruitment and training that have marked so many of the Latin American republics. Thus, a large pool of capable leaders can be found in the national officialdom of all the major parties, and even regional and local party leaders—though certainly uneven in their leadership skills—tend to be surprisingly well endowed with leadership qualities.[137]

[137] However, the Christian Democrats, who experienced such a sudden growth, did encounter some difficulty in staffing all their party offices and at the same time fielding a slate of congressional candidates. Still, their ability to

Despite certain organizational strengths, the record of internal party discipline and cohesion is somewhat mixed. All the parties have experienced occasional leadership defections and they have had to invoke expulsion proceedings from time to time. Most commonly, these have occurred because of doctrinal and personality differences and, then, the disagreements usually break out over one or more candidates the controlling portion of the party favored or because of electoral pacts it has entered. Very rarely is membership expunged for defalcation or other personal improprieties. Still, discipline is remarkably good within the congressional parties, which work out policy and strategy lines behind closed doors and in subsequent legislative processes tend to adhere to those directives.

A final dimension of the Chilean political parties to be discussed here regards their finances. Actually, it is very difficult to obtain more than the sketchiest details about party revenue sources and expenditures. Nevertheless, a few conclusions can be drawn from scattered bits of information. Money enters party coffers at the national level through both regular and sporadic channels. On the regularized side, each party's representatives in Congress pledge to return 10 per cent of their salaries each month; likewise, party directors pay a specified quota monthly to the party treasury. In the case of the Liberals, this amounted to a total of approximately $3,500 to $4,000 annually during the early 1960's;[138] of course, this amount would vary up or down with other parties depending upon the number of congressmen and the size of the quota levied on directors.

Membership dues constitute a grey area in terms of regularized financial sources. That is, the parties specify a monthly quota each member is requested to pay. Typically, the amount is determined on the basis of one's economic status and thus is highest, say, for the wealthy businessman, less for the middle-class professional, and least for the laborer. In fact, even the 3 to 15¢ a month asked of the worker is commonly beyond his financial means and, so, by no stretch of the imagination can the anticipated return from dues be computed strictly

---

draw from so large a number of middle-class technical and professional people undoubtedly contributed to the generally high quality of their officers.

[138] Interviews with Ivan Urzua A. and Oscar Fuenzalida E.

on the number of members in the party. Voluntary contributions thus assume a commensurately greater importance and necessarily accrue almost solely from the middle and upper classes.[139]

Of course, during electoral campaigns, when voter interest runs high and costs mount appreciably, special devices are developed to tap greatly augmented revenue sources. For the 1964 election, the Christian Democrats launched an "Escudos for Frei" drive, in which people paid an escudo (roughly 35¢ U.S. at the time) for a ticket as a donation to Frei's campaign. Half the money garnered went to local party organization and half was sent to national headquarters. The sales motivation was enhanced by pitting cities against each other in terms of the number of tickets per capita they could sell. Other promotion schemes were employed by the Frapistas and Duranistas and it was widely held that all three presidential candidates received financial assistance from abroad.[140]

In the matter of party financing, the Communists seem to be a special case. Apparently, they underwrite a larger number of full-time directors and staff than the other parties. Many non-Marxists maintain that this is possible because of a steady flow of financial aid from Eastern Europe. Whatever the case, it is likely that a good deal of their revenues originate in Chile proper. For example, great quantities of books, magazines, and pamphlets of all kinds are sold at several Communist bookstores in the center of Santiago. Other profit-making enterprises, such as soft-drink and snack stands, also are believed to contribute to Communist coffers.

By and large, local party units must seek out their own revenues. This approach possesses obvious merit in that the primary party bases

[139] In 1963, the Christian Democrats requested adherents to give the equivalent of one day of salary to the party. This brought in E°50,000, or, about $17,000 U.S. (interview with José de Gregorio).

[140] It was generally thought that Allende's organization received money from Eastern Europe by way of Cuba; Frei was believed to have obtained money from Christian Democratic groups in Western Europe and, after Curicó, to have tapped some U.S. sources; and, while he still seemed to be in the running (that is, before Curicó), Durán probably was helped by U.S. money. One rumor insisted that Durán, on his return trip from the United States, carried suitcases filled with dollars unopened through Chilean customs.

are closer to local money sources and a local group survives only if it can rally its own resources. Still, as one observer put it, "many of these bases are scratching for funds with their fingernails."[141] Of course, during an electoral campaign the national party headquarters does provide certain types of aid to its local units. At the very least, it offers quantities of posters, pamphlets, and other propaganda items and may send out speakers whose costs are defrayed nationally. At best, the national party organization additionally may pay for the rent and electricity of the local office. Undoubtedly, this kind of underwriting paid off for the Christian Democrats in the 1964 campaign. In Valdivia, for example, the Christian Democrats scored a stunning victory against impressive odds due to a combination of many circumstances. Nevertheless, the fact that the national organization invested in renting a local building early in the campaign clearly got the Christian Democratic efforts off the ground very quickly and built up local optimism and activism to a high self-sustaining level; in contrast, the Democratic Front, which traditionally had been very influential in the region, six months before the election still had not found funds to get the organization moving.[142]

In some areas, the local groups have maintained their own physical facilities by giving them a social as well as a political function. The conservative parties especially created a sort of private-club atmosphere in many local headquarters. While this helped somewhat to cement party relationships among militants, the exclusive nature of such an atmosphere kept out the workers, who by the 1960's had emerged as a sizable political force. In contrast, the Marxist parties held their doors open to the poor and the name given to local headquarters,

[141] Interview with Ivan Urzua A. A similar comment was made by Osvaldo Yáñez Rivas, director of the newspaper *Correo de Valdivia,* in Valdivia, March 9, 1964.

[142] Interviews with General (retired) Alfonso Cañas Ruiz Tagle, president of the Christian Democrats' Provincial Command of Valdivia, in Valdivia, March 9, 1964; and with Heribarto Vivanco Cuecha, secretary general, and Luis E. Frías Valverde, secretary of the Political Department—both of the Democratic Front's Provincial Command of Valdivia, in Valdivia, March 9, 1964.

Casa del Pueblo, or the People's House, was a far more inviting welcome to the laboring classes.

At any rate, most party bases rely very heavily on volunteer help and typically they are able to take on a few hired workers—such as one or two secretaries and a public relations man—only during a campaign. Of course, national headquarters are maintained on a day-to-day basis—each party being housed in its own building in downtown Santiago and staffed with a number of paid secretaries and the like. In 1964, FRAP and the Christian Democrats also rented additional offices for their extensive political activities. In the case of the Marxists, a separate building contained their elaborate planning group, OCEPLAN (Oficina Central de Planificación, or Central Planning Office), which labored to create a coherent economic and social program for the campaign and for Allende's administration if he achieved the presidency. The Christian Democrats' second headquarters was an expensive suite of offices remote to the rank and file of the party, but a beehive of high-ranking officers and scores of assistants.

As has been mentioned, it is virtually impossible to estimate either the ongoing costs of a party in its regular activities or the expenditures necessary to carry out a very costly campaign like that of 1964. No public accounting is made and the parties generally are understandably secretive about such matters. (The secretary general of the small PADENA party did confide that it required about $1,600 U.S. a month to run his party and one source estimated the Christian Democrats' monthly operating expenses to be at least $18,500 U.S.).[143] In any event, costs are considerable. Although television remains in its formative stages, radio and newspaper propaganda as well as the ubiquitous posters and other visual presentations take a large chunk of campaign finances. Vote buying, a standard expense earlier, has been declining, as the Christian Democrats and the Marxists prefer to provide food, clothing, and medical-dental services to prospective voters and to reduce the conservatives' ability to purchase votes outright.

[143] Interview with Lautaro Ojeda H.; George W. Grayson, Jr., "Significance of the Frei Administration for Latin America," *Orbis* 9, no. 3 (Fall 1965): 760–779.

The middle 1960's were especially exciting years for Chilean politics. The nation continued to be rent with grave economic and social difficulties that demanded resolution; and the heat of the contest of political groups competing to control the administration of government in order to deal with those problems was particularly intense. Some old solutions were revamped in new forms and the emergence of newer political groups and doctrinal offerings stimulated hope for reforms. The 1964 presidential election spotlighted this process and brought a determinedly reformist regime to power. Subsequent events, however, raised serious questions about the Chilean political system—whatever its admitted strengths—and its ability to convert groups' claims into effective policy formation and greater group satisfactions. The mid-1960's also brought out the sobering reminder that Chile has a long record of devouring reformers.[144]

[144] Bray, "Chile," p. 96.

CHAPTER SIX

Conclusion: The Dialogue between Order and Change

IN ORDER TO PULL TOGETHER the threads of group politics in Chile, it seems useful at this juncture to discuss three particularly eventful episodes in recent Chilean history. One of these, the health workers' strike of 1963, exemplifies the causes of political alienation among an important segment of the urban working class; it also sheds light on group methods and relationships in, as well as governmental response to, a crisis situation. Second, the elections of 1964 and 1965 are interesting in the way groups interact and contend as they react to deep societal frustrations in a period of heightened political activity. Finally, the subsequent reformist administration of President Eduardo Frei demonstrates difficulties inherent in the existing Chilean political system that deter any sudden resolution of endemic social and economic problems.

The Health Workers' Strike of 1963

For a number of years prior to the 1963 strike, the health workers had enunciated grievances about their working conditions and low pay.[1] Periodically, they initiated wildcat strikes to publicize these grievances; often they were charged with committing acts of sabotage during work stoppages in the hospitals and clinics where they were employed. For example, in the first six months of 1961 alone, twenty walkouts took place and, in the process, the conservative press claimed that the strikers turned off the heat in one hospital causing an explosion, that they stopped giving anaesthesia during surgery, that workers inserted ground glass in doctors' and nurses' surgical gloves, and that they committed additional reprehensible acts. The health workers countered that such accusations were baseless lies served up to inflame public opinion against them and to inhibit legitimate unionist activities. Frequently, when the heat of argument built toward its climax, the government granted a few concessions in the form of a small bonus and the rescinding of threatened disciplinary proceedings against the workers. Customarily, also, the minister of health and a few congressmen called for an overhaul of the entire National Health Service—a proposal that was forgotten in the aftermath of the dispute.

Then, in June, 1963, work stoppages broke out in several Santiago hospitals for mainly noneconomic reasons.[2] The government berated alleged acts of sabotage and went so far as to assign policemen to the affected hospitals to guard against additional improper actions. This simply further aggravated the workers, who left their jobs in even

[1] For a sympathetic treatment of the health workers' situation between 1961 and 1963, see Partido Comunista, *La salud de Chile: Un problema gremial y un problema nacional.*

[2] One of these was a solidarity strike for the families of four doctors killed in an explosion and for several nurses who were mutilated in the same explosion. The employees of the Arriaran Hospital did not consider the compensation to be paid by the government as sufficient. Another strike, in Borja Hospital, was in protest against the chief surgical nurse, whom the workers wanted transferred or fired.

larger numbers to protest the government's accusations and the measures levied against them. As tempers heated in the next weeks, the Health Workers' Federation once again brought up the basic economic injustices they suffered and, on August third, a rash of wildcat strikes erupted in many of Santiago's hospitals. Although not apparent at the time, this event was to lead into one of the most bitterly contested, longest, and most crippling strikes in the history of the National Health Service.[3]

As a background to the ensuing happenings, several aspects of the over-all situation need to be explained. To begin with, health workers are employed by the National Health Service (SNS), a governmental agency under the Ministry of Health.[4] Chile was the first Latin American country to institute a compulsory health insurance program for workers and, by the 1960's, three-fourths of the nation's population was cared for by the SNS. The SNS runs 80 per cent of the hospital beds in Santiago and 90 per cent throughout the country generally.[5] Thus, not only is the bulk of the citizenry dependent upon public medicine and thus adversely affected by a work stoppage, but also the number of workers who potentially could be involved in a strike against the National Health Service is unusually large.

SNS workers, being public employees, are legally not permitted to associate in unions. However, this injunction against government workers is notoriously ignored in Chile and, in fact, the health workers are organized into the Federación Nacional de Trabajadores de Salud (FNTS). Furthermore, FNTS is a component of CUT, Chile's major labor central. As the strike bore on, this relationship would prove only moderately helpful in strengthening the health workers' collective bar-

[3] Research for this section is based upon conversations with a number of the participants in the strike as well as upon files in the press-clipping service of the Chilean Library of Congress. In the latter category, the following Santiago newspapers and magazines were perused for August and September, 1961, and for June through December, 1963: *La Nación*, *El Diario Ilustrado*, *La Tercera de la Hora*, *El Mercurio*, *El Siglo*, *Las Ultimas Noticias*, *Clarín*, *Las Noticias de Ultima Hora*, *Ercilla*, *Vistazo*, and *Vea*.

[4] Robert Alexander, *Labor Relations in Argentina, Brazil, and Chile*, pp. 274–276.

[5] Kalman H. Silvert, *Chile: Yesterday and Today*, pp. 156–157.

gaining position, though CUT's ties with leftist parties would prove decisive in later political negotiations.

In 1963, it would have been difficult to disagree with the health workers' contention that they were not very generously paid for their labor. The issue centered more on whether they were any worse off than other workers and, even if they were, where could the government find revenues to raise their salaries. The director general of SNS, A. L. Bravo, insisted that the health workers actually had been rather well treated, noting that the number of health service employees had increased 25 per cent between 1958 and 1963, whereas the total salary increase for all health workers had jumped 250 per cent in the same period. On the other hand, he failed to mention that inflation had robbed that salary increase of very much meaning. And, even admitting to some improvement over those years, the minimum monthly pay for nonspecialized workers still was only about E°80 and for technical help, E°103 (roughly $26 and $34 U.S. respectively).[6]

Early in the strike, the conservative press set the tone of opposition to the health workers' walkout. *El Diario Ilustrado* editorialized that, instead of being just an economic matter, the strike was managed by leftists who sought to harass the government and to instill fear in the hearts of the people with an end to bringing down the government and establishing their own regime of tyranny. Hence, *El Diario Ilustrado* rejected "these illegal and sudden work stoppages" and it opposed the strikers "because of the threatening nature of the petitions they present to Public Authorities or to private enterprises; because the petitions are unjust or inopportune; because they are contrary to the Labor Code; because especially, they harm the general public—criminal!"[7] The newspaper itself was somewhat threatening when it reminded the workers of the futility of their acts, since there was no money to be found anywhere to increase salaries, and that they would lose their pay for the days they did not work.[8] For their part, *El Mercurio* and *La Nación* tallied the mounting numbers of workers who left their posts in the hospitals and stressed the dangers to the ill imposed by the strike.

[6] *El Mercurio* (Santiago), August 24, 1963.
[7] *El Diario Ilustrado* (Santiago), August 3, 1963.
[8] *Ibid.*, August 18, 1963.

President Jorge Alessandri (1958 to 1964) was a no-nonsense type of executive who demanded honesty and dedication from his staff. His administration—while comprising Conservatives, Liberals, and Radicals—was supposed to be "above politics," and his primary goal in governing seemed to be the maintenance of stability in the country at the same time that he endeavored to reduce the ruinous rate of the inflationary spiral. Toward the latter, he looked with great dismay at wage increases as deleterious in the long run to the worker and to the economy.

Not surprisingly, then, the government's approach to the strike was unyielding and tough. Bravo immediately moved members of the armed forces, police, Red Cross, Civil Defense, and other voluntary agencies into as many of the jobs left vacant by the striking workers as he could find personnel to fill them. In addition, he issued a strongly worded edict ordering hospital directors to dock a striker's pay for every day he failed to appear on the job and threatened summary dismissal to any worker absent from his post for more than three days without just cause.

Meanwhile, the leftist political parties, in unanimous support of the strikers, came up with ways to finance a salary hike for the health workers. On August fifth, Communist deputies met with Minister of the Interior Sótero del Río and suggested that taxes be enlarged by 5 per cent on corporations, by 10 per cent on corporation executives, and by 10 per cent on private banks, and that the steel factory at Concepción (Compañía de Acero del Pacífico) be removed from its tax-free status. The plea fell on unsympathetic ears and the government stood firm in refusing to allow any wage relief for the SNS.

To the health workers all this was a too-familiar pattern; to the government there was no way to satisfy the health workers. Thus, what began on August second as a four-hour work stoppage in a number of Santiago hospitals, on August nineteenth commenced a four-day walkout in most Santiago hospitals. At the close of the four-day period, the strike was renewed for another ninety-six hours, and so on; from Santiago the strike reached out into more and more of the provinces. For a moment, on August twenty-second, it seemed as though three senators —Salvador Allende for the Socialists, Jaime Barros for the Communists, and Luis Bossay of a rebel Radical wing—had reached a solution to the impasse in conversation with the minister of the interior.[9] But this favorable report proved premature and the failure of the negotiations only toughened the stand of the Federation of Health Workers, who now ordered even its hospital emergency crews to leave their posts. The following day, strikers attempted to keep nonstriking personnel from entering the hospitals; police, however, kept the entrances open and several strikers were taken into custody.

After one week of the strike, the director general of SNS reversed an earlier threat to close the hospitals if the workers did not return and instead indicated that the situation had normalized. Bravo observed that in the various regions of the country, either the strike movement had never gotten off the ground, it had been halted, or military and civilian help were maintaining necessary hospital services. (Actually, the hospitals were operating at perhaps 50 per cent of capacity.)

The next day the strike spilled over into downtown Santiago for the first time. Strikers ran through the streets calling "Long live the hospital strike" and occasional sympathetic bystanders echoed their slogan.

On September first, the strike had dragged on for two weeks and the antistrike forces had not budged. President Alessandri flatly rejected any pay increase. He was backed by Liberals and Conservatives in his cabinet and in Congress; management overwhelmingly approved his anti-inflationary stance; and a few other groups, such as hospital supervisory personnel (i.e., the Federación Nacional Hospitalaria de Chile), expressed their reservations about the walkout.

For the time being, the health workers' position seemed untenable in the face of Alessandri's posture in the matter and his apparent majority control of both houses of Congress. Still, the health workers were not without friends. Employees in the administrative headquarters of the health department (i.e., in the Dirección General de Salud) began a twenty-four–hour sympathy strike on August twenty-ninth and then continued to follow the health workers' lead by staying away from their jobs in sequential four-day periods. Early in the strike, an association of medical doctors, the Federación Médica, proffered their

[9] *Las Noticias de Ultima Hora* (Santiago), August 22, 1963.

moral support to the health workers; then on September second, leaders of Federación Médica agreed to contribute financially to the health workers and the president of the federation announced that he had received a number of requests from doctors that they also go out on strike. Indeed, doctors at the Psychiatric Hospital did leave their jobs for four days beginning September thirteenth.

Moreover, on September second, Salvador Allende, himself a doctor and a former minister of health, returned to Santiago from campaigning in the southern provinces. Allende quickly moved to take command of the pro–health workers' forces and called for all doctors and teachers to support the strike. The leftist press made much of his popping up at several open-air soup kitchens, which fed thousands of the strikers every day. At one of these *ollas comunes*, Allende said, "I see that you are firm. For our part, we shall continue doing everything possible to find a just solution to the conflict." Then he went up to an old nurse who had worked with him for a half-dozen years in one of Santiago's hospitals; after they embraced each other, the nurse exclaimed, "This time for sure we will elect you President. We consider you one of us."[10]

As a component of CUT, the health workers had every reason to expect support from that organization. In point of fact, however, the big labor confederation was having troubles of its own. At the end of August, CUT's president, Oscar Núñez, announced his confederation's complete backing to the health workers and threatened a national strike that would halt all activities in the country if the government did not come up with a satisfactory solution "in the next few days."[11] On September second, a meeting of CUT's National Directive Council considered the possibility of a forty-eight–hour solidarity strike involving thirty-five federations and 750,000 workers.[12] Two days later, the Council reassembled to discuss such a strike, but no definite conclusion was reached. Several federations were not represented at the conference

[10] *El Siglo* (Santiago), September 11, 1963.
[11] *Clarín* (Santiago), August 30, 1963.
[12] This was an exaggerated claim. If all of CUT's membership were to go on strike—an unlikely possibility at any time—the total would probably be less than half the number cited.

and disagreement developed among those who were present over the advisability of proclaiming a nation-wide work stoppage. Nevertheless, they did unite in addressing a lengthy letter to President Alessandri, signed by the heads of all the federations comprising CUT, in which they reminded the President that he had admitted that the workers were improperly remunerated. Indeed, the CUT leaders insisted, they were not paid enough to provide the barest necessities for their families, that their cause was just, and that if the strike were not settled equitably quite soon the health of all the working-class families of Chile would be severely endangered. Alessandri replied that he already had done everything possible for the workers in granting an average increase of 30 per cent during 1962. He repeated that no funds existed in the present fiscal year to do any more; the best he could suggest was that the situation be reassessed in 1964.[13]

Since CUT could not reach accord on a walkout, on September fourth the Communist-controlled Federación Minera declared its own solidarity strike for forty-eight hours.[14] On September sixth, CUT reiterated its total allegiance to the health workers' cause, vowed to redouble its monetary and food contributions to the strikers, and instructed its federations to be ready to launch a great general strike soon. The call never came. Some of the weaker federations feared a general strike would only further reduce their bargaining effectiveness; the active participation of political parties in the negotiations caused some union splits along partisan lines; and, although there existed general sympathy for the health workers' gaining a salary raise, many industrial workers made less in wages, recognized the futility of the strike, and suffered the most from the limited hospital services available.

Paralleling these developments, a torrent of congressional debate had also been concerned with all aspects of the strike and an almost continuous flow of congressional party leaders beat at the doors of high-ranking executive officials. A debate in the Chamber of Deputies on the night of September fourth typified the major parties' positions

[13] *El Mercurio* (Santiago), September 4, 1963.

[14] The miners also tossed in some grievances of their own relating to conditions in the Atacama region.

regarding the strike.[15] For their part, the Liberal party members argued that the strike was the wrong way to settle the problem because it caused inadequate hospital care—a 10 per cent jump in the infant mortality rate already being apparent. Furthermore, the Liberals contended that the strike was contrary to the right of freedom to work, since the strikers impeded others from reaching their jobs. Conservatives supported this viewpoint, claiming that the strike was not legitimate, that the strikers should have looked for other means to resolve their differences with the government, and that the effects of the strike were ruinous on the care of the sick—figures suggesting that the mortality rate for all ages in the hospitals had leaped by 50 per cent.

Of all the parties, the Radicals found themselves in the most enigmatic position. From one standpoint they should have supported the health workers fully, since government workers in large measure adhered to the Radical party. On the other side, the Radicals still formed part of Alessandri's coalition and thus were obliged to stick with the chief executive's policies. As a consequence, they argued a middle position. The Radicals recognized that the needs of the health workers were sizable and required sympathetic attention. Nevertheless, little could be done for them immediately inasmuch as the National Health Service treasury suffered from a deficit of nearly 24 million escudos. Instead, the Radicals declared they were forwarding a plan to President Alessandri that requested consideration of a law for 1964 to balance the budget of the National Health Service and to seek some method for implanting a new wage scale for the health workers more appropriate to the important services they performed. In the meantime, they proposed that the strike be terminated by authorizing a loan of E°100 to each health worker and by agreeing to pay all wages for the period of the walkout.

The rest of the political parties lined up solidly against the government's decision to deny the health workers any remunerative improvement during 1963. Christian Democrats asserted that eighteen thousand employees of the National Health Service earned less than the

[15] The official version of the debate appeared in *La Nación* (Santiago), September 6, 1963.

base salary necessary to minimally provide for a family. When legally permitted deductions were accounted for, their wages appeared even more paltry. For example, a monthly salary of E°79 dropped to E°66 after deductions. Therefore, the Christian Democrats recommended an across-the-board salary increase of E°24 per month and demanded that no reprisals be invoked against those out on strike.

The parties in FRAP lambasted the government for its obduracy. PADENA lashed away at officials who traveled to Europe and the United States at public expense, but who could not come up with money for the workers. PADENA also branded the Radical party solution an absurd one; how, they asked, could loans be offered to people not receiving a just salary in the first place? The Socialists took the government to task for lying about the health workers' actual wages, for dismissing them as unimportant menial functionaries, and for instituting a "siege of hunger" against the strikers. Communists decried an official policy that favored a handful of monopolies, latifundists, and Yankee imperialists. They resubmitted their earlier proposal to raise taxes on corporations, corporation executives, and banks and to begin taxing the steel plant at Concepción. By taking these measures, more than E°12 million would accrue to the public coffers, a sufficient amount to lift the health workers to a viable economic status.

In mid-September, the stalemate persisted with no hope in sight for an early end to the walkout. Then, on the twenty-fifth day of the strike matters came to a head. For several weeks, governmental intransigence and deepening frustrations among the strikers increasingly moved the locus of strike activity into the center of Santiago. At first, gatherings of SNS workers and members of fraternal unions assembled at the confluence of Alameda and Dieciocho streets in order to communicate on the latest happenings and to plot strategy. But as tempers heated, the strikers turned to parading along other streets to rally support to their cause. Soon they were joined by students and sympathetic workers from CUT. Perhaps inevitably, on September ninth the mounting numbers of demonstrators clashed with police. At noon the following day, several hundred persons came together in the gardens of the national Congress; following instructions they next broke up into groups and quickly moved throughout the downtown streets disconnecting the cables of the trolleybuses. The resulting traffic congestion brought the intervention of police, who tried to unsnarl the mess. Then, some protestors hurled missiles at the police, who retaliated by ordering water trucks to the scene and shot streams of water at the demonstrators. Nearly twelve hours were required to untangle the traffic and to return the city to normalcy. By the end of the day, twenty-five protestors had been arrested; of those detained, seven worked for the National Health Service.

No important transgressions of the peace were repeated during the following day. Around noon a few clusters of protestors appeared briefly; and at seven o'clock in the evening, several youths and adults sat in the street at a busy intersection, though when the police diverted traffic along other avenues, they departed without incident.

At noon on September twelfth, just a block from the President's offices in the Palacio Moneda, rioting broke out once more. Protestors hurled rocks and refuse at commercial buildings and at public transportation vehicles. For a moment, Chief of Police Colonel Joaquín Chinchón H., speaking through a megaphone, succeeded in quieting the mob; the police then started the demonstrators moving out of the area of conflict. But one block beyond, the protestors encountered another group of demonstrators and the combined force renewed their violent acts. Several nonstrikers leaped on the chief of police and hurled him to the ground; a police lieutenant, who tried to free Colonel Chinchón, was grounded as well. With this, the police brought out their full antiriot weaponry, covering everyone within range with streams of water and tear gas. Unfortunately, a water truck's span of visibility is limited and in the hectic circumstances one of the drivers failed to observe a striker by his truck and accidentally ran over him. The fallen man turned out to be Luis Becerra, a principal leader of the health workers, who died a few minutes later on his way to the hospital.

With this tragic turn of events, practically all the protestors dispersed and the police were able to restore order by two o'clock in the afternoon. That the demonstrations had led to death sobered most unionists as well as the political party leaders who had helped to convert what originally was a strike with economic goals into a political cause célèbre. Now, the Radical congressmen broke ranks with the Alessandri coalition to force through a legislative enactment aimed at ending the strike deadlock. Although Allende led the fight in the Senate on behalf of the proposed law, the legislative bill comprised proposals similar to ones the Radicals had put forth somewhat earlier. That is, a loan of E°200 was granted to each SNS worker (to be paid in two installments and based upon a loan from the Central Bank to the SNS), workers were paid for the period of the walkout, and no reprisals were to be launched against any strikers. Finally, it was requested that a commission be formed in 1964 to uncover a definitive solution to the plight of the health workers. In record time, the Senate passed the bill and sent it immediately to the Chamber of Deputies where it was handled with equivalent dispatch and passed with a large majority.[16] In both chambers, only Conservatives and Liberals voted in opposition on the grounds that the measure was unconstitutional. Eduardo Frei retorted that, while the measure was not ideal, it was "an emergency solution to an emergency situation" and that when there was death in the streets there no longer was time to debate over constitutional niceties.[17]

Thus, a strike of twenty-five days finally was resolved by the Congress in a couple of hours and the following day strikers began returning to their jobs. As a face-saving device, CUT called for a brief work stoppage to enable workers to attend Becerra's funeral. Unquestionably, there never was any thought that all of CUT's components would actually leave their jobs; but the gesture was aimed at assuaging any hurt feelings by showing that the health workers had not been neglected by the big labor confederation.

In the wake of the strike settlement, Alessandri's cabinet collectively offered to resign in order to free the chief executive's hands to deal

[16] The bill was approved in the Senate by a vote of 13 to 3 and in the Chamber of Deputies by a majority of 46 to 14. The bill was printed in *Las Ultimas Noticias* (Santiago), September 13, 1963.

[17] *Ibid.*

with residual complexities growing out of the crisis. In fact, Radicals in the cabinet went so far as to condemn the Radical congressmen for abandoning Alessandri's position and for backing the health workers' loan. Accordingly, the Radical party's CEN assembled, severely chastised the Radical ministers for their comments, and voted to pull out of the Alessandri government. (Nevertheless, they still favored staying with the Conservatives and Liberals in the Democratic Front in its campaign for Julio Durán for the presidency.) As a result of CEN's decision, Alessandri was forced to reconstitute his cabinet as a "nonpolitical" one made up of Conservatives, Liberals, and independents.

The response of the press to these events followed along characteristically partisan lines. *La Nación* evaluated Congress' handling of the strike as an inflationary act that would cause the cost of living to leap ever higher; *El Mercurio* viewed the congressional action as a grave "transgression of the principle of authority."[18] The leftist newspapers labored to characterize the ending of the strike and the fall of Alessandri's cabinet as blows for the people that presaged victory in the upcoming presidential election. Hence, on the day of Becerra's funeral, *El Siglo* exclaimed: "Today the people will march to the Cemetery. Tomorrow to Power."[19]

For the time being an uneasy calm fell over the political scene. At last, the crippling strike had ended and the political parties could concentrate their resources directly on higher stakes, the presidential election. In fact, very few Chileans obtained satisfaction from the outcome of the strike and neither the government camp nor the health workers and their allies settled anything. And whatever the justice of one side or another in the dispute, ever-enlarging segments of the population concluded that the incumbent type of administration could not or would not effectively deal with endemic social and economic problems. The bulk of the population answered this situation by demanding change.

[18] Quoted in *El Siglo* (Santiago), September 14, 1963. Also, see *El Mercurio* and *La Nación* for the same day.

[19] *El Siglo* (Santiago), September 14, 1963.

The Elections of 1964 and 1965[20]

The Chilean voter is called upon to express his electoral choice for four types of officeholders—the municipal councilmen (*regidores*), national congressmen (both deputies and senators), and the nation's President.[21] The President is chosen by direct popular vote every six years (e.g., 1958, 1964, 1970). However, if no candidate obtains an absolute majority of the ballots cast, the decision as to who is the winner falls to the Congress, which assembles in a joint session with each deputy and senator voting as an individual. Then the Congress chooses between the two candidates who secured the highest popular pluralities; historically, this has always meant that the leading candidate received congressional approval. In 1964, the Frapistas, who had a definite minority of congressional seats, claimed that, should their nominee win a plurality but not a majority of the popular votes, the center-right would violate tradition and pick the second man on the list. Numerous Marxist labor and political leaders threatened to "go to the streets" if that should occur. Since the Christian Democrats' Eduardo Frei actually carried an absolute majority the issue did not arise.

Municipal councilmen and congressmen are selected by direct popular vote on the basis of the d'Hondt type of proportional representation. Thus, each electoral district produces several officeholders for the representative bodies. Commonly, most municipal councils are composed of five *regidores*, but departmental capitals have seven, provincial centers nine, and Valparaíso and Santiago twelve and fifteen, respectively. The electoral districts for the Chamber of Deputies select a more varied number, with three to five being the most common, though rising to eighteen in Santiago's first district. Senators are elected

20 Most of this section originally appeared in Ben G. Burnett and Kenneth F. Johnson, *Political Forces in Latin America*, pp. 360–365.

21 Regarding Chilean election procedure, see Mario Bernaschina González, *Cartilla electoral*; Ricardo Cruz-Coke, *Geografía electoral de Chile*; Frederico G. Gil, *Chile: Election Factbook*; República de Chile, *Ley General de Elecciones*. Additional information was obtained from M. Eugenia Soler Manfredini, executive secretary of the National Electoral Registration Secretariat, in Santiago, April 8, 1964.

from nine districts, each having five senate seats. All deputies and approximately half the senators stand election every four years (e.g., 1961, 1965, 1969); elections for *regidores* used to occur in three-year intervals, but beginning in 1967 they have taken place every four years. Since the municipalities are virtually powerless, elections for councilmanic posts attract primary interest as a bellwether of political party strength.

Generally, electoral procedure has evolved into a democratic and meaningful process in modern times. Still, it has not been completely devoid of problematic aspects. Under the 1925 Constitution literate males twenty-one years or more were obliged to register and vote though the compulsory feature was largely ignored. In 1949, women gained the franchise. One grave shortcoming of the registration process reduced the citizenry's voting capacity: registration offices were open for only a very few hours. During the 1950's, offices were open for only about 4 per cent of the average work time in Chile. This proved to be a particular handicap for the working classes, who found it difficult to obtain a release from their employment in order to register. If there was a line-up, they often had not been granted sufficient time to complete the registration process.[22] This difficulty affected as many as 26 per cent of those legally entitled to vote. Improvements in the system were finally enacted in 1962 when permanent registration was created, and at about the same time a longer period in which to register was ordered.

For the most part, the balloting process itself is conducted under fair and impartial boards of scrutiny, and vote counting is carried out honestly. Any political party can list its candidates on the ballot once it has filed the necessary information with electoral authorities. The principal requirement, that a party must be endorsed by the signed petition of ten thousand registered voters, is not a serious deterrent to such groups. Only independent candidates at times find it difficult to acquire the requisite number of signatures, of which two thousand for a deputy, five thousand for a senator, and twenty thousand for President are needed. Violence is not unknown but is uncommon.

[22] *Ercilla* (Santiago), August 22, 1956.

Certain coercive techniques have been part of the stock in trade of traditionalist elements. In the rural areas especially, landowners ordered qualified voters on their estates to cast ballots for conservative candidates, and frequently votes were purchased. Similar practices could be found in some urban-management situations. As recently as the Curicó by-election of 1964, the conservative electoral front banked a large sum of cash with the intent of spreading the largesse for vote buying. On learning of this move, the Christian Democrats joined with the Marxists to keep the rightists physically from entering the bank to make a withdrawal. Such techniques are rapidly becoming passé as reformist parties play upon working-class demands for fundamental change instead of on just a bread-and-circus approach at election time.

An intriguing electoral phenomenon in recent years has been the expanding number of citizens expressing their wishes at the polls. The proportion of those who registered grew from roughly one-eighth of the total population in the 1940's to more than a third in the 1960's. This increase can be explained partly by the addition of women's votes after 1949 and partly by improved registration procedures. In addition, swelling alienation from what many considered to be "do-nothing" regimes undoubtedly had its impact on election turnouts. Statistics on the percentage of the total population who actually voted in the last four presidential elections dramatically substantiate this trend: in 1946, 8.73 per cent voted; in 1952, 15.95 per cent; in 1958, 17.90 per cent; and in 1964, 31.82 per cent.

The 1964 presidential election was remarkable from the opening of the campaign to the announcement of the voters' decision. In Chile the formal campaign process may not begin until six months before the date of the presidential election (two months in the case of congressional and municipal elections), but by that time many things will have already transpired. Shortly after the April 7, 1963, municipal elections were concluded, four candidates actively sought support for their presidential aspirations. Right-wing elements of the Radical party succeeded in carrying the Radicals into an electoral alliance with the Liberals and Conservatives. Calling themselves the Frente Democrático (FD, or Democratic Front), the alliance nominated the right-wing Radical Julio Durán, who had come up from his party's youth movement to be a deputy and then a senator since 1957. Durán demonstrated excellent stage presence and youthful vigor (he was forty-six years old in 1964), and the fact that the front's three component groups had won slightly over 46 per cent of the votes cast in the 1963 municipal elections engendered optimism among FD members that their candidate held the inside track to victory.

The Socialists and the Communists, along with the small hanger-on PADENA (Partido Democrático Nacional), had coalesced into FRAP (Frente de Acción Popular or Popular Action Front) and now renominated their 1958 standard-bearer, Salvador Allende Gossens, a physician and Socialist senator who only narrowly lost to Jorge Alessandri in 1958. Allende at fifty-six was the oldest of the candidates and, though a Marxist, came from the professional upper class. Some critics considered him rather foppish, an image he sought to dispel by shaving off his mustache and appearing in a less flamboyant manner. Still, his followers prized him as one of their own, a man of means with a genuine social conscience.

The logical choice of the Christian Democrats for their presidential nominee, Eduardo Frei Montalva, had helped to found the Christian Democratic party (known as the Falange Nacional in earlier times) when a number of youths broke away from the Conservative party. Frei had alienated many of the upper class by this act. Moreover, he continually attacked the upper class as well as the conservative regime of Jorge Alessandri (1958–1964). Undoubtedly his background as a law professor and senator helped Frei gain a reputation as a notable opponent in debate and, together with a stately appearance and manner, marked him as a formidable campaigner. He had been the first member of his party to gain a seat in the Senate, he had chalked up 21 per cent of the vote in the 1958 presidential election, and now at fifty-three years of age he would become Latin America's first Christian Democratic president.

The candidacy of the far rightist, Jorge Prat Eschaurren, held only nuisance value for the campaign. A follower of the *caudillo* Carlos Ibáñez, in whose administration Prat had served as minister of finance, his posture was personalist and independent, against politics, big business, and the United States. Some concern existed that the forty-six–

year–old candidate might cut into one of the other three front runners' voting strength.

The campaign unfolded in typical Chilean style as the candidates scurried throughout the republic developing organization, seeking financial aid, and talking to anyone who would listen. All the media were filled with their wanderings, charges and countercharges, and estimates of their relative standing among the voters. Then, in the otherwise minor special election for deputy held in the rural district of Curicó in March, 1964, the tone of the campaign altered. All three major candidates staked a great deal on the outcome of the Curicó race and converted it into a micropresidential election. Durán announced that, if the Democratic Front did not win, he would withdraw his candidacy—seemingly a safe statement, since the front had previously accumulated almost as many votes as the total of Frapist and Christian Democratic ballots. Meanwhile, FRAP had been registering increasingly strong inroads into the rural areas, considered the Frapist chances to be very good in Curicó, and so accepted the election as a welcome proof of superior national strength. The Christian Democrats unwillingly entered a candidate of their own in the contest as well; Prat refused to do so and, standing on the side lines, attacked the entire process.

When the last ballot was counted, the Democratic Front's pre-election claim of 56 per cent of the votes proved absurd, as it received only 32.5 per cent. The Frapist candidate won with 39.5 per cent. Now the Democratic Front collapsed like a house of cards. Durán resigned though later was compelled to re-enter the campaign in order to try to hold the Radical party together. The Liberals and the Conservatives faced a critical dilemma. They disliked Frei but feared that, if they backed Prat, they might permit Allende to sneak into the presidency by a small plurality. Hence, they ended up throwing their weight to Frei, and Prat stepped out of the running—effectively reducing the race to a contest between Frei and Allende.[23]

[23] Among several good studies of the 1964 campaign, see Federico G. Gil and Charles J. Parrish, *The Chilean Presidential Election of September 4, 1964*, and Orville G. Cope, "The 1964 Presidential Election in Chile: The

The most important change in the campaign in subsequent months was the increasing emphasis on Allende's being controlled by the Communists and the recurring propaganda asking Chileans if they wanted to go the way of Cuba. This evoked images of dictatorship, executions, and children being taken from their mothers and sent off to the Soviet Union.[24] Actually, the two candidates' programs possessed elements of great similarity; both candidates attacked the incumbent, do-nothing Alessandri regime and demanded the deepest political, economic, and social reforms. Indeed, both insisted that only revolution would answer Chile's needs. However, Frei denounced the Frapist revolution as being "with dictatorship" and instead offered his own "revolution in freedom." Allende countered with the claim that the Christian Democrats would really bring "exploitation in freedom," the Frapistas planning a "revolution without blood."

Most significant here is the stress upon revolution. The conservatives had to support Frei as the lesser of two very unpleasant evils, and more of the conservatives probably liked Allende but were fearful of his Marxist beliefs and Communist ties. This left the Christian Democrats comparatively free to pursue their reformist program and capture the allegiance of the poor, among whom dissidence was ubiquitous.

By and large, Frei's campaign appeared to be more professionally managed than Allende's. The Christian Democrats emulated a number of party practices followed in the United States and it was believed that the top party officials had been avid students of the 1960 Kennedy campaign.[25] For example, whereas the Frapistas interviewed a number

Politics of Change and Access," *Inter-American Economic Affairs* 19, no. 4 (Spring 1966): 3–29.

[24] One especially notorious poster that was directed against alleged Communist control of Allende was issued by the Durán camp, but ultimately contributed to Frei's anti-Communist propaganda. It pictured the arm of communism stamping the hammer and sickle on a child's forehead. The caption read, "Chilean Mother: Fidel Castro sent 15,000 children to Russia, tearing them from their mothers' arms. If you don't want to lose your children, vote for Durán."

[25] Certainly, many Christian Democratic leaders read Theodore H. White's *Making of the President 1960,* with more than passing interest.

of slum dwellers in largely pro-Allende neighborhoods without regard to scientific sampling techniques and then announced the results for their propaganda impact, the Christian Democrats undertook selective scientific polling in a few areas with a purpose to appraise their own ability to reach voters and then, where appropriate, they adjusted their campaign strategy and organization accordingly.

Furthermore, while both camps labored vigorously for their nominees, the atmosphere within Allende's national campaign headquarters differed markedly from that of Frei's. The Allende campaign forces were centered in FRAP's Casa del Pueblo in downtown Santiago.[26] An air of informality permeated the headquarters: working-class people circulated freely through the shabby old building and rubbed elbows with party officials. Senator Allende himself maintained his office in the Casa and frequently appeared in the corridors and stopped for a moment to chat with bystanders.

In contrast, the Christian Democrats operated out of two buildings —both in the central section of the capital. One of these, like the Casa del Pueblo, was an old building; it housed the party's secretariat and various departments and it was here where people off the street mingled with mostly lower-echelon party workers. On the other hand, Senator Frei and practically all his high-ranking campaign strategists were quartered in a suite of offices in a modern building several blocks away. This arrangement encouraged a close budgeting of Frei's time and kept him aloof from the chance and informal contacts with people that characterized Allende's style.[27]

[26] FRAP did maintain another group of offices. However, it was for OCEPLAN, its body of research-and-planning specialists who were preparing governmental programs should Allende be elected President.

[27] The author was privileged to interview both candidates in May, 1964. In Allende's case, the interview was set up quite simply. The senator's secretary was away from her desk, so the author knocked on Allende's office door and was invited in; Senator Allende agreed to a meeting in three days. Arranging a conversation with Senator Frei proved more complicated. At the conclusion of an interview with the Christian Democrats' secretary general, José de Gregorio, in the party's main headquarters, the author requested an interview with Mr. Frei. Indicating that this would be difficult, if not impossible, Gregorio did call campaign headquarters and set up a meeting for a couple of days later. It turned out that the initial contact actually was with a receptionist

Election day on September 4, 1964, passed devoid of improprieties. In line with Chile's generally unbroken democratic tradition, the government remained scrupulously impartial and the voting process was carried out in total honesty. In the end Christian Democracy recorded a clean sweep: Frei garnered 56.1 per cent of the vote (1,409,012 votes), Allende followed with 38.9 per cent (977,902 votes), and Durán could only pull in 5 per cent (125,233 votes). Frei carried nineteen of Chile's twenty-five provinces, narrowly lost in five of the remaining six, overwhelmingly won in Santiago and Valparaíso (Allende's district), and captured 60.5 per cent of the women's vote (compared to Allende's 35.7%). Unexpectedly, the Christian Democrats defeated FRAP among rural workers, did exceedingly well in the urban slums, found a large following among northern miners (a long-standing leftist stronghold), and even mustered a majority in Valdivia, which the Freista hierarchy had viewed in advance as a certain loss. Frei's magnetism, strong organizational base, doctrinal dynamism, and, very importantly, the Communist issue all contributed to the extraordinary Christian Democratic victory.

From another viewpoint, the 1964 election seemed to manifest widespread and growing insistence upon change. For one reason or another, 95 per cent of Chileans voted for revolution—either Christian Democratic or Marxist. This move to the left was repeated in the equally incredible and perhaps more revealing congressional elections held in March, 1965.[28] The popularity of Christian Democracy continued to climb to precedent-shattering heights. The Christian Democrats won 82 of 147 deputies' seats—strikingly more than their own most optimistic prediction of 60. Christian Democracy was the first political party to hold a majority in the Chamber of Deputies in well

who paved the way for an introduction to a secretary. She in turn worked out a date to come back. This time the author met with Frei's aide-de-camp, Juan de Dios Carmona, who politely refused the request. Fortunately, the previous interview with Salvador Allende caused him to reverse his decision and, on the following Monday morning, a very pleasant interview with Senator Frei took place.

[28] For an excellent study of the 1965 congressional election, see Charles J. Parrish, Arpad J. von Lazar, and Jorge Tapia Videla, *The Chilean Congressional Election of March 7, 1965: An Analysis.*

over a century. They only put up candidates for 12 senatorial seats and won all 12. Nevertheless, including a carry-over of one senator, the party controlled but 13 of the Senate's 45 seats—a minority situation that would act as a serious barrier to Christian Democratic reform efforts. Meanwhile, the Socialists and Communists survived the election in an even stronger position with 33 deputies, compared to 28 in the previous congressional election. Of course, the recipients of the voters' wholesale rejection of old styles and outdated solutions were the former partners of the Democratic Front. Their combined representation in the Chamber of Deputies toppled from 84 to 29; the Radicals had only half their former strength, and the Liberals-Conservatives collapsed to one-fifth. Clearly Chile had shifted to the left. Now the remaining question hinged on what Frei could do with such an apparent mandate in the way of translating his program into action.

FREI'S "MINI-REVOLUTION"[29]

There can be no question about Frei's sincerity in wanting to restructure society along lines he had elaborated in the 1964 and 1965 electoral campaigns. But obstructionist tactics by his political enemies and perhaps the inevitable inadequacies that derive from a government comprised of many inexperienced officials left a record of administration that fell short of total success.

The tip-off as to what Frei would experience as normal relationships with the Congress came as early as October 24, 1964, when Congress was supposed to proclaim Eduardo Frei the newly elected President. A congressional boycott by all the Socialists and Communists and by most of the Radicals forced a postponement of the proclamation until the following day when the law demanded legislative action. True, this was a lame-duck Congress in which the Christian Democrats constituted a minority grouping; but even after the Christian Democratic sweep of the 1965 congressional elections, their minority position in the Senate guaranteed enormous difficulties for Frei in his endeavors to convert proposals into deeds.

[29] This heading was suggested by James Becket's interesting article, "Tempest in a Copper Pot: Chile's Mini-Revolution," *Commonweal*, December, 1967, pp. 406–408.

In his first few weeks as Chile's chief executive, Frei antagonized the Right as well as the Left by the content of his demands for reform. The conservatives reacted negatively to fiscal proposals to increase income taxes, to reevaluate the bases of property assessments, and to initiate an austerity period in order to reduce inflation. An implied threat to institute rigid price controls also angered the Right. The Marxists saw the wind reduced in their sails by Christian Democratic demands for extensive school and housing expansion programs, by a call for the establishment of diplomatic and trade relations with Eastern nations, and by a proposal of an authentic land reform and the Chileanization of certain foreign-owned enterprises, especially in the copper mines.

Although it only held nuisance value in any practical sense, perhaps Congress' supreme insult to Frei occurred early in 1967 when, by a 23-to-15 vote in the Senate, the President was refused permission to leave the country for an official visit to the United States. The Marxists insisted that their action was solely aimed at protesting U.S. involvement in Vietnam; the Christian Democrats viewed their performance, though, as an act of monumental pettiness. Whatever the case, this event epitomized Frei's frustration in dealing with a recalcitrant Senate and pointed up the beleaguered state of his reform package. Moreover, in the following April, Christian Democratic fortunes slipped further when, after Frei stumped the country on behalf of his administration and tied the upcoming municipal elections to his own popularity, the Christian Democrats dropped more than seven percentage points from their proportion of the total vote cast in congressional elections two years before.[30]

Midway in Frei's presidency, countless observers of the Christian Democratic experiment were chronicling the "revolution with freedom" with friendly or morbid fascination. Sympathetic authors were impressed with the fact that, despite all the obstacles, some change had actually transpired; others were depressed with the only partial success of practically all of Frei's reform efforts.[31]

[30] See Michael Francis and Eldon Lanning, "Chile's 1967 Municipal Elections," *Inter-American Economic Affairs* 21, no. 2 (Autumn 1967): 23–36.

[31] A highly sympathetic view of Frei and the Christian Democrats is Leonard

Of the advances that were registered, achievements in education headed the list. The university population jumped from 35,000 to nearly 50,000 students and, whereas before 1965, approximately 25,000 new students entered the educational system each year, during Frei's first three years as President at least 450,000 youths were enrolled in the schools for the first time. Some 6,500 additional teachers and more than 2,000 new schols helped to absorb the increased school enrollments.[32] Also, a new program that provided two free meals a day in the schools ensured a higher nutritional intake for the poorer children and resulted in the added bonus of better attendance. (After nine months in operation, a rather curious decree that introduced compulsory religious education in the first two grades of all primary schools was rescinded, apparently in response to Protestant and secular pressures.)[33]

Governmental planners also recognized that a greatly invigorated public housing program was essential in order to contend with Chile's rapid population growth and to replace thousands of homes destroyed in the earthquakes of 1960 and 1965. Accordingly, almost immediately upon assuming office, the government launched an ambitious housing program that scored impressive performance levels in its first year of operation. Unfortunately, however, the burden of a top-heavy bureaucracy in the government housing agency and the early depletion of revenues for housing construction created drastic cutbacks in the public housing program. Thus, after the banner year of 1965, which totalled up 480,000 square meters of new publicly financed housing in the first four months alone, the public housing sector plummeted to 83,000

Gross, *The Last Best Hope: Eduardo Frei and Chilean Democracy*. More balanced critiques of the Frei administration at mid-passage are Becket, "Tempest in a Copper Pot"; Alan Angell, "Chile: The Christian Democrats at Midterm," *The World Today* 23, no. 10 (October 1967): 434–443; W. Raymond Duncan, "Chilean Christian Democracy," *Current History* 53, no. 315 (November 1967): 263–309; and Arpad von Lazar and Luis Quirós Varela, "Chilean Christian Democracy: Lessons in the Politics of Reform Management," *Inter-American Economic Affairs* 21, no. 4 (Spring 1963): 51–72.

[32] *New York Times*, January 22, 1968; "Los problemas de un reformador," *Visión*, May 24, 1968, p. 13.

[33] *New York Times*, March 25, 1967.

square meters in 1966 and to less than 43,000 in 1967 during comparable periods.[34] Nevertheless, the Christian Democrats boasted that 126,000 government-financed dwellings had been completed by early 1968. If this failed to fulfill their target figures—360,000 housing units had been the announced goal for 1970—it was a considerable improvement over the accomplishments of previous administrations.

Frei's record in the economic sphere also was very mixed.[35] For the three years of 1965 through 1967, the gross national product increased by 19 per cent, exceeding the 15 to 16 per cent growth rate that had been planned. Over and above that, government statistics maintained that real per capita wages rose by 41 per cent in the same period. Part of the country's improved financial position reflected inordinately high copper prices; but, in addition, the creation of sixty new industries and the greatly strengthened position of industrial exports (not counting copper and fishmeal, industrial exports in 1967 were double those between 1964 and 1966) contributed to the improved picture. On the other hand, early inroads made into cutting away at the inflationary spiral gradually weakened. In 1965, the rate of inflation was held to 26 per cent—comparing favorably with the 48 per cent of 1964—and in 1966, to 17 per cent. Still, in 1967, the rate edged up to 20 per cent and continued to rise in 1968 and 1969 to just over 27 per cent. Even at that, the situation almost certainly was worse than it appeared: "Since the government controls the prices on the items in the sample market basket, the above inflation figures are artificially low and no one in Chile believes them, a fact of some political importance."[36]

[34] Statistics on public housing are summarized in "Chile: No Work for the Building Industry," *Latin America*, September 22, 1967, pp. 168, 170, and "Los problemas de un reformador," p. 13.

[35] The following figures on economics are taken from "Chile," *Bank of London and South America Review* 2, no. 19 (July 1968): 406–410, and 4, no. 37 (January 1970): 58; "Media etapa del experimento chileno," *Visión*, November 24, 1967, pp. 12–13; "Chile: Exports Improve," *Latin America*, February 2, 1968, p. 39; and *New York Times*, October 16, 1967, and January 22, 1968.

[36] Becket, "Tempest in a Copper Pot," p. 406. Also, see Angell, "Chile," pp. 435–438; Angell makes a strong case against the more optimistic appraisals of Frei's ability to fight inflation.

In the field of taxation, while enraging the upper classes, the Frei administration scored some solid triumphs.[37] Initially, the basis for property assessment was reappraised. In 1965, it had been thirty-three years since the last assessment figures had been set out and then the Chilean peso was about four thousand times stronger. Now, property was reassessed and the appraised values rose from two to three times above the old rates. This was certainly more realistic than the levels extant for many years, though it still fell considerably below comparable taxation standards operative in Europe and the United States. By this means, and by feeding tax rolls along with the Santiago telephone book into a computer (as well as enforcing a "wealth tax" on assets held abroad and on automobiles and stocks), the government built up an increase in real tax revenues of 25 per cent per year.

Finally, on two of the most heatedly debated planks in the Christian Democratic platform—land reform and the Chileanization of certain foreign industries—achievements lagged behind promises. Frei's land reform bill was not introduced into Congress until 1965 and then close to two years of bitter struggle were required to secure its passage.[38] Meanwhile, the government was forced to rely upon the more conservative agrarian reform law passed in 1962 under Alessandri's presidency until its own measure saw the light of day. Consequently, the Frei administration at mid-passage perhaps necessarily dragged its feet in redistributing land—hardly the "massive, rapid, and drastic" process that its principal administrator, Jacques Chonchol, had promised.[39] (Indeed, late in 1968, Chonchol resigned in protest against what he considered to be the slow pace of land reform.) By the end of 1967, only about 8,000 families had acquired land of their own under resettlement procedures. Still, this rated better than the 4,480 families who were resettled between 1928 and 1962 and, then, most of the plots utilized for resettlement were carved out of unused gov-

[37] Taxation is discussed by Becket, "Tempest in a Copper Pot," p. 406, and *New York Times*, February 19, 1967.

[38] For the text of this proposed law, see Kenneth L. Karst, ed., *Latin American Legal Institutions: Problems for Comparative Study*, pp. 441–452.

[39] Jacques Chonchol, "Razones económicas, sociales, y políticas de la reforma agraria," in *Reformas agrarias en la América Latina*, ed. Oscar Delgado, p. 119.

ernment land.[40] Furthermore, the 1967 law permitted a greater number of causes for land expropriation than had been the case earlier. Now, besides inefficient land use, the government could expropriate estates because of their largeness, as a result of the social condition of their workers, and as a consequence of certain irrigation situations.[41]

Naturally, Frei found himself in a "damned-if-you-do, damned-if-you-don't" situation regarding land reform. The Right placed many obstacles in the way of any expropriation of private property, while the Marxists and many Christian Democrats favored a much stronger approach. Whatever the case, Frei's ambitious proposal on taking office to resettle 100,000 families by 1970 had to be reduced to 40,000 families and even that number seemed optimistic. Nonetheless, a start was made and, as a highly significant by-product, real impetus was given to fostering farm workers' associations. This alone could conduce measurably to restructuring the traditional nature of the rural community.[42]

Like the land reform bill, the copper bill experienced a lengthy fight for adoption. The two-fold purpose of Chileanizing copper was to increase production and to place majority control of the foreign companies' Chilean holdings in the hands of the Chilean government. Toward these ends, a copper bill was proposed to Congress at the end of 1964 and finally became law two years later.[43] In this instance, however, it was not so much limitations in the law itself that provoked opposition, but rather the government's clumsiness in negotiating with the U.S. copper companies. The upshot of the bargaining sessions was for Anaconda to retain complete control of its main investments and

[40] *New York Times*, January 22, 1968. The record of the Alessandri regime under the 1962 law was extremely mediocre. See William C. Thiesenhusen, *Chile's Experiment in Agrarian Reform*, pp. 36–45.

[41] The control of water rights, a major factor contributing to the perpetuation of *latifundia*, has been an especially difficult feature of the Chilean land system for proponents of land reform to contend. See James Becket, "Problemas de la Reforma Agraria," in *Reformas agrarias en la América Latina*, ed. Delgado, pp. 570–572.

[42] The ramifications of this development are discussed below in the concluding section on labor.

[43] At this writing Frei had reneged on his promise to Chileanize the incredibly poorly functioning foreign-owned telephone and electrical utilities.

to admit Chile only to a 25 per cent sharing in a minor holding; Kennecott agreed to Chilean control of 51 per cent of its big El Teniente mine, but won the right to continue managing its holding for eleven years, gained a more favorable tax position (actually boosting its profit margin), and reached an agreement whereby Chile and several international agencies would assume the burden of added investment for expansion. If one compares the mood of the copper companies in 1964, when they seemed threatened with nationalization by the Marxists or loss of majority control if the Christian Democrats won the election, with that of 1967, the change in circumstances could only have delighted them.[44]

In brief, by 1970, Frei's well-intentioned moves to fulfill his "revolution with freedom" had stumbled and then hesitated short of fulfillment. At best, as James Becket suggests, "the Christian Democrats have initiated a kind of New Deal."[45] And for a developing nation, it must be asked whether that is enough at this stage of its development. Arpad von Lazar and Luis Quirós Varela, commenting on the Christian Democrats as reform managers, conclude that indeed it may not be adequate:

> The example of Chile suggests that the management of socio-economic reforms is a difficult, slow and many-pronged process. Once the excitement and the halo of political victories wear off the day-to-day management and resolution of conflicts assume primary importance. Performance—the indicator of change and development—is both dependent upon capabilities and time. But time is the one that is most scarce. Unfortunately "delayed gratification" is acceptable only for a few; people want results and rewards immediately and the notion that rewards will have to be "reinvested" into the system is not a popular one.[46]

On the other hand, perhaps, that is all that can be expected:

[44] Angell, "Chile," pp. 438–439; Becket, "Tempest in a Copper Pot," p. 407; von Lazar and Quirós Varela, "Chilean Christian Democracy," p. 407. In January, 1969, the contract with Anaconda was renegotiated. As a consequence, the Chilean government assumed 51 per cent ownership of Anaconda's holdings in Chile.

[45] Becket, "Tempest in a Copper Pot," p. 407.

[46] Von Lazar and Quirós Varela, "Chilean Christian Democracy," p. 71.

But changes do occur. They occur if the government wants it, plans for it and helps to bring it about or not. . . . In this sense reform management is a tedious, undefined and exasperating process of manipulating social, economic and political forces in an essentially traditional environment. It is tedious because there are no short answers and quick solutions to problems that are the result of years of stagnation and inferiority. It is an undefined process because goals and means are often dependent upon the whims of political life, capabilities and resources. It is exasperating because it is a process that demands also conciliation and compromise.[47]

In all events, Frei can take credit for getting the country moving in several new directions and, despite failures in some areas and only partial successes in others, he has presided over the initial reallocation of scarce economic resources among wider strata of the population. And, even in the brief span of the first three years of his administration, adjustments in political role playing by various groups ensured irrevocable changes in the entire political fabric.

The Frei Era and Group Politics

One extremely important dimension of Frei's presence on the Chilean scene that often tends to get lost in the plethora of statistics about imports and exports, gross national product, and the like, has been the introduction of newly organized sectors of society into the political process at a time when traditionalists suffered a diminution of influence. The import of such modifications in group politics has obvious meaning for the relative ability of groups to issue their claims into the political system with anticipation of their satisfaction. In order to place this process in perspective, the following discussion, like the previous sequence of chapters, will review the communications media and the military, clergy, student, management, and labor elements, as well as the political parties in terms of their unfolding during the Frei years.

Communications

No dramatic innovations have altered the communication process in Chile in any substantive way, though the few changes that have taken

[47] *Ibid.*, pp. 71–72.

place are not without importance. Except for the Christian Democrats' situation, the Chilean press remained the same during the 1960's: informational and political arms of the Left and Right. Formerly dependent upon such friendly treatment as they could glean in the moderate and conservative press, the Christian Democrats gained their own newspaper, the government organ *La Nación*, when they won the presidency in 1964. The party's monthly publication, *Boletín PDC*, and Christian Democratic youth's *Ediciones Rebeldía* rounded out their polemical-informational media.

Aside from the press, radio continued to be far and away the most significant of the other mass media. Nonetheless, advances in the television industry presaged a sudden spurt in its over-all expansion. Although the content of television programming did not improve measurably—it still was plagued by a dearth of high-quality news presentations and of good domestically produced drama, with somewhere between 60 and 80 per cent of programs made up of films emanating from abroad, mostly from the United States—broadcasting stations were added at the universities in Valparaíso (Channel 8) and Antofagasta (Channel 4). The University of Concepción was authorized to start broadcasting; but by 1968 it still had not begun to do so. More important, the technical problems of broadcasting in a country sliced with mountain chains have been overcome with the installation of relay towers. These will permit the early establishment of a government-operated television station, beamed at the entire nation, which is supposed to avoid political partisanship and stress educational programs.[48]

In the realm of civil liberties, the right of free speech received a bonus from the Frei regime as well as a possible setback. On the positive side, in 1967 the more questionable features of the "Gag Law" (Ley Mordaza) were removed. Negatively, however, the government's frustrations over dealing with the obstreperousness of the Right and the Left led it to move against several political enemies in a manner that many consider excessively highhanded. Within a few months of its action liberalizing the press law, the government came down hard

[48] "Chile: Growth Aspects for Television," *Latin America*, March 22, 1968, pp. 89–90.

on leaders of the National party (a merger of the old Conservative and Liberal parties) for statements Frei construed to be seditious. The Nationals' president, vice-president, and treasurer were arrested under the Law for the Internal Security of the State; but the Santiago Court of Appeals and the nation's Supreme Court rejected the charges as without foundation.[49] Not long afterward, Socialist Senator Carlos Altamirano was charged with slandering the nation's armed forces; in this case, though, the court upheld the government's allegations and sentenced Altamirano to two months in jail.[50] Criticism of these measures was widespread, especially since the charges could not be made to stick in the case of the Nationals. The occurrences emphasized the difficulty those who govern at times have in differentiating between what can be defined as license in Chile's extremely open political environment and what the opposition insists is nothing less than the authoritative harassment of legitimate political expression. Perhaps it is revealing of the problems of governing Chile that the democratic reformer, Frei, found the distinction as elusive as had his conservative predecessor, Jorge Alessandri.

Military, Clergy, and Students

Of the military, clergy, and students, only the military might have shifted somewhat during Frei's administration from its customary relationship to the political system. In contrast, the high clergy remained committed to social and economic reform, which it advocated openly, but the political maneuvering for which it largely left to lay elements.[51]

49 "¿Una conspiración contra Chile?" *Visión*, September 29, 1967, p. 12.

50 *New York Times*, April 2, 1968.

51 Inevitably some priests, in their eagerness for reform, overstep the boundaries even of what a liberal hierarchy considers proper. Such occurred in August, 1968, when 8 priests and 3 nuns, along with 150 or so laymen, seized the Santiago cathedral and held it for fourteen hours on a Sunday in protest against the squandering of money for the Pope's upcoming visit to Bogotá and for the present Church's compromise with wealth and power. The cardinal suspended the priests for one day until they apologized for their action and accepted the authority of the Church. That they were not more harshly dealt with perhaps says a great deal about the Chilean hierarchy's progressivism—an agreement on social views, but a disagreement over tactics (*Los Angeles Times*, August 12, 1968).

In the process, the Church tended to continue to move away from its traditional allies among the upper classes and to devote greater attention to the spiritual and social condition of the lower economic strata. This was summed up in a bishops' pastoral letter, which asked forgiveness for "the haughty, un-Christian and even despotic behavior of many of its sons in the face of the social injustice of the countryside."[52]

For their part, students early responded to Frei's call for Promoción Popular, a program directed at strengthening associational ties at the grass roots, by working among the impoverished neighborhoods of Santiago and elsewhere. University students, for example, devoted part of their vacations in poverty areas teaching illiterates to read and write and helping to construct schools. Furthermore, Christian Democratic and Communist students dominated the Frente Unido de la Reforma Agraria, an interest group operating in the late 1960's to foster agrarian reform and endeavoring to counter rightist efforts to halt land redistribution. At the same time that Christian Democracy attracted great numbers of students to its fold—in 1966 at the University of Concepción, for instance, Christian Democratic students gained majority control of the only university student directorate not then in its possession—the Frei government, like many of its predecessors, encountered some of its most active adversaries among students.

In April, 1965, at a time of continuing price increases because of the inflationary spiral, the government sought to invoke a 50 per cent addition to the cost of bus fares—the students' especial bugaboo—and, hence, provoked a vigorous protest from both university and high-school students. Thousands of them demonstrated in the streets of Santiago and for a few hours several hundred students held the gardens in front of the Congress building. Related demonstrations also broke out in Concepción. A year later, students closed down the University of Concepción, insisting that Ford Foundation, Peace Corps, United Nations, and other foreigners working at the University be

[52] "Chile: Right Wing Reaction to Agrarian Reform," *Latin America*, April 26, 1968, p. 130. For a discussion of some possible dangers in the Chilean church's social philosophy, see Fredrick B. Pike, "The Catholic Church and Modernization in Peru and Chile," *Journal of International Affairs* 20, no. 2 (1966): 272–278.

ejected from the campus. Similarly, classes were suspended at the University of Chile during part of May and June, 1968, because of student protests. Despite the abundance of student activist expression, there was no fundamental modification in their tactics. Also, the catalysts propelling them into an activist posture were typical of their primary interests: in the 1965 episode, economic problems and the enormous burden that students feel if transportation becomes more costly; political-nationalistic considerations at the University of Concepción in 1966; and, at the University of Chile in 1968, as the outgrowth of a long-time fight for strong student representation on the University Council, a victory the Catholic University students had won the previous year.[53]

If student activists were to resort to more violent tactics in the near future, they would be most likely to appear as a consequence of tactical changes on the far left. A number of socialist politicians, many of whom are identified with Maoism and Castroism, have rejected peaceful methods and parliamentary democracy. Should they convert their statements into action, their student adherents could form a revolutionary vanguard that undoubtedly would embroil moderates. Still and all, there is no evidence to indicate that, except for a particularly chaotic period, any sizable proportion of students would opt for illegal and undemocratic tactical approaches.

If the clergy and students, then, mostly operated along familiar channels during the years of the Frei presidency, some doubts were raised about whether the military actually held to its customary aloofness from politics. It is exceedingly difficult to determine whether such a slippage occurred, but some evidence exists to indicate that sectors of the armed forces were growing edgy about developments late in 1967 and early in 1968.

At that time Frei faced some of the most problematic challenges of

[53] For statements by university students, faculty, and administration regarding the student movement and its role in the university and in society, see "Cincuenta años después: De Santiago," *Visión*, June 21, 1968, p. 26. By 1970, the university reform movement had succeeded in democratizing decision-making processes at the University of Chile and had stimulated the modernization of curriculum throughout the university system.

his chronically crisis-ridden presidency. The nation had barely come out of a CUT-instigated work stoppage, which brought the deaths of five persons, when a rash of strikes erupted among teachers, postal-telegraph workers, and gas and electricity employees. A rising mood of tension was heated by a proliferation of street demonstrations and by the explosion of bombs in two U.S. government offices, at the old headquarters of the Christian Democratic party, and in the home of a leading National party senator.[54] To counteract the strikes, the government sent police into schools, forcing teachers and students to vacate the premises; soldiers took over the postal system to try to break a backlog of millions of items piled up there; and sailors were called into the gas and electricity companies to keep them functioning.

During April, rumors circulated that a military takeover was imminent, inducing CUT to proclaim that "the working class, by its firmest resistance, will oppose any attempt at a coup."[55] On April thirtieth, in the heat of the crisis, troops were alerted to be ready to cope with any contingency. Then a few days later, Frei startled the nation by appointing two ranking military officers to cabinet posts ordinarily held by civilians. General Tulio Marambio became minister of defense and General Jorge Quiroga was selected to head up the postal and telegraph ministry. By this move Frei settled matters at least for the moment. Almost immediately, postal-telegraph workers accepted the government's wage proposal and other strikers started back to work as well. Moreover, Frei's sudden action forestalled a major military move toward the centers of power—if, indeed, such an occurrence were even contemplated.[56]

Whatever the case, all this served to remind "Chile-watchers" that

[54] "Chile: Contentando para seguir adelante," *Economist* (Edición para Latino América), April 19, 1968, pp. 11–12.

[55] Quoted in "Los problemas de un reformador," p. 12.

[56] It was reported that some junior officers were unhappy with the government's reluctance to grant them more substantial salary increases and that informal discussions had been initiated to consider ways of handling the matter ("Chile: Coup de Main or Coup d'État," *Latin America*, May 10, 1968, pp. 146, 148). Additional flare-ups involving small military units goaded on by retired officers occurred in October, 1969, and March, 1970. They were easily put down, and most of the armed forces seemed satisfied with pay raises of 80 to 100 per cent and with the purchase of new equipment.

the military's generally admirable history of keeping out of the governing process is not necessarily immutable and that moments arise when the military may have to be reckoned with and placated. Nonetheless, the "cataclysmic event" that might have triggered such a radical departure from the military's traditional ways as an outright assumption of governmental control did not transpire in the April-May crisis of 1968.

Management

Prior to Frei's election in 1964, management associations constituted the single most powerful agglomeration of pressure activity in Chile. Their enormous resources, the ability to tie themselves to a substantial collection of sympathetic congressmen, and their preferential representation on government agencies (a kind of "quasi-corporatism" that positioned them at the center of administrative decision making) secured for management a preeminent role in policy formation.[57] If on occasions their legislative or administrative requests were rebuffed, more often than not the associations could delay or moderate decisions not completely to their liking. Indeed, until the 1920's, the Sociedad Nacional de Agricultura itself seems to have authored every legislative item that affected agriculture.

On the other hand, during the period between the 1920's and 1960's several developments were congealing that inevitably would reduce managerial effectiveness in the political system if a less than friendly administration reached government. For example, neither the military nor the clergy, allies of moneyed elements in other countries and in earlier times in Chile, could now be looked to for support. Also, an enlarging constituency in the middle and lower classes demanded reforms. And the constitutional system, becoming increasingly democratic, almost definitely guaranteed that reform-minded sectors who could put together a popular plurality would be permitted to govern.[58]

57 For an excellent study that examines some of these aspects of business in government, see Constantine C. Menges, "Public Policy and Organized Business in Chile: A Preliminary Analysis," *Journal of International Affairs* 2, no. 2 (1966): 343–365.

58 See Robert Kaufman, *The Chilean Political Right and Agrarian Reform*, pp. 5–6.

This, of course, is what happened in the elections of 1964 and 1965. Frei brought with him to office an assemblage of experts who put together their own legislative projects and planned their own administrative programs with practically no participation by the business community. Such an approach, together with the policies formulated, inaugurated a fundamental rearrangement in the allocation of political resources and inflamed more than one conservative to vow that they would never again be able to vote for the Christian Democrats in this century.

Commenting on how the climate of management and government relationships under the Christian Democrats differed from previous years, Minister of Economy Domingo Santamaría said: "It used to be that the directors and managers of banks and corporations always had highly placed friends and relatives in Government. If they had a problem they would just call them on the phone. Now it is different and they sit and fret."[59] This probably represented something of an overstatement of the actual situation, since a few opportunistic government officials seemed to exchange favors for managerial largesse. Still and all, management associations as political pressure groups suffered a distinct erosion of influence. This fact became manifest at the National Convention of the Confederación de Producción y Comercio, meeting in Santiago in April, 1968. Management leaders berated the government for excluding them from their long-time representation on official agencies, for augmenting governmental authority by means of laws and decrees, and for facilitating the expropriation of land under the agrarian reform law. President Frei attempted to mollify the convention delegates by taking a moderate, procapitalist stand when he asserted that "private initiative and private enterprise are the fundamental and indispensable elements for the full development of the country"; but Christian Democratic Deputy Luis Maira undoubtedly spoke for a large section of Christian Democracy when he attacked the private sector, claiming that "there has never been an economic experiment which has been advanced by means of capitalistic development."[60]

One of the most bitter points of contention between management

[59] Quoted in *New York Times*, November 7, 1966.

[60] "Unión empresario," *Visión*, April 26, 1968, p. 17.

and government has been the agrarian reform law and related labor law changes that enormously improved the ability of farm workers to unionize. At first, Big Agriculture showed signs of adjusting somewhat to the new regime. In 1965, it selected a comparatively progressive young man, Luis Larraín, as president of the Sociedad Nacional de Agricultura and in the next months a few landowners actually signed labor contracts with newly organized unions of rural workers. But as the pace of land reform quickened under a tougher land law, the landed interests reverted to their old image and solidified their opposition to the government land-acquisition program. This was reflected in the conservative media—especially, *El Diario Ilustrado*, *El Mercurio*, and Radio Sociedad Nacional de Minería—which assailed Frei for his discriminatory and confiscatory policies.

One episode that typified the impasse between the latifundists and the government took place on the Longotoma *fundo* in Aconcagua. Quite simply, when officials of the Agrarian Reform Corporation arrived at Longotoma to initiate the expropriation and division of the estate among the peasantry, they were halted in their tracks by armed *fundo* workers. The Right cited the event as positive proof that the farm laborers themselves opposed land redistribution; government spokesmen saw the incident differently, claiming instead that it had been a contrived arrangement set up by landowners.[61]

In short, propertied interests in both rural and urban areas now had to bargain with what, from their standpoint, was an extraordinarily difficult administration. They still possessed a great reservoir of power, though it was nowhere nearly as considerable as previously. And the expansion of reformist and revolutionary political parties together with the activation of the associational and political proclivities of rural workers characterized an inexorable process in the late 1960's that could only conduce to management's lessening influence in the political system.

[61] "Chile: Right Wing Reaction to Agrarian Reform," p. 130. For an interesting study of a peasant seizure of an estate, see Terry L. McCoy, "The Seizure of 'Los Cristales': A Case Study of the Marxist Left in Chile," *Inter-American Economic Affairs* 21, no. 1 (Summer 1967): 73–93.

Labor

Unquestionably, the farm workers constituted the most important single beneficiary of the reforms implanted by the Frei regime. In particular, changes in the Labor Code finally enabled rural laborers to organize freely, unfettered by the countless restrictions that previously hemmed them in so severely. Now, under an act promulgated on April 26, 1967, associational and collective-bargaining rights were greatly extended.[62] The legitimate functions of agricultural workers' associations were recognized to include arranging collective contracts; representing union members (and, when the union should agree, persons under individual contracts) in collective disputes; fostering educational endeavors; establishing cooperatives; and representing laborers on public and private agencies.

A minimum of one hundred workers may form a union, though under special circumstances the minimum number may drop to twenty-five. If a single farm does not contain the necessary number of laborers, workers of neighboring farms are permitted to organize together and negotiate with the respective employers. Special regulations protect the union in its formative stage and rules exist to shield candidates for union offices from the employers' harassment or arbitrary firing. Moreover, employers are obligated to provide a place for the union to assemble, to arrange time for union officers to perform their associational duties, and to collect a minimum of 2 per cent of both union and nonunion workers' wages—as well as contributing an equivalent amount themselves—for union funds. Employers are prohibited from attempting to delimit union activities, to break up unions, or to dominate workers' organizations. Indeed, only the courts are granted the authority to dissolve a trade union. Local unions may federate and the resultant federations will enjoy the same protection as local labor associations.

Finally, the law notes that collective claims need the approval of 51 per cent of the affected workers and it permits workers to initiate a

[62] This law, Act No. 16625, also elaborated rights of employers. The act is summarized in "Organisation of Rural Workers in Chile," *International Labour Review* 96, no. 4 (October 1967): 420–421.

strike if a majority, in secret balloting, is in agreement and understands that it must continue to conserve crops, fruit, and livestock during the work stoppage. Should the occasion warrant such action, Special Permanent Conciliation boards—comprising labor, employer, and neutral members—are authorized to adjudicate disputes.

As a direct result of liberalizations in the Labor Code and of the passage of a new minimum wage law that tripled farm workers' income, the rural labor force acquired a greatly enhanced economic position, which spilled over into measurably augmented political power. Thus, the process of incorporating the peasantry into the political system, which had its origins in the 1950's, increased rapidly in tempo during the 1960's. And, although the Christian Democrats' efforts to underwrite rural labor's associational propensities was legally stalled until 1967, in fact Frei had given instructions soon after becoming President that public officials should perform as though the bill had already become law.[63] The effect of this policy was dramatic. Whereas between 1952 and 1964, only about two dozen rural unions obtained legal status, in the first half of 1966 alone some 300 farm workers' unions came into existence and unionists were able to negotiate collective contracts with 150 landowners.[64] Much of this was possible because the government did not just give lip service to farm labor's associational needs, but fully backed them. This prolabor stance even went so far as to confiscate a farm that had dismissed a number of union organizers; the government justified the seizure by declaring that it was essential for the defense of state security.[65]

Figures on the true number of farm workers who have been incorporated into trade unions, like so much data about organized labor generally, are difficult to verify. One source suggests that the Confederación Nacional de Campesinos (CNC), an agricultural workers' central loosely associated with the Christian Democrats, had registered a total of fifty thousand members by 1967; Marxists were reputed to

63 McCoy, "The Seizure of 'Los Cristales,'" p. 83.

64 Sidney Lens, "Chile's 'Revolution in Liberty,'" *Progressive* 30, no. 10 (October 1966): 35.

65 *Ibid.*

have organized some ten thousand rural laborers during a one-year period running up to September, 1967.[66] Part of the Christian Democrats' success stems from the rather peculiar involvements of Jacques Chonchol's Instituto de Desarrollo Agropecuario (INDAP). INDAP's agents not only were charged with the land redistribution program, but also directly fostered the unionization of many thousands of farm workers—an action that some Christian Democratic trade-union leaders construed to be an improper governmental intrusion into their own province.[67]

The intense competition prevailing between the Christian Democrats and the Marxists in their attempts to unionize the countryside closely resembled the highly politicized nature of the older urban unions. One of the CNC's directors, Mario Alarcón, accused the Marxists of not just sending their regular union organizers into the rural areas to form unions, but of having assembled teams of teachers who entered remote areas in order to inculcate Marxism along with formal educational subjects. Furthermore, Alarcón contended that Marxist militants moved out into the fields among the *campesinos*, offering help to those in need and, after winning their friendship, inducing them to join Marxist study groups and ultimately to form Marxist unions.[68] Of course, the Christian Democrats' hands were not completely clean of political manipulations either. In fact, some of the party's more leftist elements believed that the CNC devoted too much of its efforts to bread-and-butter activities and not enough to political indoctrination.

In all events, farm labor had received an unprecedented boost in its economic and political fortunes, which even the installation of a repressive, antilabor regime in government could only temporarily threaten. It merely remained to be seen whether the Christian Democrats or the Marxists ultimately would win a hegemony over this newly activated segment of society.

In the urban areas, there were no substantial modifications in trade

[66] *New York Times*, September 15, 1967. Another estimate placed 82,000 farm workers in 952 unions by early 1969 (*Times of the Americas*, January 15, 1969).

[67] Lens, "Chile's Revolution in Liberty," p. 34.

[68] *New York Times*, September 15, 1967.

unionism's lot that paralleled happenings among the farm workers. Neither the professional nor the industrial unions improved their position vis-à-vis the Labor Code and many of the same organizational shortcomings (e.g., financial weaknesses) that inhibited their full associational expression prior to Frei still prevailed. In large measure, this was due to the perpetuation of factionalism within organized labor. Additionally, however, the same antagonisms existing between the Christian Democrats and the opposition parties in Congress, which commonly hamstrung the legislative process, also conduced to a failure to act on an overhaul of the Labor Code.

Nevertheless, Frei's policies were not without their impact on the urban working classes. Ending management's preeminent position on public agencies clearly disadvantaged employers both in policy formation and in policy effectuation and, consequently, removed a club that they had held for so long over labor. The government also sought to impose alterations in the working day by instituting the unified work day (*jornada única*); furthermore, it pushed for a stronger sense of work discipline, restricted the sale of liquor during certain hours of the day, and initiated other measures aimed at revamping age-old workers' habits.[69]

Actually, some of Frei's most troublesome challenges came from organized labor and, in particular, from the big Marxist-run central, CUT. Strikes and labor violence became a chronic problem during the Frei presidency. At times, they seemed to represent little more than political opposition to the government; certainly this appeared to be the case with the rash of work stoppages that broke out among the copper workers. On the other hand, despite certain political overtones, CUT's general strike late in 1967 clearly carried economic justification. At that time, as part of its anti-inflationary program, the Frei administration called for the establishment of a Workers' Capitalization Fund to be based upon compulsory savings taken from workers' salaries. CUT held that this was an effrontery to the workers; even more, it would constitute a grievous injury to societal elements least able to afford it, the already underpaid workers.

[69] Von Lazar and Quirós Varela, "Chilean Christian Democracy," pp. 69–70.

Within the national trade-union movement itself the picture remained cloudy. The election of the Christian Democrats to office had spurred Christian Democratic unionists to redouble their efforts to seize control of the organized labor movement and a number of Christian Democrats broke away from CUT. Nevertheless, the formation in 1968 of a new trade-union central, the Unión de Trabajadores de Chile (UTRACH), in direct opposition to CUT, did not win universal approval in the Christian Democratic party nor among the party's trade unionists. Accordingly, the Christian Democrats' National Council at least tacitly went along with a motion from those of its labor leaders who opposed the existence of UTRACH by indicating its disfavor with the creation of such an organization. Certainly, the record of separatist Christian Democratic trade-union centrals had not been a very inspiring one and the prospects for a new Christian Democratic central being any more viable than its predecessors seemed remote. In point of fact, by 1969, even those Christian Democrats who had broken away from CUT appeared to be moving toward a rapprochement with the big central.[70]

In short, the bulk of Chile's unionized workers still followed the leadership of highly politicized union officers and the main prize in the organized labor movement continued to be the control of CUT. Developments in the political parties, many of whose trade-union militants sat on CUT's councils, ensured a prolongation of the struggle for ascendancy over organized labor and an uncertainty about its eventual outcome.

Political Parties

The 1964 election and the subsequent period of Eduardo Frei's presidency had a profound impact on all of Chile's political parties. The old parties of the Right, the Conservatives and the Liberals, who had been suffering a decline in popularity at the polls for a number of years and who now felt threatened by the Christian Democratic reforms, determined to bury the minor differences separating them in order to preserve a viable political vehicle for the aristocracy. As a con-

[70] In 1969, CUT also gained a major boost with the affiliation of CEPCH and the National Association of Government Employees.

sequence, in 1965, they merged into the Partido Nacional, or National party. Their initial electoral appearance was not a great success, however, as they dropped from a combined total of 24.6 per cent of the votes cast in the 1963 municipal elections to only 13.1 per cent in the 1965 congressional elections. Nevertheless, the Nationals held their own in the 1967 municipal elections—edging up to 14.6 per cent of the vote—and scored a spectacular increase to 20.9 per cent of the ballots cast in the 1969 congressional elections.[71]

In the Chilean Congress, the National party's tactical position was to stand solidly against the government's reform measures, while occasionally supporting the Frei regime on some of its more moderate proposals—especially, any that could be construed as favoring economic restraint. Electorally, they hoped that many middle-class elements who had deserted them in 1964 would have become so disenchanted with the Christian Democrats by the 1970 presidential election that there would be a massive return to the National fold. With this prospect in mind, they resurrected the name of Jorge Alessandri, whom they had helped to elect as President in 1958 and whom they believed still held wide popular appeal. Thus, when the National party's deputy from the province of Cautín died, a by-election in July, 1968, to fill that vacancy seemed a particularly propitious moment to send up a trial balloon on Alessandri's behalf. Víctor Carmine, the Nationals' nominee for deputy, tied his candidacy to a possible Alessandri presidential race with the slogan, "A vote for Carmine is a vote for Alessandri."[72] In fact, the National party's optimism for a resurgence of strength behind the Alessandri banner at least for the moment was dashed to the ground when Carmine came in last.[73]

On the other hand, congressional elections only nine months later

[71] Figures in this section regarding the 1967 election are taken from Michael Francis and Eldon Lanning, "Chile's 1967 Municipal Elections," *Inter-American Economic Affairs* 21, no. 2 (Autumn 1967): 23–36; statistics on the 1969 congressional elections can be found in "De Santiago," *Visión*, March 28, 1969, p. 13.

[72] "Chile: A Bonus for Frei," *Latin America*, July 12, 1968, pp. 217–218.

[73] Earlier, in the mayorality election in Santiago, the National party's candidate, an outspoken pro-Alessandri supporter, had been overwhelmingly defeated.

reversed this trend and infused feelings among the jubilant Nationals that Alessandri's chances of returning to the presidency had soared. Clearly, the "mummies," as the other parties labeled the Nationals, still possessed considerable vitality and the mercurial quality of Chilean politics had served them a new lease on life.

Like the Nationals, the Radical party suffered a slippage in the 1965 elections—dropping 8 per cent from their proportion of the vote in 1963; they then recouped some of their loss in 1965 by posting an increase of 3.2 per cent in 1967 and secured a relatively stronger base in most regions of the country. In part, the Radicals' improved position was credited to a shift to the left, beginning in 1965, which lifted the liberal Senator Hugo Miranda to head the party. The new leftist predominance in the Radical party led to voting alliances with the Communists in the Chilean Congress and, late in 1967, permitted Miranda to negotiate for Communist backing of Professor Alberto Baltra, a Marxist Radical, who was running for a seat in the Senate. Baltra's narrow victory in the by-election encouraged a number of Radicals—including their 1964 standard-bearer, Julio Durán—to openly advocate an alliance with FRAP in anticipation of the 1970 presidential campaign. Baltra was singled out as a suitable person to lead such a Popular Front into power.

On the other hand, a measurable portion of the Radicals' right wing refused to accept the party's thrust to the left without a fight. Many of the rank and file had balked at Baltra's candidacy and they increased their pressure on national party leadership, demanding that the party stay clear of any entanglements with the Marxists. In an effort to placate the right-wing Radicals and hopefully to woo them into an eventual coalition with the Marxists, Miranda offered a senatorial candidacy to Raúl Rettig, a prominent leader of the party's conservative wing.

Miranda's maneuver infuriated the left-leaning Radical youth organization as well as many other party leftists, who vowed to boycott Rettig's campaign if he were kept on as a Radical candidate. Moreover, it was doubtful if the conservatives in the Radical party were sufficiently satisfied to be willing to take the long step toward a coalition with FRAP, and the Radicals' disastrous showing in the 1969 congressional election, when they dropped to 13.4 per cent of the vote, reinforced that stance. In all events, the Radical party continued to show itself as an exceptionally heterogeneous grouping whose chronic factionalism would ensure some agonizing infighting in any attempt to move the party into a national electoral alliance, whether it be to the left or to the right.

Just as Radical party leaders were sounding out FRAP about the possibility of an electoral alliance and experiencing factional opposition in the process, FRAP itself was undergoing structural disintegration due to partisan factionalism. The small PADENA group had broken away and, to all intents and purposes, was relocated in the Christian Democratic camp. This was evidenced in two by-elections in the Cautín area when PADENA endorsed the Christian Democratic candidates and in the fact that, in 1968, Frei chose a PADENA adherent for the cabinet post of minister of lands and settlement.

Far more injurious to FRAP's ability to survive, however, were a split in Socialist ranks and increasingly abrasive relations between the Socialists and the Communists. Personal differences between Raúl Ampuero and Aniceto Rodríguez, the new secretary general of the Socialist party, finally reached a climax late in 1967 when Ampuero led his faction out of the party. Together with the high-ranking CUT officer, Oscar Núñez, as well as with Senator Tomás Chadwick and six deputies, Ampuero established the Popular Socialist party (Partido Socialista Popular, or PSP), which at its inception boasted a generally good working organization throughout Chile.[74]

Actually, aside from a personality clash between the leaders, there was little dividing the PSP from Rodríguez' Partido Socialista de Chile; both groups clung to a militant brand of Marxism and promoted Castroite tactics, though the PSP was less formally tied to Cuba than the PSC. Nonetheless, the rift was a bitter one. Immediately upon completion of the split in Socialist ranks, Rodríguez' forces launched a campaign to destroy the PSP as a viable political movement. It threw up a number of stumbling blocks aimed at keeping the PSP from acquiring legal status as a political party; furthermore, with Communist

[74] See "Chile: Defeat for the Government," *Latin America*, February 9, 1968, pp. 41–42.

help, the old-line Socialists succeeded in suspending six PSP members from their official posts in CUT. PSP responded vigorously, pushing aside all barriers to the attainment of legal recognition and exerting great pressure in CUT to have its ousted officers reinstated.

Meanwhile, deteriorating relations between the Communist and Socialist parties threatened to sever the few remaining links that bound them together in FRAP. Fundamentally, the Communists and Socialists disagreed over tactics.[75] The Communists had been the architects of the *vía pacífica* and, following the Christian Democrats' electoral victories in 1964 and 1965, the Communists evinced a willingness to cooperate with the Frei regime regarding matters of mutual concern. This was in line with current Soviet policy, which encouraged Latin America's Communist parties to collaborate with nationalist reform parties and thereby contribute to the United States' isolation from Latin America.[76] Indeed, in 1965 at their Thirteenth National Congress, the Communists clearly favored siding with the Christian Democrats in Congress in order to bring about what they considered to be vital economic and social reforms; but the Socialists would have none of it and, instead, called for total congressional opposition to the Frei government.

Confronted with the Socialists' intransigence, more and more the Communists found common cause with the Radicals, merging their congressional blocs to vote with the Christian Democrats on those statutory proposals with which they agreed and which they construed as improving their electoral positions.[77] Of course, this only irritated

[75] The recent municipal and congressional elections had not provided any clear-cut answer to which tactical approach, the Communists' *vía pacífica* or the Socialists' advocacy of greater militancy, was more likely to carry the Marxists to power, since both parties fared similarly. The two parties carried almost the identical voting percentages in 1963 and 1965 and both augmented their electoral support between 1965 and 1967—the Communists rising from 12.4 per cent to 15 per cent and the Socialists from 10.3 per cent to 14.2 per cent.

[76] Herbert S. Dinerstein, "Soviet Policy in Latin America," *American Political Science Review* 61, no. 1 (March 1967): 80–90.

[77] Early in 1968, the Communists voted for the government's *reajuste* bill —an annual workers' cost-of-living increase, which is bitterly fought over by all elements across the party spectrum—whereas the Socialists opposed it. The awkwardness of the Communist-Socialist split was reflected in CUT, whose Socialist leaders wanted to call a general strike against the government and

those Socialists who took their cues from Havana and who simply could not abide associating with the "bourgeois" Radicals.

In addition to all these challenges to the survival of FRAP, the picture was further obscured by another complication. Even elements within the Partido Socialista de Chile did not fall into a neat package over the issue of an electoral entente with the Radicals. Thus, when the Communists requested all Marxists to underwrite Baltra's senatorial campaign, Rodríguez firmly opposed such an endorsement, whereas Salvador Allende announced his "spiritual support" of Baltra. Then Rodríguez went so far as to release to the press word that the party had given "a fraternal but firm box on the ears to comrade Salvador Allende" for backing the "bourgeois" Baltra.[78] Still, when Baltra won the election, such far-left Socialists as Clodomiro Almeyda and Carlos Altamirano gave every indication that they were shifting their stance to one more amenable to a rally of the Left that would include the Radicals. The Socialists' daily newspaper in Santiago, *Ultima Hora*, demonstrated a similar interest in the leftist grouping, provided the Radicals clarified their position and agreed to back a Marxist presidential candidate.

Since it was founded in 1956, FRAP had never fallen into an abyss more wracked with dissension. The cleavages among the Socialists were compounded by mounting bitterness between the Communists and Socialists, whose youths responded to the interparty tensions by battling each other in the streets, and the 1969 congressional elections —in which the Communists moved up to 16.6 per cent of the vote and the PSC carried 12.8 per cent (while the miniscule vote recorded by Ampuero's Socialists threatened them with extinction)—only intensified the antagonism. Obviously, only the most arduous and delicate of negotiations could conceivably reunite FRAP into anything approaching an operative electoral unit.

Although the Frei administration could take some comfort in the

---

whose Communist leaders were obligated to oppose such action, since their members in Congress had supported the measure. The upshot was to call a "selective" work stoppage by certain unions. The solution satisfied very few of CUT's followers.

[78] "Chile: Frei's Attitude to Marxists," *Latin America*, January 5, 1968, p. 7.

nearly atomized state of their Marxist opposition, the Christian Democrats also were beset with internal power struggles that endangered their own solidarity as they headed into the 1970 presidential campaign. Christian Democratic leadership roughly divided into three cliques. A moderate group, the *oficialistas*, remained loyal to Eduardo Frei and favored both the priorities and the pace of his reform program. On the left of the party stood an element that was impatient with Frei for not carrying out the "revolution in freedom" either rapidly enough or far enough; known as the *rebeldes*, or rebels, its members pumped for a "noncapitalist" road to economic development. In between these two groups were the *terceristas*, or third-liners, who generally promoted more reform, but who also endeavored to bridge the rift between the *oficialistas* and the *rebeldes*.

In a sense, the 1967 municipal elections marked a turning point in the Christian Democrats' ability to keep their differences within the family. For, when the party failed to win the massive majority that Frei had solicited from the voters, the rebels' frustrations broke the surface. They immediately reiterated their earlier demand that a *modus operandi* be created with FRAP and insisted that the Christian Democrats must compromise with the Marxists in order to establish the long-promised Neighborhood Councils (Juntas de Vecinos) and thus facilitate the politicization of the Chilean masses.[79]

Then, at the Christian Democrats' National Committee meeting in July, 1967, the *oficialistas* were outwitted in an intraparty leadership struggle. The third-liners gained a concession from the rebels that the latter would soften their attacks on the Frei administration. This enabled the two factions to offer a joint slate of officers for party leadership, headed by Senator Rafael A. Gamucio, that won by a majority of 47 out of 441 votes. The new officers then drew up a statement in which they praised much of the Frei regime's program—especially with regard to education, copper, and agrarian reforms—while at the

[79] The Juntas de Vecinos were part of Frei's program for uplifting the Chilean lower economic classes through Promoción Popular. FRAP indicated that it might support the creation of the Juntas de Vecinos if they were taken out of Promoción Popular, thus removing the overwhelming political advantage that the Christian Democrats would have enjoyed.

same time berating the government for its labor policy, for not nationalizing certain industries, and for too moderate a tone in dealing with the nation's conservative forces.

Despite the leftists' initial success in grabbing control of the top party apparatus, the *oficialistas* were better prepared to contend with the rebels when the party met in a special session of its National Council (Junta Nacional Extraordinaria) in January, 1968. After a vigorous debate, Gamucio's camp was ousted and a new bank of officers, led by a strong Frei backer and major Christian Democratic ideologist, Jaime Castillo Velasco, assumed hegemony over the party.

For the moment, the *oficialistas* carried the day and Frei's insistence that a "government cannot live with two heads and two opinions" seemed to be answered.[80] Still, the new unity between party and government was more apparent than real. In August, 1968, at a meeting of the Christian Democratic National Council, a caretaker administration assumed party leadership in anticipation of the congressional elections scheduled for March, 1969. To heal party wounds, Jaime Castillo Velasco was, with some difficulty, talked into relinquishing his hold on the party presidency; in his place, a *tercerista*, Senator Renán Fuentealba, was installed as party president with the understanding that he simply would administer the party and not attempt to gain advantages for *tercerista* programs.

A month later, at a meeting of Christian Democratic youths from all over Latin America, an acrimonious debate erupted between two factions of Chilean Christian Democratic youths in which the argument was not so much between moderates and leftists as between a faction seeking to tie up with the Communists and another element that derided the Communists as too conservative and that demanded arrangements with more radical political groups. After the 1969 congressional election, when the Christian Democrats fell to 31.1 per cent of the vote and lost twenty-six seats in the Chamber of Deputies (especially among the leftists), most Christian Democratic leaders rallied behind Radomiro Tomic as their preferred presidential nominee in

[80] "Chile: Frei's Attitude to Marxists," p. 7. For a summary of *oficialista* views on taking over party leadership, see "Chile: Frei Turns the Tables on the Rebels," *Latin America*, January 12, 1968, pp. 9–10.

1970 and agreed to a somewhat more leftist platform,[81] though a recalcitrant minority, referred to as the *rupturistas*, or "rupturists," held out for an alliance with the Marxists. In any event, the party's standard-bearer in 1970 would have his work cut out for him attempting to hold the several disparate factions of the party together.

Although the pressure of presidential campaigns often enables party factions to pull together behind a candidate long enough to get through the election, at first the intensity of party cleavages offered little hope that this would be the case in 1970. No fewer than eight party leaders surfaced as candidates: Jorge Alessandri (National party), Radomiro Tomic (Christian Democratic party), Salvador Allende (Socialist party), Jacques Chonchol (Popular Action movement), Alberto Baltra (Radical party), Julio Durán (Democratic Radical party), Pablo Neruda (Communist party), and Rafael Tarud (independent leftist).

Then, as party politics have a way of doing in Chile, by February, 1970, the race narrowed down to three candidates—Alessandri, Tomic, and Allende—the Marxian and non-Marxian left largely joining with Allende in Unidad Popular, or Popular Unity. Unidad Popular seemed to be a tactical success for the Communists who, arguing for the importance of program rather than candidate, swung support from the Baltra, Chonchol, and Tarud camps—along with the Communist party—behind Allende.

Still, unless additional coalitions developed, the 1970 presidential campaign almost certainly presaged a minority winner in the election and an even greater abrasiveness between the chief executive and Congress than Frei had suffered for six years. On the other hand, wider electoral alliances (as between the Nationals and the Christian Demo-

[81] In April, 1968, Radomiro Tomic returned to Chile from his post as ambassador to the United States to take charge of the Christian Democrats' campaign in the upcoming congressional elections and almost certainly to seek the party's presidential nomination. Almost at once he became embroiled in party controversies. His strategy seemed to be to avoid an attachment to any one faction and to attempt to meld the party back together. In this regard, he refused to endorse the noncapitalist road to economic progress, so urgently desired by the rebels, though he did call for a "union of the popular forces in the country which really want change" ("Chile: Tomic Returns," *Latin America*, May 3, 1968, p. 143).

crats, or between Popular Unity and the Christian Democrats), while creating the possibility of a statistical majority in Congress, also would produce a highly contentious governing group as a result of the ideologically diversified nature of the coalition. Indeed, rampant factionalism in the parties, coupled with an excess of immobilism in government, persisted as an endemic feature of the Chilean political system.

CONCLUSION

In its pressure politics, Chile still falls short of having evolved to the status of a highly developed society. Harry Eckstein briefly defines such a society, assuming the presence of voluntary association, as one where can be found "not only large numbers of social groupings and associations, but groupings and associations with well-articulated structures, large masses of members, wealthy treasuries, specialized administrators, and well-functioning channels of communications; these things make for power. . . . Authority becomes less rooted in tradition, less sacred, distant, and awesome, while policy becomes more rationally calculated and changeable. These things also increase the willingness and capabilities of social groups to play a role in politics."[82] Among the Latin American republics, Chile probably comes as close as any to approximating this model. Moreover, although management and labor —the most continuously and intensively active interest groups contending in the political process—do not possess equal power as rivals, the recent developments mentioned earlier have narrowed the gap somewhat in their competitive capabilities.

Chile's evolution to an approximation of the model of a highly developed society revolves around several factors.[83] Certainly, the nation's long and generally unbroken record of constitutional democracy created an environment promotive to the development of regularized group penetration of the political system.

Furthermore, the growth of government's social functions makes

[82] In Harry Eckstein and David E. Apter, eds., *Comparative Politics: A Reader*, p. 395.

[83] Largely adapted from *ibid.*, pp. 395–396. Also, see Harry Eckstein, *Pressure Group Politics*, pp. 15–39.

the authoritative decision-making process in any open society a target of the most profound interest-group attention. This, of course, has been the case in Chile where the government not only is involved in a great many economic operations and regulatory activities, but also has undertaken responsibility for providing a large proportion of the country's medical and other social services. Under such circumstances, pressure groups' stake in both governmental policy formation and policy effectuation is greatly heightened.

Finally, Chile's pressure groups undoubtedly are operative at a higher stage of development than in most of Latin America because of the nature of its governmental organization: "The significance of pressure groups may reflect the structure of government no less than its policy or underlying political culture. More specifically, it seems to be relatively great in highly pluralistic structures of government and relatively small in highly monolithic ones."[84] Thus, while on paper practically all of Latin America's constitutions have provided for a separation of powers, in only a very few of the actual governing systems can one find a truly functioning legislative body that shares governmental power with the executive. In fact, Chile's Congress is probably the most powerful legislature in Latin America and, along with the executive branch of government, the Chilean Congress stands as a vital focal point for group pressure.

Naturally, the mere existence of a number of pressure groups and their generally regularized penetration of the political system does not ensure the automatic satisfaction of their claims in the conversion process. Throughout, this study has endeavored to evaluate the comparative strengths and weaknesses of interest groups in the political process. In this regard, Almond and Powell quite properly warn us about passing judgment on the effectiveness of the decision-making process simply because it does not seem to respond properly to groups with whom we feel some attachment.[85] This study has tried to avoid falling into such a trap and hopefully no such bias has crept into the discussions. Rather, the author's purpose has been to describe and ana-

[84] Eckstein and Apter, *Comparative Politics*, p. 396.

[85] Gabriel Almond and G. Bingham Powell, Jr., *Comparative Politics*, p. 106.

lyze group politics in Chile in terms of the relative ability of interest groups to penetrate the policy-making process and to gain resultant satisfactions, whoever they may be.

Insofar as group styles or tactics are concerned, Chilean groups in the aggregate seem to have preferred peaceful methods of action in the political system. Nevertheless, large elements of society have demonstrated their frustration over what they considered to be the slowness of decision makers to bring changes they favored; others, of course, have been equally disturbed about the nature as well as the pace of change. For this reason, the years of the Frei administration witnessed an intensification of political activity, especially by economic groups, as labor sectors sought to speed up the rate of passage of various aspects of the Frei reform program at a time when management brought its power to bear on slowing down the enactment of many of the same reforms.

Intensified group political activity also resulted from the close interrelationships of political parties with pressure groups. Management's peak interest organizations largely controlled the old Conservative and Liberal parties and customarily left most of the open political bargaining to the parties, whereas representatives of the management structures themselves mostly were content to operate out of the public limelight as they exercised their influence in and on governmental agencies, especially in the executive branch of government. However, the diminution of their direct influence upon executive agencies during the Frei regime, together with the threats they felt from taxation, agrarian, and related reforms, coincided until 1969 with a decline in the electoral strength of management's political party outlets. As a consequence, the central organizations of management moved more openly into politics. This manifested itself variously, but it could be exemplified in the Sociedad Nacional de Agricultura's public attacks against the agrarian reform program and the SNA's growing willingness to openly reveal its political posture and activities.

Labor's situation was somewhat different in that political parties historically exercised a major sway over such trade-union centrals as CUT and, more recently, moved into the fledgling peasant union movement. In instances where associational interest groups, such as trade unions, lack autonomy, certain tendencies can be observed. One outgrowth of this arrangement has been to submerge many of labor's economic goals under immediate political objectives.[86] Hence, what the bulk of trade-union members might think are the important issues may be set aside in favor of what political parties consider to be more significant in their efforts to mobilize popular support behind their cause. Almond and Powell observe that when political parties (or other social institutions) deny interest structures avenues to independent lines of action, this condition may provoke anomic outbreaks.[87] In fact, while non-violent tactics have been Chilean labor's most common stock in trade, often when violence has developed out of labor strategy it has resulted from the entrance of political parties into labor's policy-forming councils.

Indeed, the keen political rivalry so characteristic of the Frei era periodically exploded into anomic actions. Peasant land seizures occurred on several occasions, including the celebrated examples of the Fundo Los Cristales in 1965 and of the Hacienda San Miguel in 1968.[88] On both occasions, leftist party leaders incited and led the seizures. In addition, clashes between CUT (or its components acting individually) and the government increased in number and severity as left-wing parties promoted their political ends in the midst of basically economic issues. Thus, copper workers went out on strike twenty times during Frei's first sixteen months in office and, in March, 1966, the series of work stoppages culminated in a violent interchange between miners and soldiers that left eight dead and several dozen wounded.[89] In November, 1967, a CUT-sponsored general strike ended with five dead and more than a score injured. The frequency and gravity of these and other anomic eruptions marked the period of Frei's administration as one of the most intensively competitive and bitterly fought political epochs in recent Chilean memory.[90]

[86] *Ibid.*, pp. 78–79.

[87] *Ibid.*

[88] The Los Cristales' episode has been well described and documented in McCoy, "The Seizure of 'Los Cristales,'" pp. 73–93.

[89] Gross, *The Last Best Hope*, pp. 151–153.

[90] Previous violent episodes of major proportions occurred in 1938, when many people were killed in altercations between Popular Front and Nazi ele-

The nature of political conflict in the late 1960's reflected a substantial modification in the customary dialogue between order and change. Until the demand for change reached a crescendo in the 1964 and 1965 elections, traditionalist elements bulked large in the decision-making process and maneuvered to preserve the status quo; the parties of change often, like the Marxists, diluted their power through divisiveness or, like the Radicals, suffered from ambivalence on reformist questions. Personal contacts, pragmatic bargaining, and elections characterized the group process; though from time to time when the traditionalists regarded their opposition as too obstreperous, they turned to coercive measures (e.g., their enacting the Laws for the Defense of Democracy) to silence them. Typically, as Robert Scott observes, the traditionalists have been unwilling to compromise with the newly emerging groups in society through reorganizing party structures and adjusting their doctrines in order to accommodate them. Instead, the "traditional leaders tend to reinforce their historic positions, to try to freeze the status quo [and this] forces the challengers into equally extreme activities, into alienation from the existing political system, into anomic demonstrations and physical retaliation."[91]

The Christian Democrats, initially a break-away group from the traditionalist camp, stepped into this situation and tried to enlarge societal participation in government decision making, to create a reformist environment, and still to adhere to peaceful, orderly methods for accomplishing their objectives. Frei's problems with the Senate and his own handling of some of the proposed reforms antagonized many of his followers and served as ammunition for his leftist enemies. Many Socialists and others on the far left, along with elements among the increasingly politicized masses, espoused violent tactics and evinced

ments; in 1946, when six people lost their lives in a clash between nitrate workers and their supporters and the police; in 1959, when twenty-six people fell in skirmishes involving Communist-led construction workers and the police; and in 1957, when twenty-one died in violence that broke out in the nation's three largest cities when students and Marxists demonstrated against a government-decreed raise in bus fares.

[91] Robert E. Scott, "Political Parties and Policy-Making in Latin America," in *Political Parties and Political Development*, ed. Joseph La Palombara and Myron Weiner, p. 339.

a varying disenchantment with the parliamentary process. This created a mood for less dialogue and more anomie.

In short, the old dialogue between order and change had been converted, among most of the dominant sectors in society, into demands either for substantive and rapid reforms or for an authentic structural and procedural revolution. Whatever the outcome of this struggle, it was certain to have wide ramifications throughout Chile's entire social system.

Postscript

As this study was going to press, the years of Christian Democratic governance shuddered to a halt. For on September 4, 1970, after three previously unsuccessful bids for the presidency, Salvador Allende secured a plurality of the vote. Unofficial returns gave Allende 36.3 per cent of the total ballot, Jorge Alessandri 35.9 per cent, and Radomiro Tomic only 27.8 per cent.

In a campaign uncharacteristically marred by several acts of violence, Alessandri presented to the voters the known image of a rather conservative and honest nationalist. On the other hand, Tomic found difficulty establishing a comfortable ideologic position. Despite the legacy of Frei's considerable popularity, Tomic largely eschewed the Frei program until the last minutes of the campaign. Consequently, the largest portion of the women's vote went to Alessandri and an even larger fraction of the men's vote fell to Allende.

If nothing impedes Allende's assumption of presidential power, he has promised to convert Chile into a socialist society along the lines of Cuba. This means the nationalization of all large industrial, commercial, and financial institutions; the socialization of educational curricula; and the replacement of Congress with a unicameral People's Assembly. Of course, Chile's long history of factionalized political parties—and in Allende's case, an exceptionally contentious gathering—offered no guarantee that rhetoric could be translated into accomplishment. Nevertheless, as had occurred in 1964, a sizable majority of voters—whether for Allende or Tomic—expressed their preference for a regime committed to deep societal change.

SELECTED BIBLIOGRAPHY

Books

Acton, Rudolph P. *The Latin American University*. Bogota: Editorial ABC, 1966.

Aguilar Vidal, Oscar. *Geografía económica de Chile y geografía económica general*. Santiago: Editorial Nascimento, 1963.

Aguilera, Angel. *Las tierras fiscales de Chile*. Santiago: Instituto de Capacitación e Investigación en Reforma Agraria, 1966.

Ahumada, Jorge. *La crisis integral de Chile*. Santiago: Editorial Universitaria, 1966.

———. *En vez de la miseria*. Santiago: Editorial del Pacífico, 1958.

Alba, Víctor. *El militarisimo*. Mexico City: Universidad Nacional Autónoma de México, 1959.

Alexander, Robert J. *Communism in Latin America*. New Brunswick, N. J.: Rutgers University Press, 1957.

———. *Labor Relations in Argentina, Brazil, and Chile*. New York: McGraw-Hill Book Co., 1962.

———. *Latin American Politics and Government*. New York: Harper and Row, Publishers, 1956.

———. *Organized Labor in Latin America*. New York: Free Press of Glencoe, 1965.

Almeyda, Clodomiro. *¿Reforma agraria?* Santiago: Prensa Latinoamericana, 1962.

Almeyda Arroyo, Elías. *Geografía agrícola de Chile*. Santiago: [Imprenta San Francisco, 1957].

Almond, Gabriel, and G. Bingham Powell, Jr. *Comparative Politics*. Boston: Little, Brown and Company, 1966.

Alvarez Andrews, Oscar. *Chile: Monografía sociológica.* Mexico City: Instituto de Investigaciones Sociales, Universidad Nacional, [1968].

Ampuero Díaz, Raúl. *1964, año de prueba para la revolución chilena.* Santiago: Prensa Latinoamericana, 1964.

Amunátegui, Domingo. *Objetivos del socialismo en Chile.* Santiago: Editorial Nascimento, 1936.

Andrade Geywitz, Carlos. *Elementos de derecho constitucional chileno.* Santiago: Editorial Jurídica de Chile, 1963.

Arteaga Undurraga, Ignacio, comp. *Partido Conservador XIV—Convención Nacional—1947.* Santiago: Imprenta Chile, 1947.

———. *Reseña histórica de las XVI Convenciones del Partido Conservador.* Santiago: Imprenta Chile, 1947.

Baltra Cortés, Alberto. *Pedro Aguirre Cerda.* Santiago: Editorial Orbe, 1962.

———, Felipe Herrera, and René Silva. *El futuro económico de Chile y de América Latina.* Santiago: Editorial Universitaria, 1957.

Baraona, Rafael, Ximena Aranda, and Roberto Santana. *Valle de Putaendo: Estudio de estructura agraria.* Santiago: Editorial Universitaria, 1961.

Barría Serón, Jorge. *Trayectoria y estructura del movimiento sindical chileno, 1946–1962.* Santiago: Instituto de Organización y Administración, Universidad de Chile, 1963.

Barría Soto, Francisco. *El Partido Radical, su historia y sus obras.* Santiago: Editorial Universitaria, 1957.

Bascuñán Valdez, Aníbal. *Universidad: Cinco ensayos para una teoría de la universidad latinoamericana.* Santiago: Editorial Andrés Bello, 1963.

Bello Codesido, Emilio. *Recuerdos políticos.* Santiago: Editorial Nascimento, 1954.

Benham, F[rederick], and H. A. Holley. *A Short Introduction to the Economy of Latin America.* London: Oxford University Press, 1961.

Bernaschina González, Mario. *Cartilla electoral.* Santiago: Editorial Jurídica de Chile, 1958.

———. *Los Constituyentes de 1925.* Santiago: Editorial Universitaria, 1945.

———. *Derecho municipal chileno.* 3 vols. Santiago: Editorial Jurídica de Chile, 1952.

———. *Manual de derecho constitucional.* Santiago: Editorial Jurídica de Chile, 1955.

Boizard B., Ricardo. *La Democracia Cristiana en Chile.* Santiago: Editorial Orbe, 1963.

Bowen, J. David. *The Land and People of Chile.* New York: J. B. Lippincott Co., 1966.

Braun L., Juan, and José Luis Federici R. *Algunas características de la población inactiva en Chile.* Santiago: Instituto de Economía, 1965.

Bravo, Leonidas. *Lo que supo un auditor de guerra.* Santiago: Editorial del Pacífico, 1955.

Bravo Lavín, Mario. *Chile frente al socialismo y al comunismo.* Santiago: Editorial Ercilla, 1934.

Bryce, James. *South America.* New York: Macmillan Co., 1923.

Burnett, Ben G., and Kenneth F. Johnson. *Political Forces in Latin America.* 2nd ed. Belmont, Calif.: Wadsworth Publishing Co., 1970.

Butland, Gilbert J. *Chile: An Outline of Its Geography, Economics, and Politics.* 3rd ed. London: Oxford University Press, 1956.

Cabero, Alberto. *Chile y los chilenos.* Santiago: Editorial Lyceum, 1948.

———. *Recuerdos de don Pedro Aguirre Cerda.* Santiago: Editorial Nascimento, 1948.

Cámara Central de Comercio de Chile. *Memoria y balance.* Santiago: Cámara Central de Comercio de Chile, 1964.

Campos Harriet, Fernando. *Desarrollo educacional, 1810–1960.* Santiago: Editorial Andrés Bello, 1960.

———. *Historia constitucional de Chile.* Santiago: Editorial Jurídica de Chile, 1946.

Castillo Velasco, Jaime. *El problema comunista.* Santiago: Editorial del Pacífico, 1955.

Castro, Baltazar. *¿Me permite una interrupción?* Santiago: Editorial Zig-Zag, 1963.

Center of Latin American Studies. *Statistical Abstract of Latin America.* Los Angeles: University of California Press, 1965.

Cereceda, Raúl. *Las instituciones políticas en América Latina.* Madrid: FERES, 1961.

Chonchol, Jacques, *et al. Proposiciones para una acción política en el período 1967–70 de una vía no capitalista de desarrollo.* Santiago: Separata Especial de PEC, 1967.

Cohen, Alvin. *Economic Change in Chile, 1929–1959.* Gainesville: University of Florida Press, 1960.

Comisión Económica para América Latina. *Antecedentes sobre el desarrollo de la economía chilena, 1925–1952.* Santiago: Editorial del Pacífico, 1954.

Comité Interamericano de Desarrollo Agrícola. *Chile: Tenencia de la tierra y desarrollo socio-económico del sector agrícola.* Santiago: CIDA, 1966.

Confederación Marítima de Chile. *Conclusiones seminario.* Valparaíso: COMACH, 1963.

Confederación de Trabajadores de Chile. *II Congreso Nacional de la Confederación de Trabajadores de Chile.* Santiago: CTCH, 1944.

Confederación de Trabajadores de Chile. *II Congreso Nacional de la Confondo.* Santiago: CUT, 1962.

———. *Segundo Congreso Nacional Ordinario.* Santiago: CUT, 1959.

———. *Tercer Congreso Nacional Ordinario, Convocatoria.* Santiago: CUT, 1962.

Corbalán, Salomón. *El Partido Socialista.* Santiago: Imprenta Atenea, 1957.

Corporación de Fomento de la Producción. *Geografía económica de Chile.* Vols. III and IV. Santiago: Talleres Gráficos "La Nación," 1962.

Correa Prieto, Luis. *Aspectos negativos de la intervención económica, fracasos de una experiencia.* Santiago: Editorial Zig-Zag, 1955.

Correa Vergara, Luis. *Agricultura chilena.* 2 vols. Santiago: Imprenta Nascimento, 1938.

Corvalán, Luis. *Chile hoy: La lucha de los comunistas chilenos en las condiciones del gobierno de Frei.* Buenos Aires: Editorial Anteo, 1965.

Crawford, William R. *A Century of Latin-American Thought.* Rev. ed. Cambridge: Harvard University Press, 1961.

Croxato, Héctor, *et al. La universidad en tiempos de cambio.* Santiago: Editorial del Pacífico, 1965.

Cruz-Coke, Ricardo. *Geografía electoral de Chile.* Santiago: Editorial del Pacífico, 1952.

Cunill, Pedro. *Geografía de Chile.* Santiago: Editorial Universitaria, 1963.

Dahl, Robert A. *Modern Political Analysis.* Englewood Cliffs, N.J.; Prentice-Hall, 1965.

D'Antonio, William V., and Fredrick B. Pike, eds. *Religion, Revolution, and Reform.* New York: Frederick A. Praeger, 1964.

Daugherty, Charles H., ed. *Chile:Election Factbook.* Washington, D.C.: Institute for the Comparative Study of Political Systems, 1963.

Davis, Harold E., ed. *Government and Politics in Latin America.* New York: Ronald Press Co., 1953.

Delgado, Oscar, ed. *Reformas agrarias en la América Latina.* Mexico City and Buenos Aires: Fondo de Cultura Económica, 1965.

Desarrollo de Chile en la primera mitad del siglo XX. 2 vols. Santiago: Editorial Universitaria, [1951?].

Díaz Salas, Juan. *Legislación social: Código del trabajo.* 10 vols. Santiago: Editorial Nascimento, 1962.

Di Domenico, Rafael. *Yo fuí candidato.* Santiago: Imprenta Alfa, 1961.

Domínguez C., Oscar. *Aspiraciones de los inquilinos de la Provincia de Santiago.* Santiago: Instituto de Capacitación e Investigación en Reforma Agraria, 1966.

———. *El campesino chileno y la Acción Católica Rural.* Madrid: FERES, 1961.

———. *El condicionamiento de la reforma agraria.* Louvain: E. Warny, 1963.

Donoso, Ricardo. *Alessandri, agitador y demoledor.* Mexico City: Fondo de Cultura Económica, 1953.

———. *Desarrollo político y social de Chile.* Santiago: Imprenta Universitaria, 1943.

———. *Las ideas políticas en Chile.* Mexico City: Fondo de Cultura Económica, 1946.

Dorner, Peter. *Issues in Land Reform: The Chilean Case.* Madison: Land Tenure Center, University of Wisconsin, 1965.

Durán Bernales, Florencio. *El Partido Radical.* Santiago: Editorial Nascimento, 1958.

———. *La política y los sindicatos.* Santiago: Ediciones Andes, 1963.

Eckstein, Harry. *Pressure Group Politics.* Stanford: Stanford University Press, 1960.

———, and David E. Apter, eds. *Comparative Politics: A Reader.* New York: Free Press of Glencoe, 1963.

Edelmann, Alexander T. *Latin American Government and Politics.* Homewood, Ill.: Dorsey Press, 1964.

Edwards Vives, Alberto. *La fronda aristocrática.* Santiago: Editorial del Pacífico, 1952.

———. *La organización política de Chile.* Santiago: Editorial del Pacífico, 1943.

———, and Eduardo Frei. *Historia de los partidos políticos chilenos.* Santiago: Editorial del Pacífico, 1949.

Encina, Francisco. *Historia de Chile.* 3 vols. Santiago: Editorial Nascimento, 1949.

———. *Nuestra inferioridad económica, sus causas, sus consecuencias.* Santiago: Imprenta Universitaria, 1912.

———. *La reforma agraria.* Santiago: Editorial Nascimento, 1962.

———. *Resumen de la historia de Chile.* 3 vols. Santiago: Editorial Zig-Zag, 1963.

Escobar Cerda, Luis. *Organización para el desarrollo económico.* Santiago: Editorial Universitaria, 1961.

Estévez Gazmuri, Carlos. *Elementos de derecho constitucional.* Santiago: Editorial Jurídica de Chile, 1949.

Extensión Cultural de la Biblioteca Nacional. *Chile: Su futura alimentación.* Santiago: Ediciones de la Biblioteca Nacional, 1963.

Eyzaguirre, Jaime. *La fisonomía histórica de Chile.* Santiago: Editorial del Pacífico, 1948.

———. *Historia constitucional de Chile.* Santiago: Editorial Universitaria, 1955.

Federación de Sindicatos Profesionales de Estibadores Marítimos de Chile. *La Asamblea Anual de 1963.* Valparaíso: FEMACH, 1963.

Fernández Pradel, Jorge. *Hacia un nuevo orden por un catolicismo social auténtico.* Santiago: Editorial del Pacífico, 1952.

Fetter, Frank W. *Monetary Inflation in Chile.* Princeton: Princeton University Press, 1931.

Fichter, Joseph H. *Cambio social en Chile: Un estudio de actitudes.* Santiago: Editorial Universitaria Católica, 1962.

Finer, Herman. *The Chilean Development Corporation.* Montreal: International Labour Office, 1947.

Frank, Andrew Gunder. *Capitalism and Underdevelopment in Latin America: Historical Studies of Chile and Brazil.* New York: Monthly Review Press, 1967.

Fredes, Carlos. *Curso de economía: Elementos de economía chilena.* Santiago: Editorial Universitaria, 1962.

Freedman, Ronald, ed. *Population: The Vital Revolution.* Garden City: Doubleday & Co., 1964.

Frei Montalva, Eduardo. *Chile desconocido.* Santiago: Ediciones Ercilla, 1937.

———. *Chile, 1964–1970.* Santiago: Editorial del Pacífico, 1964.

———. *Pensamiento y acción.* Santiago: Editorial del Pacífico, 1958.

———. *La política y el espíritu.* Santiago: Ediciones Ercilla, 1940.

———. *Sentido y forma de una política.* Santiago: Editorial del Pacífico, 1951.

———. *El social cristianismo.* Santiago: Editorial del Pacífico, 1951.

———. *Tercer mensaje del Presidente de la República de Chile al inau-*

gurar el período de sesiones ordinarias del Congreso Nacional. Santiago: Departamento de Publicaciones de la Presidencia de la República, 1967.

———. *La verdad tiene su hora*. Santiago: Editorial del Pacífico, 1955.

Frías Valenzuela, Francisco. *Geografía de Chile*. Santiago: Editorial Nascimento, 1963.

———. *Manual de historia de Chile*. Santiago: Editorial Nascimento, 1950.

Gajardo, Samuel. *Alessandri y su destino*. Santiago: Editorial Universitaria, 1951.

Galdames, Luis. *A History of Chile*. Translated and edited by Isaac J. Cox. Chapel Hill: University of North Carolina Press, 1941.

Gandarillas M., Guillermo. *Curso de educación cívica*. Santiago: Imprenta "La Nación," 1963.

García Gajardo, Oscar. *Chile guerrero*. [Santiago]: Artes y Letras, 1955.

Gerassi, John. *The Great Fear in Latin America*. New York: Collier Books, 1965.

Gil, Federico G. *Chile: Election Factbook*. Washington, D.C.: Institute for the Comparative Study of Political Systems, 1965.

———. *The Political System of Chile*. Boston: Houghton Mifflin Co., 1966.

———, and Charles J. Parrish. *The Chilean Presidential Election of September 4, 1964*. Washington, D.C.: Institute for the Comparative Study of Political Systems, 1965.

Gill, Clark C. *Education and Social Change in Chile*. Washington, D.C.: U.S. Department of Health, Education and Welfare, Office of Education, 1966.

Girard, Alain, and Raúl Samuel. *Situación y perspectivas de Chile en septiembre de 1957: Una investigación de opinión pública en Santiago*. Santiago: Editorial Universitaria, 1958.

Goldenberg, Gregorio. *Después de Frei ¿Quién?*. Santiago: Editorial Orbe, 1966.

Gómez Millas, Juan. *Tradición y tarea universitaria*. Santiago: Impresos Planet, 1963.

Góngora, Mario. *Origen de los "Inquilinos" de Chile central*. Santiago: Editorial Universitaria, 1960.

González, José. *Curso elemental sobre el partido*. Santiago: Impresora Horizonte, [1962?].

Gregory, Peter. *Industrial Wages in Chile*. Ithaca: New York State School of Industrial and Labor Relations, Cornell University, 1967.

Gross, Leonard. *The Last Best Hope: Eduardo Frei and Chilean Democracy.* New York: Random House, 1967.

Guilisasti Tagle, Sergio, ed. *Partidos políticos chilenos.* Santiago: Editorial Nascimento, 1964.

Halperin, Ernst. *Nationalism and Communism in Chile.* Cambridge: M.I.T. Press, 1965.

Hamuy, Eduardo, *et al. El problema educacional del pueblo de Chile.* Santiago: Editorial del Pacífico, 1961.

Hanke, Lewis. *South America.* Rev. ed. Princeton: Van Nostrand Co., 1967.

Hanson, Earl Parker. *Chile, Land of Progress.* New York: Reynal and Hitchcock, 1941.

Heise González, Julio. *Historia constitucional de Chile.* Santiago: Editorial Jurídica de Chile, 1954.

Herrick, Bruce H. *Urban Migration and Economic Development in Chile.* Cambridge: M.I.T. Press, 1965.

Hirschman, Albert O. *Journeys toward Progress.* New York: The Twentieth Century Fund, 1963.

Houtart, François, and Emile Pin. *The Church and the Latin American Revolution.* New York: Sheed & Ward, 1965.

Hübner Gallo, Jorge Iván. *Los católicos en la política.* Santiago: Editorial Zig-Zag, 1959.

Hudeczek, Carl. *Economía de Chile, rumbos y metas.* Santiago: Editorial del Pacífico, 1956.

Iglesias, Augusto. *Alessandri, una etapa de la democracia en América.* Santiago: Editorial Andrés Bello, 1960.

Instituto de Economía de la Universidad de Chile. *Desarrollo económico de Chile, 1940–1956.* Santiago: Editorial Universitaria, 1956.

James, Preston E. *Latin America.* New York: Odyssey Press, 1942.

Jiles Pizarro, Jorge. *Partido Comunista de Chile.* Santiago: Academia de Ciencias Políticas, 1957.

Jobet, Julio César. *Ensayo crítico del desarrollo económico-social de Chile.* Santiago: Editorial Universitaria, 1955.

———. *Recabarren: Los orígenes del movimiento obrero y del socialismo chilenos.* Santiago: Prensa Latinoamericana, 1955.

———. *Socialismo y comunismo.* Santiago: Editorial Espártaco, 1952.

Johnson, John J. *The Military and Society in Latin America.* Stanford: Stanford University Press, 1964.

———. *Political Change in Latin America.* Stanford: Stanford University Press, 1958.

———, ed. *Continuity and Change in Latin America.* Stanford: Stanford University Press, 1964.

———, ed. *The Role of the Military in Underdeveloped Countries.* Princeton: Princeton University Press, 1962.

Kaempffer Villagrán, Guillermo. *Así sucedió, 1850–1925, sangrientos episodios de la lucha obrera en Chile.* Santiago: Arancibia Hnos., [1961?].

Kaplan C., Oscar. *Geografía de Chile.* Santiago: EDIGRAF, 1963.

Karst, Kenneth L., ed. *Latin American Legal Institutions: Problems for Comparative Study.* Los Angeles: University of California Press, 1966.

Kaufman, Robert R. *The Chilean Political Right and Agrarian Reform.* Washington, D.C.: Institute for the Comparative Study of Political Systems, 1967.

Keller R., Carlos. *Un país al garete.* Santiago: Editorial Nascimento, 1937.

Lafertte, Elías. *Vida de un Comunista.* Santiago: Talleres Gráficos Horizonte, 1961.

Lagos Escobar, Ricardo. *La concentración del poder económico, su teoría, realidad chilena.* Santiago: Editorial del Pacífico, 1961.

Landsberger, Henry, Manuel Barrera, and Abel Toro. *El pensamiento del dirigente sindical chileno.* Santiago: Instituto de Organización y Administración, Universidad de Chile, 1963.

La Palombara, Joseph, and Myron Weiner, eds. *Political Parties and Political Development.* Princeton: Princeton University Press, 1966.

León Echaíz, René. *Evolución histórica de los partidos políticos chilenos.* Santiago: Editorial Ercilla, 1939.

Lieuwin, Edwin. *Arms and Politics in Latin America.* New York: Frederick A. Praeger, 1961.

Lipset, Seymour Martin, and Aldo Solari, eds. *Elites in Latin America.* New York: Oxford University Press, 1967.

McBride, George M. *Chile: Land and Society.* New York: American Geographical Society, 1936.

Macdonald, Austin F. *Latin American Governments and Politics.* New York: Crowell Books, 1954.

Mac Eoin, Gary, *Latin America: The Eleventh Hour.* New York: P. J. Kenedy & Sons, 1962.

Maitland, Francis J. *Chile: Its Land and People.* London: F. Griffiths, 1914.

Mallory, Walter, ed. *Political Handbook and Atlas of the World.* New York: Harper & Row, 1964.

Mamalakis, Markos. *The Changing Structure and Roles of the Chilean Agricultural Sector.* New Haven: Economic Growth Center, Yale University, 1967.

———, and Clark W. Reynolds. *Essays on the Chilean Economy.* Homewood, Ill.: Richard D. Irwin, 1964.

Marienberg F., Ralph. *Algunas sugerencias respecto a combinaciones de medios de propaganda en Chile.* Santiago: Memoria de Prueba, Universidad de Chile, 1960.

Marín Balmaceda, Raúl. *Derechas o izquierdas.* Santiago: n.p., 1948.

Martínez Candia, Marcelo. *Ni marxismo ni liberalismo: Social-cristianismo.* Santiago: Editorial del Pacífico, 1952.

Mecham, J. Lloyd. *Church and State in Latin America.* Rev. ed. Chapel Hill: University of North Carolina Press, 1966.

Millas, Orlando. *Los comunistas, los católicos y la libertad.* Santiago: Editorial Austral, 1964.

Montecinos Rozas, Edmundo. *Apuntaciones para el estudio de la evolución de los partidos políticos chilenos y de su proyección jurídica.* Santiago: Imprenta Dirección General de Prisiones, 1942.

Moody, Joseph N., ed. *Church and Society.* New York: Arts, Inc., 1953.

Morris, James O. *Élites, Intellectuals, and Consensus: A Study of the Social Question and the Industrial Relations System in Chile.* Ithaca: Cornell University Press, 1966.

———, Roberto Oyaneder C., *et al. Afiliación y finanzas sindicales en Chile, 1932–1959.* Santiago: Instituto de Organización y Administración, Universidad de Chile, 1962.

Moulian, Tomás. *Estudio sobre Chile.* Santiago: Editorial Orbe, 1965.

Movimiento Unitario de Trabajadores de Chile. Santiago: Sopech, n.d.

North, Liisa. *Civil-Military Relations in Argentina, Chile, and Peru.* Berkeley: Institute of International Studies, University of California, [1966].

Núñez, Oscar. *Diez años de los trabajadores chilenos.* Santiago: Impresora Horizonte, 1963.

Olavarría Bravo, Arturo. *Chile bajo la Democracia Cristiana.* Santiago: Editorial Nascimento, 1966.

———. *Chile entre dos Alessandri.* 2 vols. Santiago: Editorial Nascimento, 1962.

Pacheco Gómez, Máximo. *La Universidad de Chile.* Santiago: Editorial Jurídica de Chile, 1953.

Parrish, Charles J., Arpad J. von Lazar, and Jorge Tapia Videla. *The Chilean Congressional Election of March 7, 1965: An Analysis.* Washington, D.C.: Institute for the Comparative Study of Political Systems, 1967.

Partido Comunista. *Estatutos.* Santiago: Impresora Horizonte, 1962.

———. *Hacia la conquista de un gobierno popular: Documentos del XII Congreso del Partido Comunista de Chile.* Santiago: Impresora Horizonte, 1962.

———. *El Partido Comunista de Chile y el movimiento comunista internacional.* Santiago: Impresora Horizonte, [1963?].

———. *Programa del Partido Comunista de Chile.* Santiago: Impresora Horizonte, 1962.

———. *La salud de Chile: Un problema gremial y un problema nacional.* Santiago: Impresora Horizonte, 1963.

———. *Una línea inquebrantable de conducta ideológica: El Partido Comunista de Chile y el movimiento comunista internacional.* Santiago: Impresora Horizonte, [1963?].

Partido Conservador. *Declaración fundamental, programas y estatutos del Partido Conservador, XVII Convención General, 1961.* Santiago: Talleres Claret, 1961.

———. *Estatutos del Partido Conservador.* Santiago: Talleres Claret, 1959.

Partido Demócrata Cristiano. *Estatutos del Partido Demócrata Cristiano.* Santiago: Editorial "El Imparcial," 1963.

Partido Democrático Nacional. *Declaración de principios, programa fundamental, y estatutos.* Santiago: Graphik, 1962.

Partido Liberal. *Estatuto orgánico del Partido Liberal.* Santiago: Imprenta Lathrop, 1959.

———. *Programa y estatuto orgánico del Partido Liberal.* Santiago: Imprenta Lathrop, 1962.

Partido Radical. *Estatutos.* Santiago: Vera y Gianini, 1961.

Partido Socialista. *Estatuto del Partido Socialista.* Santiago: Prensa Latinoamericana, 1962.

———. *La Polémica socialista-comunista.* Santiago: Prensa Latinoamericana, [1964?].

———. *Programa del Partido Socialista, XX Congreso General Ordinario Celebrado en Concepción, febrero, 1964.* Santiago: Prensa Latinoamericana, 1964.

Pastoral. Santiago: Editorial Arniz, 1965.

Pattee, Richard. *Catholicism in Latin America.* Washington, D.C.: National Catholic Welfare Conference, 1945.

Perceval. *¡Ganó Allende!* Santiago: Editorial Universidad Católica, 1964.

Pike, Fredrick B. *Chile and the United States, 1880–1962.* Notre Dame: University of Notre Dame Press, 1963.

———, ed. *The Conflict between Church and State in Latin America.* New York: Alfred A. Knopf, 1964.

Pinto Santa Cruz, Aníbal. *Chile: Un caso de desarrollo frustrado.* Santiago: Editorial Universitaria, 1959.

———. *Hacia nuestra independencia económica.* Santiago: Editorial del Pacífico, 1953.

Pizarro Navea, Eduardo. *Victoria al amanecer: La huelga de enero y febrero de 1950 de los empleados particulares.* Santiago: Imprenta "La Sud-América," 1950.

Poblete, Renato. *La iglesia en Chile.* Madrid: FERES, 1961.

Poblete Troncoso, Moisés. *La organización sindical en Chile.* Santiago: R. Brias, 1926.

———, and Ben G. Burnett. *The Rise of the Latin American Labor Movement.* New York: Bookman Associates, 1960.

Poppino, Rollie E. *International Communism in Latin America.* New York: Free Press of Glencoe, 1964.

Prado Valdés, José Miguel. *Reseña histórica del Partido Liberal.* Santiago: Imprenta "Andina," 1963.

El programa de estabilización de la economía chilena y el trabajo de la Misión Klein y Saks. Santiago: Editorial Universitaria, 1958.

Próspero. *Visión espectral de Chile.* Santiago: Editorial Universitaria, 1954.

Ramírez Necochea, Hernán. *Historia del movimiento obrero en Chile—antecedentes—siglo XIX.* Santiago: Talleres Gráficos Lautaro, 1956.

———. *Origen y formación del Partido Comunista de Chile.* Santiago: Editorial Austral, 1965.

———. *El Partido Comunista y la universidad.* Santiago: Editorial Aurora, 1964.

Recent Church Documents from Latin America. Cuernavaca: Center of Intercultural Formation, 1962–1963.

Rentería Uralde, Julián, ed. *La iglesia y la política.* Santiago: Ediciones Paulinas, 1963.

República de Chile. *Código de justicia militar.* Santiago: Editorial Jurídica de Chile, 1957.

———. *Ley general de elecciones.* Santiago: Editorial "La Nación," 1962.

Retamal González, Waldo. *El servicio militar del trabajo*. Santiago: Memoria de Prueba, Universidad de Chile, 1958.

Rioseco Maureira, Eduardo. *Derechos, deberes, prohibiciones, y responsabilidades de los empleados públicos ante la jurisprudencia*. Santiago: Memoria de Prueba, Editorial Universitaria, 1958.

Ríos Ladrón de Guevara, Ivan. *La dirección general del trabajo*. Santiago: Memoria de Prueba, Universidad de Chile, 1960.

Riquelme Pérez, Jorge, *et al*. *Estudio de recursos humanos de nivel universitario en Chile*. Santiago: Instituto de Organización y Administración, Universidad de Chile, 1962.

Rodríguez Mendoza, Emilio. *El golpe de estado de 1924*. Santiago: Editorial Ercilla, 1938.

Rogers Sotomayor, Jorge. *Dos caminos para la reforma agraria en Chile, 1945–1965*. Santiago: Editorial Orbe, 1966.

Rosso, Luis, ed. *Ley No. 15,576 sobre normas de publicidad escrita y oral*. Santiago: Cepeda y Rodríguez, [1964].

Saavedra E., Enrique. *La educación en una comuna de Santiago: Comuna de San Miguel*. Santiago: Instituto de Educación, Universidad de Chile, 1965.

Sáez, Raúl. *Chile y el cobre*. Santiago: Departamento del Cobre, 1965.

Sáez Morales, Carlos. *Recuerdos de un soldado*. 3 vols. Santiago: Editorial Ercilla, 1934.

———. *Y así vamos*. Santiago: Editorial Ercilla, 1938.

Sampaio, Plinio, *et al*. *Organización, planificación y coordinación de las instituciones del sector público agrícola de Chile, a nivel de terreno*. Santiago: Instituto de Capacitación e Investigación en Reforma Agraria, 1966.

Sanfuentes Carrión, Marcial. *El Partido Conservador*. Santiago: Editorial Universitaria, 1957.

Schramm, Wilbur. *Mass Media and National Development*. Stanford: Stanford University Press, 1964.

Scott Elliot, G. F. *Chile*. London: T. Fisher Unwin, 1911.

Sepúlveda S., Carlos. *Los indicadores económicos*. Santiago: Instituto de Economía, Universidad de Chile, 1965.

Serrano Palma, Horacio. *¿Por qué somos pobres?* Santiago: Editorial Universitaria, n.d.

Silva Cimma, Enrique. *Derecho administrativo chileno y comparado*. Santiago: Editorial Jurídica de Chile, 1954.

Silva Yoacham, Manuel. *Legislación y realidades económicas.* Santiago: Editorial del Pacífico, 1960.

Silvert, Kalman H. *Chile: Yesterday and Today.* New York: Holt, Rinehart, & Winston, 1965.

———. *The Conflict Society: Reaction and Revolution in Latin America.* New Orleans: Hauser Press, 1961.

Steinberg, S. H., ed. *Statesman's Yearbook.* New York: St. Martin's Press, 1964.

Stevenson, John R. *The Chilean Popular Front.* Philadelphia: University of Pennsylvania Press, 1942.

Steward, Julian H., and Louis C. Faron. *Native Peoples of South America.* New York: McGraw-Hill Book Co., 1959.

Subercaseaux, Benjamín. *Chile: A Geographic Extravaganza.* New York: Macmillan Company, 1943.

TePaske, John, and Sydney N. Fisher, eds. *Explosive Forces in Latin America.* Columbus: Ohio State University Press, 1964.

Thiesenhusen, William C. *Chile's Experiments in Agrarian Reform.* Madison: Land Tenure Center, University of Wisconsin Press, 1966.

Tomasek, Robert, ed. *Latin American Politics: Studies of the Contemporary Scene.* Garden City: Doubleday & Co., 1966.

Truman, David B. *The Governmental Process.* New York: Alfred A. Knopf, 1951.

Urzúa Valenzuela, Germán. *El Partido Radical, su evolución política.* Santiago: Academia de Ciencias Políticas y Administrativas, 1961.

U.S. Department of Labor. *Labor in Chile.* Washington, D.C.: Bureau of Labor Statistics, Division of Foreign Labor Conditions, 1962.

Varas C., Guillermo. *Derecho administrativo.* Santiago: Editorial Nascimento, 1948.

Vergara Vicuña, Aquiles. *Tres años en el frente político.* Santiago: Imprenta Universidad, 1925.

Vial, Carlos. *Cuaderno de comprensión social.* Santiago: Editorial del Pacífico, 1952.

———. *Cuaderno de la realidad nacional.* Santiago: Editorial del Pacífico, 1952.

Vicuña Fuentes, Carlos. *La cuestión social ante la Federación de Estudiantes de Chile.* Santiago: Imprenta Lito. y Enc. Selecta, 1922.

Vitale, Luis. *Los discursos de Clotario Blest y la revolución chilena.* Santiago: Imprenta Victoria, 1961.

———. *Esencia y apariencia de la Democracia Cristiana.* Santiago: Arancibia Hnos., 1964.

Vuskovic, Sergio, and Osvaldo Fernández. *Teoría de la ambigüedad: Bases ideológicas de la Democracia Cristiana.* Santiago: Editorial Austral, 1964.

Waiss, Oscar. *Presencia del socialismo en Chile.* Santiago: Ediciones Espártaco, 1952.

Walker Linares, Francisco. *Nociones elementales de derecho del trabajo.* Santiago: Editorial Nascimento, 1957.

Ward, Robert E., and Roy C. Macridis, eds. *Modern Political Systems: Asia.* Englewood Cliffs, N.J.: Prentice-Hall, 1963.

Whitaker, Arthur P. *Nationalism in Latin America.* Gainesville: University of Florida Press, 1962.

White, Theodore H. *Making of the President 1960.* New York: Atheneum Publishers, 1961.

Wilgus, A. Curtis, ed. *Argentina, Brazil and Chile since Independence.* New York: Russell & Russell, 1963.

Williams, Edward J. *Latin American Christian Democratic Parties.* Knoxville: University of Tennessee Press, 1967.

Articles, Dissertations, and Mimeographed Material

Agor, Weston. "Senate vs. CORA: An Attempt to Evaluate Chile's Agrarian Reform to Date." *Inter-American Economic Affairs* 22, no. 2 (Autumn 1968): 47–53.

Allende, Salvador. "Significado de la conquista de un gobierno popular para Chile." *Cuadernos Americanos* 23, no. 5 (September–October 1964): 7–24.

Angell, Alan. "Chile: The Christian Democrats at Mid-term." *The World Today* 23, no. 10 (October 1967): 434–443.

Arroyo, Gonzalo. "Reforma agraria en Chile." *Mensaje* no. 146 (January–February 1966): 2–15.

Asenjo, Alfonso. "La universidad y el trabajo." *Anales de la Universidad de Chile* 121, no. 127 (May–August 1963): 42–69.

Barrera R., Manuel J. "Participation by Occupational Organizations in Economic and Social Planning in Chile." *International Labour Review* 96, no. 2 (August 1967): 151–176.

———. "Trayectoria del movimiento de reforma universitaria en Chile." *Journal of Inter-American Studies* 10, no. 4 (October 1968): 617–636.

Becket, James. "Tempest in a Copper Pot: Chile's Mini-Revolution." *Commonweal*, December 29, 1967, pp. 406–408.

Blanksten, George. "The Aspiration for Economic Development." *Annals of the American Academy of Political and Social Science* no. 334 (March 1961): 10–19.

Bonilla, Frank. "The Student Federation of Chile: 50 Years of Political Action." *Journal of Inter-American Studies* 2, no. 3 (July 1960): 311–334.

Bray, Donald W. "Chile: The Dark Side of Stability." *Studies on the Left* 4, no. 4 (Fall 1964): 85–96.

———. "Peronism in Chile." *Hispanic American Historical Review* 47, no. 1 (February 1956): 38–49.

Cabieses Donoso, Manuel. "La ley mordaza." *Aurora* 1, no. 1 (January–March 1964): 96–99.

Carter, Roy E., Jr., and Orlando Sepúlveda. "Some Patterns of Mass Media in Use in Santiago de Chile." *Journalism Quarterly* 41, no. 2 (Spring 1964): 216–224.

Chilcote, Ronald. "The Press in Latin America, Spain, and Portugal." *Hispanic American Report* (Special Issue, [1963?]): xxix–xxxii.

"Chile." *Bank of London and South America Review* 2, no. 19 (July 1968): 406–410.

Congreso de Planificación Regional. "Informa Final." Mimeographed. Concepción, 1963.

Cope, Orville G. "The 1964 Presidential Election in Chile: The Politics of Change and Access." *Inter-American Economic Affairs* 19, no. 4 (Spring 1966): 3–29.

Cox, Isaac J. "Chile." In *Argentina, Brazil, and Chile since Independence*, edited by Curtis A. Wilgus, pp. 279–369. New York: Russell & Russell, 1963.

Dinerstein, Herbert S. "Soviet Policy in Latin America." *American Political Science Review* 61, no. 1 (March 1967): 80–90.

Duncan, W. Raymond. "Chilean Christian Democracy." *Current History* 53, no. 315 (November 1967): 263–309.

"Estatutos de la Federación de Estudiantes de Concepción." Mimeographed. Concepción, 1963.

Feliú Cruz, Guillermo. "Durante la república. Perfiles de la evolución política, social, y constitucional." In *La Constitución de 1925 y la Facultad de Ciencias Jurídicas y Sociales*, pp. 59–305. Santiago: Editorial Jurídica, 1951.

Francis, Michael, and Eldon Lanning. "Chile's 1967 Municipal Elections." *Inter-American Economic Affairs* 21, no. 2 (Autumn 1967): 23–36.

Frei, Eduardo. "Christian Democracy in Theory and Practice." In *The Ideologies of the Developing Nations*, edited by Paul E. Sigmund, pp. 308–320. New York: Frederick A. Praeger, 1964.

———. "Paternalism, Pluralism, and Christian Democratic Reform Movements in Latin America." In *Religion, Revolution, and Reform*, edited by William V. D'Antonio and Fredrick B. Pike, pp. 27–40. New York: Frederick A. Praeger, 1964.

Gil, Federico G. "Chile: 'Revolution in Liberty,'" *Current History* 51, no. 303 (November 1966): 291–295.

———. "Chile, Society in Transition." In *Political Systems of Latin America*, edited by Martin C. Needler, pp. 351–379. New York: D. Van Nostrand, 1964.

Glazer, Myron. "The Professional and Political Attitudes of Chilean University Students." Ph.D. dissertation, Princeton University, 1965.

Goldrich, Daniel, Raymond B. Pratt, and C. R. Schuller. "The Political Integration of Lower Class Urban Settlements in Chile and Peru." *Studies in Comparative International Development* 3, no. 1 (1967, 1968): 1–22.

Gray, Richard B., and Frederick R. Kerwin. "Presidential Succession in Chile: 1817–1966." *Journal of Inter-American Studies* 11, no. 1 (January 1969): 144–159.

Grayson, George W., Jr. "Christian Democrats in Chile." *SAIS Review* 9, no. 2 (Winter 1965): 12–20.

———. "Significance of the Frei Administration for Latin America." *Orbis* 9, no. 3 (Fall 1965): 760–779.

Jobet, Julio César. "Acción e historia del socialismo chileno." *Combate* 2, no. 12 (September–October 1960): 32–45.

———. "Teoría y programa del Partido Socialista de Chile." *Arauco* 3, no. 27 (April 1962): 9–24.

Johnson, Kenneth. "Causal Factors in Latin American Political Instability." *Western Political Quarterly* 17, no. 3 (September 1964): 432–446.

Lens, Sidney. "Chile's 'Revolution in Liberty,'" *Progressive* 30, no. 10 (October 1966): 32–35.

Lieuwin, Edwin. "The Changing Role of the Military in Latin America." *Journal of Inter-American Studies* 3, no. 4 (October 1961): 559–569.

Luksic Savoia, Zarko. "La política económica demócratacristiana." *Política y Espíritu* 21, no. 298 (January–March 1967): 108–123.

McAlister, Lyle N. "Civil-Military Relations in Latin America." *Journal of Inter-American Studies* 3, no. 3 (July 1961): 341–350.

McCoy, Terry L. "The Seizure of 'Los Cristales': A Case Study of the Marxist Left in Chile." *Inter-American Economic Affairs* 21, no. 1 (Summer 1967): 73–93.

Menges, Constantine C. "Public Policy and Organized Business in Chile: A Preliminary Analysis." *Journal of International Affairs* 20, no. 2 (1966): 343–365.

Moreno, Rafael. "Resultado de los asentamientos." *Política y Espíritu* 21, no. 300 (June 1967): 81–85.

Nery Ríos, Bertilio J. "Estudio de una institución burocrática en Chile." *Ciencias Sociales* 1, no. 2 (June 1964): 183–224.

"Ninth National Congress of the Christian Workers' Confederation of Chile." *International Labour Review* 96, no. 1 (July 1967): 110–113.

Nunn, Frederick M. "Chile's Government in Perspective: Political Change or More of the Same?" *Inter-American Economic Affairs* 20, no. 4 (Spring 1967): 73–89.

"Organisation of Rural Workers in Chile." *International Labour Review* 96, no. 4 (October 1967): 420–421.

Partido Demócrata Cristiano. "Congreso de planificación regional: Informe final." Mimeographed. Concepción, November 1963.

Petras, James. "After the Chilean Presidential Election: Reform or Stagnation?" *Journal of Inter-American Studies* 7, no. 3 (July 1965): 375–384.

———, and Maurice Zeitlin. "Miners and Agrarian Socialism." *American Sociological Review* 32, no. 4 (August 1967): 578–586.

Pike, Fredrick B. "The Catholic Church and Modernization in Peru and Chile." *Journal of International Affairs* 20, no. 2 (1966): 272–288.

———. "Chile." In *Latin America and the Caribbean: A Handbook*, edited by Claudio Véliz, pp. 59–73. New York: Frederick A. Praeger, 1968.

Sánchez, Luis Alberto. "The University in Latin America: The University Reform Movement." *Américas* 14, no. 1 (January 1962): 13–16.

Sievers W., Hugo K. "La expansión urbana de Santiago y sus consecuencias 1941–1960." *Mapocho* 1, no. 3 (October 1963): 30–55.

Sigmund, Paul E. "Christian Democracy in Chile." *Journal of International Affairs* 20, no. 2 (1966): 332–342.

Silvert, Kalman H. "Nationalism in Latin America." *Annals of the American Academy of Political and Social Science* no. 334 (March 1961): 1–9.

———. "Some Propositions on Chile." *American Universities Field Staff Report* 11, no. 1 (January 1964): 43–57.

Smith, David H. "A Psychological Model of Individual Participation in Formal Voluntary Organizations: Application to Some Chilean Data." *American Journal of Sociology* 72, no. 3 (November 1966): 249–266.

Snow, Peter. "The Political Party Spectrum in Chile." *South Atlantic Quarterly* 62, no. 4 (Autumn 1963): 474–487.

Soares, Glaucio, and Robert L. Hamblin. "Socio-economic Variables and Voting for the Radical Left: Chile, 1942." *American Political Science Review* 61, no. 4 (December 1967): 1053–1065.

Soto, Lionel. "El XIII Congreso del Partido Comunista de Chile." *Cuba Socialista* 5, no. 52 (December 1965): 25–44.

Soza, Héctor. "The Industrialization of Chile." In *Latin America and the Caribbean: A Handbook*, edited by Claudio Véliz, pp. 614–621. New York: Frederick A. Praeger, 1968.

Sunkel, Osvaldo. "Change and Frustration in Chile." In *Obstacles to Change in Latin America*, edited by Claudio Véliz, pp. 116–144. London: Oxford University Press, 1969.

Thiesenhusen, William C. "Agrarian Reform and Economic Development in Chile: Some Cases of Colonization." *Land Economics* 43, no. 3 (August 1966): 282–292.

———. "Chilean Agrarian Reform: The Possibility of Gradualistic Turnover of Land." *Inter-American Economic Affairs* 20, no. 1 (Summer 1966): 3–22.

———. "Latin American Land Reform: Enemies of Promise." *Nation*, January 24, 1966, pp. 90–94.

Trellez, Amarildo. "En los caminos de la reforma agraria." *Política y Espíritu* 21, no. 296 (October 1966): 79–87.

von Lazar, Arpad, and Luis Quirós Varela. "Chilean Christian Democracy: Lessons in the Politics of Reform Management." *Inter-American Economic Affairs* 21, no. 4 (Spring 1968): 51–72.

Weatherhead, Richard, and Joseph Maier. "Augurio político para la América Latina? La Democracia Cristiana y la victoria de Frei en Chile." *Foro Internacional* 5, no. 2 (October–December 1964): 212–224.

Weekly, James K. "Christian Democracy in Chile—Ideology and Economic Development." *South Atlantic Quarterly* 66, no. 3 (Autumn 1967): 520–533.

Willems, Emilio. "Protestantism and Culture Change in Brazil and Chile." In *Religion, Revolution, and Reform*, edited by William V. D'Antonio and Fredrick B. Pike, pp. 91–108. New York. Frederick A. Praeger, 1964.

Winnie, W. F., Jr. "Communal Land Tenure in Chile." *Annals of the Association of American Geographers* 55, no. 1 (March 1965): 67–86.

Wyckoff, Theodore. "The Role of the Military in Latin American Politics." *Western Political Quarterly* 3, no. 3 (September 1960): 745–763.

Zeitlin, Maurice. "Determinates sociales de la democracia política en Chile." *Revista Latinoamericana de Sociología* 2, no. 2 (July 1966): 223–236.

INDEX